THE POLITICAL ECONOMY OF
MONETARY REFORM

Also by Robert Z. Aliber

THE INTERNATIONAL MARKET
  FOR FOREIGN EXCHANGE (*editor*)
THE INTERNATIONAL MONEY GAME
NATIONAL MONETARY POLICY
  AND THE INTERNATIONAL
  FINANCIAL SYSTEM (*editor*)

THE POLITICAL
ECONOMY OF
MONETARY REFORM

Edited by
ROBERT Z. ALIBER

LANDMARK STUDIES
Allanheld, Osmun & Co. Publishers
Universe Books

ALLANHELD, OSMUN AND CO. PUBLISHERS, INC.
19 Brunswick Road, Montclair, N.J. 07042

Published in the United States of America in 1977
by Allanheld, Osmun and Co. and by Universe Books
381 Park Avenue South, New York, N.Y. 10016
Distribution: Universe Books

LIBRARY OF CONGRESS CATALOGING IN
   PUBLICATION DATA
The Political economy of monetary reform.
   (Land mark studies)
   Based on the proceedings of a conference held in
Racine, Wis., in 1974.
   Includes index.
   1. International finance – Congresses. 2. Monetary
policy – Congresses. I. Aliber, Robert Z.

HG3881.P58   332.4′5   76–26692
ISBN 0–87663–810–8

Printed in Great Britain

Contents

Foreword by RICHARD N. ROSETT   vii

Introduction by ROBERT Z. ALIBER   ix

I   RULES AND MONETARY ARRANGEMENTS   1

   1   Monetary Rules and Monetary Reform   3
       ROBERT Z. ALIBER

   2   On the Political Economy of Monetary Integration:
      A Public Economics Approach   13
       KOICHI HAMADA

   3   Current Account Targets and Managed Floating   32
       ANNE O. KRUEGER

   4   Beyond Fixed Parities: The Analytics of
      International Monetary Agreements   42
       RONALD I. McKINNON

II   MONETARY INTERDEPENDENCE AND
    MONETARY POLICY   57

   5   Stability and Exchange Rate Systems in a Monetarist
      Model of the Balance of Payments   59
       STANLEY FISCHER

   6   International Investment and Interest Rate Linkages
      under Flexible Exchange Rates   74
       PENTTI J. K. KOURI

   7   New Cambridge Macroeconomics, Assignment Rules
      and Interdependence   97
       JOHN SPRAOS

   8   Capital Mobility and Portfolio Balance   106
       RUDIGER DORNBUSCH

   9   Interrelations Between Domestic and International
      Theories of Inflation   126
       ROBERT J. GORDON

III THE EMPIRICAL SIDE OF MONETARY
INTERDEPENDENCE   155

   10 The Interdependence of Monetary, Debt and Fiscal
       Policies in an International Setting   157
       JOHN HELLIWELL *and* ROBERT McRAE

   11 Monetary Interdependence among Major European
       Countries   179
       PAUL DE GRAUWE

   12 International Reserves and Capital Mobility   205
       K. L. MAHAR *and* M. G. PORTER

   13 World Inflation, International Relative Prices and
       Monetary Equilibrium under Fixed Exchange Rates   220
       MICHAEL PARKIN

Summary of the Discussion   243
List of Participants   262
Index   263

Foreword

Studies of international monetary relationships have been conducted for many years at the University of Chicago. Over the past decade, the Graduate School of Business has sponsored four international conferences which have brought together scholars and government officials of leading Western nations for a close examination of current theory and developments in the field. These meetings were organised and directed by Robert Z. Aliber, Professor of International Economics and Finance and Director of the Program of International Studies in Business.

Each of the conferences has resulted in a published volume, as noted by Professor Aliber in his Introduction to the present work, itself an outgrowth of the most recent meeting. Together, these volumes constitute an important contribution to our understanding of the international monetary system and its role in the world economy.

RICHARD N. ROSETT, *Dean*

Graduate School of Business
The University of Chicago

Introduction

Robert Z. Aliber

The shocks to the international financial arrangements in the early 1970s were the most severe since the Great Depression. The rules of the Bretton Woods system embodied in the Articles of Agreement of the International Monetary Fund (IMF) were ignored and became obsolete. The Articles were designed to avoid a repetition of the 1930s experience with competitive exchange rate changes; member countries were committed to a pegged exchange rate. In 1973 the major countries permitted their currencies to float, for the first time in fifty years. The Committee for Twenty (C–20), a negotiating group within the IMF established in 1972 to develop a plan for a new international monetary arrangement, proved unsuccessful. For the first time in nearly thirty years, no treaty-based rules governed the international financial transactions of particular countries, and there was no prospect for such rules. In 1973 and 1974 the international economy was subject to the most persistent peacetime inflation in the twentieth century; the world price level increased by more than 10 per cent in both years. By late 1974 the world economy was into the most severe recession since the Second World War, commodity price levels were continuing to rise, but at a less rapid rate, and there was concern that a depression was not impossible.

The breakdown of the Bretton Woods system, the worldwide inflation, and the aborted C–20 monetary negotiations were related. The inflation – and the efforts of particular countries to maintain price increases less rapid than those in other countries, especially the United States – was a significant factor in the demise of the Bretton Woods system. The band-aid approach to altering monetary arrangements, which had held the system together in the 1960s when the problem was one of inadequate levels of reserves, proved inadequate to deal with the exchange rate implications of divergent rates of inflation among the major countries. Floating exchange rates were adopted in the absence of a feasible alternative; no other exchange rate arrangement could cope with divergent rates of inflation. Moreover, central bankers no longer retained credibility in their statements about exchange rate stability. The C–20 negotiations initially leaned toward recommending a more flexible form of pegged rates. The historical experiences of the 1920s and 1930s, and those of the nineteenth century, suggest floating exchange rates are inevitable as long as price level movements in various countries diverge. Until relative price stability is achieved, the guidelines for floating rates developed by the C–20 may provide the basis for international monetary stability. These guidelines are useful, but they lack legal force and permanency. Reaching an agreement on a new set of monetary arrangements was complicated by the changed perception of the US role in the international economy. In the early 1940s, when the Bretton Woods Agreement was negotiated, the United States was very dominant and at the centre of the industrial economies; it was very large, rich, and relatively unaffected by the war. In contrast, war battles were still continuing in Europe and the Pacific, and both economies and the political processes were under tremendous stress.

By the mid-1960s, some countries felt that the United States played too dominant a role in international monetary arrangements. In the early 1970s, the United States sought to move away from the centre role, and any special responsibilities it may have acquired, willingly or unwillingly, earlier in the postwar period. Germany and Japan had emerged from defeat and occupation to become major economic powers in the world economy. The United States felt that it had greater responsibility and less freedom under the Bretton Woods system than other countries did. While there was an apparent agreement on the need for a change in the US role, there was no agreement on what the new role should be, and whether this role could be determined in a negotiation.

In the next few years, a new set of negotiations will be initiated to establish international monetary rules, either to formalise the operation of the floating rate system or to provide the basis for a return to a pegged exchange rate. The historical experience suggests that there will be a move to some type of a pegged rate arrangement when that system is feasible. A pegged system might then develop on an *ad hoc* basis, or it might result from a major multinational negotiation.

This volume and the Conference on which it was based centre on international monetary reform, including the role and content of rules in monetary arrangements and the relation of the rules to the structure of trade and payments among national economies.

The 1974 Conference is the fifth on international monetary questions sponsored by the University of Chicago since 1966. The themes and formats of these several Conferences differ somewhat; the common element involves bringing academicians and government officials to-gether to discuss current policy issues in the light of comtemporary theory. The 1966 Conference in Chicago (*Monetary Problems of the World Economy*, University of Chicago Press, 1959) examined a wide array of problems and issues that were inherent under the Bretton Woods system, including the interrelationships between monetary and fiscal policies, seignorage involved in the production of international money, the links between exchange rate policy, commercial policy, and the relationships between the International Monetary Fund, the International Bank for Reconstruction and Development, and the interest of the developing countries in monetary reform. The 1967 Conference at Ditchley Park, England (*The International Market for Foreign Exchange*, Praeger, 1968), focused on the technical characteristics of the organisation, the unity of the market foreign exchange in national financial centres like London, New York, and Zurich; a central question was how the objectives of firms engaged in international trade and finance might be reconciled with the objectives of national banks. The 1970 Conference in Madrid (*The Economics of Common Currencies*, Allen & Unwin, 1973) focused on the merits of a pegged exchange rate and floating exchange rates systems, especially in the context of the newly revived monetary theory of the balance of payments.

The 1972 Conference, held at the Johnson Foundation Conference Center, Wingspread (*National Monetary Policies and the International Financial System*, University of Chicago, 1974), and the 1974 Conference focused on the interrelationship of national monetary policies and the international system; the focus was the theoretical arguments about national financial relationships linked with empirical findings. At the time of the 1972 Conference, the pegged exchange rate system was still operative, although battered. While national price levels were increasing, the major inflationary surge was still to come, and inflation as a generalised phenomena not anticipated; the inflation rate in 1973 and again in 1974 was twice that in 1972. Nevertheless there was a belief that the inexorable working of market forces meant that the pegged rate system would not last long. Indeed the concluding statement in the 1972 volume was that 'the system has passed the point of no return in the move away from the pegged exchange rate; so much flexibility has been accepted that it is now impossible to go back to pegged exchange rates. Moreover, it is impossible to stop where we are. The existing movement is bringing us nearer to floating rates.'*

The first group of papers in this volume involves institutional issues, especially the role of rules in international financial arrangements. In the absence of monetary rules, each currency would float. Exchange rates would be determined by market forces together with the *ad hoc* intervention policies of various central banks to induce their currencies

---

* Statement of Jurg Niehans, *National Monetary Policies and the International Financial System* (University of Chicago Press, Chicago, 1974) p. 314.

to appreciate or depreciate, either to dampen increases in their domestic price level or to stimulate employment. Countries may intervene in the exchange market at cross-purposes; their targets may be inconsistent. Hence rules are desired to achieve consistency. My paper deals with the content of monetary rules, the conditions that must be satisfied if rules are to be adopted, the source of gains from monetary rules and their distribution among participating countries, and the relation of monetary agreements to the political relationships among the major participating countries. The paper by Koichi Hamada discusses the conditions that must be satisfied if currency areas are to unite, and then examines the monetary unifications of Germany, Italy and Japan in the nineteenth century in terms of these conditions. Anne Krueger's paper evaluates two competing explanations for the breakdown of the Bretton Woods system – one asserts that the breakdown was inherent in the structure of the system, while the second believes the system would have continued in the absence of the inflation. Her paper emphasises that the conflict among countries that led to the breakdown of the pegged rate system is also inherent in the floating rate system. Ronald McKinnon's paper emphasises a monetary rule that individual countries might follow that would recognise their economic diversity, especially the differences in their potential rates of economic growth, and yet provide the basis for a pegged or fixed exchange rate regime.

The second group of papers are theoretical. John Spraos's paper considers a new theory about the monetary relationships developed in Cambridge, England; this theory questions one of the basic assumptions underlying most analysis of the relation of policy instruments to employment and exchange rate targets. Pentti Kouri's paper examines the relationships among interest rates on similar assets denominated in different currencies under alternative exchange rate regimes; the model provides the basis for evaluation of the proposition that central banks have greater monetary independence under floating rate regimes than under pegged rate regimes. The paper by Stanley Fischer compares the responses of the economy to a variety of monetary and non-monetary disturbances under both exchange rate regimes. Rudiger Dornbusch's paper examines the impact of changes in financial regulations – as opposed to monetary policies – on trade in financial assets. The paper by Robert Gordon examines two theories of the inflation – a domestic theory associated with a Phillips curve trade-off between price stability and full employment, and an international theory of the balance of payments – under fixed and floating exchange rates and in an inflationary context. The underlying assumptions of the two theories are examined, and the two theories are reconciled. Michael Parkin's paper seeks to explain the relation between the national rates of inflation and balance of payments positions of different countries under the pegged rate system of the 1950s and the 1960s.

The papers in the third group are empirical. John Helliwell and Robert McRae present a simulation study of US–Canadian trade, capital and migration relationships, and their response to variations in monetary, debt and fiscal policies. Paul De Grauwe's paper examines the relationships between the monetary bases in European countries, and the impact of domestic sterilisation policies on the stability of the system. The paper by K. L. Mahar and M. G. Porter considers the relation of trade imbalances and capital flows to natural monetary policies; thus trade imbalances are largely self-financing.

The concluding section of the paper summarises the discussion at the final session of the Conference.

The Conference was made possible through the generous support of the Johnson Foundation that extended both the use of Wingspread and a grant to help defray the travel costs of overseas participants, the Norman Waite Harris Foundation of the University of Chicago and the Ford Foundation Grant to develop international studies in the university.

Part I

RULES AND MONETARY ARRANGEMENTS

1 Monetary Rules and Monetary Reform

Robert Z. Aliber

INTRODUCTION

For much of the fifteen years, the central concern in international finance has been monetary reform. Numerous proposals were advanced for the production of new international reserve assets and for changes in exchange market arrangements, especially in the mid-1960s. The modifications to the Bretton Woods system were extensive, beginning with The General Arrangements To Borrow and continuing with Special Drawing Rights, central bank swaps, the widening of support limits around parities, and the demonetisation of gold. Yet the Bretton Woods system was not saved; the pegged exchange rates re-established in the Smithsonian Agreement lasted for little more than a year. The negotiations for a new monetary arrangement of the Committee of Twenty (C–20) proved unsuccessful.

While there are now guidelines for central bank behaviour under the floating rates system, no rules now constrain the international monetary behaviour of individual countries, especially their intervention in exchange markets. The International Monetary Fund expands in membership and staff, but it functions as a research institution, a modest lender and a forum; the Fund no longer is a guardian of rules and order in international finance. International monetary arrangements are characterised by extensive 'ad hocery' about exchange market intervention practices of various nations.

An explanation is needed for the contrast between the many varied proposals for reform of international monetary arrangements and the disarray in international financial relations. The subject matter of monetary reform includes national monetary policies, exchange rate policies, exchange controls, and extension of credit among national monetary authorities, both bilaterally and through international institutions. As a political process reform involves obtaining agreement on rules about national monetary policies, exchange market intervention, and the extension of credits from one national monetary authority to another. These rules deal with the causes of payments imbalance with their consequences, and with the adjustment toward payments equilibrium.

The rule-making process involves nation-states, which compete for power, influence and leadership roles. Each set of rules has implications about the distribution of power and influence among the countries, and for the standing of various national governments in their constituencies.

In the absence of rules, each national monetary authority would follow the monetary, fiscal and exchange rate policies deemed most likely to achieve its national objectives. Whether a particular country achieves a payments deficit or surplus or whether its currency appreciates or depreciates, depends on the fit of its policies with those of foreign monetary authorities, and their exchange market intervention policies. Without rules, adjustments to payments imbalances occur continuously and automatically as a result of changes in relative prices, incomes, interest rates and exchange rates.

That so much concern has been given to monetary reform suggests that there are gains if the adjustment process operates within the context of established rules. In a system with rules, the adjustment paths of particular countries are constrained. The interests of each country – or at least of the policy makers in these countries – usually are advanced by minimising the external constraint on their choice of financial policies and the external influences on the performance of their economies. Nevertheless countries accept these constraints because of the advantages attached to having other countries accept similar constraints. The sources of these gains and the distribution of these gains among countries must be identified.

The next section of this paper deals with the economic gains associated with monetary reform, and the scope for reform. The various types of monetary rules and the ways in which rules can be combined in hierarchies are considered in the second section. The structure of rules in the various major monetary arrangements, such as the gold standard and the Bretton Woods system, are discussed in the third section. The political implications of different sets of rules are considered in the last section.

RULES AND MONETARY REFORM

The cosmopolitan motivation for monetary reform is that net benefits result for countries as a group from their adherence to a set of rules which may deal with monetary expansion, exchange market intervention, and international credit transfers. In the absence of rules, countries would follow the monetary policies, the exchange rate policies, and the international credit transfer policies they deem in their interests; payments imbalances would result, and countries would change their exchange rates and their exchange controls to advance their own interests. As a consequence, some countries might 'export' substantial shocks to the trade balances, the employment levels, and the price levels of their trading partners. Rules constrain the ability of countries to follow 'beggar-thy-neighbour' policies.

Adjustment to payments imbalances may occur automatically or in response to the measures taken by countries in payments surplus and countries in payments deficit. Imbalances have implications for changes in price levels and employment levels in the countries in payments deficit and those in payments surplus. Measures to reduce imbalances might be pursued by the countries in deficit and those in surplus.

The rules may affect the distribution among countries of economic shocks and disturbances, as well as the distribution of the costs of measures associated with the move to payments equilibrium. Rules affect the selection of measures that governments might adopt to modify their international payments position, including their monetary policies. Rules are primarily of several types. Some rules compel the governments to take certain measures – measures they might have taken in the absence of these rules. Thus the rules tend to formalise the pattern of behaviour that might otherwise occur – one reason countries accept the rules is that the cost of abiding by their commitments is low.

To the extent that the measures taken by countries in a system with rules are those that otherwise they might have taken in their absence, the rules reduce the uncertainty that each government inevitably has about the policies that its trading partners might adopt. The reduction in uncertainty may mean that each country can be better off at the same time. To the extent that the measures taken by countries in a system with rules are those they would not otherwise have taken in the absence of rules, the rules change the distribution among countries of the costs associated with adjustment, both those involving economic welfare and those involving decision costs.

Some rules may prevent countries from adopting particular measures in certain circumstances. To the extent that countries would not have adopted these measures, the rules reduce uncertainty. To the extent they would have adopted such measures, the rules affect the distribution among countries of the costs of adjusting to imbalances.

Whereas all countries may gain as a result of the reduction of uncertainty, some countries may be worse off in a situation with rules than in one without, because of the distributional impact. Their acceptance and adherence to the the rules reflects that they believe the gains from the reduction of uncertainty dominates any immediate distributional costs.

The impact of rules on particular countries differ. Some countries are more likely than others to export shocks, perhaps because of their size, openness, or domestic economic policies. The more likely a country is to export shocks, the more likely that its trading partners might wish to constrain its policies by rules. The less likely a country is to export shocks – the less interested other countries will be in constraining its behaviour. Consequently, the major beneficiaries of the reduction in uncertainty from imposition of rules are likely to be smaller countries, while the costs or constraints are likely to be felt by the larger countries.

Rules are negotiated and embodied in a treaty. Usually the rules are general; each participating country accepts the same set obligations, at least in a formal sense, because sovereign nations are deemed equals. Thus the IMF rules contained the same set of obligations on each country about exchange market intervention. Commitments about credit transfers were scaled to the size of the country through a quota formula. Even though the economic circumstances of the individual countries differ, the rules are rarely country-specific; they are legal rather than economic.

Nevertheless various participating countries in monetary arrangement may encounter quite different costs of following the rules in the same circumstances, depending on their economic structures. Consequently as long as the rules are not country specific, then the rules must be sufficiently broad to cover countries in quite different circumstances so as to induce these countries to accept the rules.

Formalising a set of rules is the necessary condition for reducing uncertainty. The sufficient condition is that individual countries have confidence in the willingness and ability of other participating countries to abide by the constraints embodied in the rules. Adherence to the rules may incur substantial costs for particular countries. Hence the confidence that any one government can place in a monetary agreement depends on its perception of whether other governments might slight their commitments because continued adherence incurs high costs to their domestic objectives. The more frequently that any one government fails to adhere to its commitments, the less confidence that other governments will have about its adherence to its commitments in the future – and the less effective the rules will be in reducing uncertainty. To the extent that individual nations are likely to ignore the commitments, the rules may have only a modest effect in reducing uncertainty.

The confidence that each country can place in the rules is inversely related to their comprehensiveness – to the severity of their constraints. The higher the cost that any one country might be expected to incur in adhering to the rules, the less likely it will abide by these constraints. Hence the smaller the confidence that others will place in the rules, and the less effective the rules in reducing uncertainty.

Designing and negotiating a set of monetary rules involves optimisation in two dimensions. The more comprehensive the set of rules, the greater the potential reduction in uncertainty, for the smaller the leeway that the national governments have in varying their domestic and international policies. The more comprehensive the rules are, the more likely that the rules may be broken and the smaller the confidence that the authorities can have in the credibility of the rules. Hence, the rules are likely to be more effective in reducing small uncertainties rather than large uncertainties.

Moreover, newly established rules are likely to have only a modest initial impact in reducing uncertainty; the credibility of a set of rules can only be established with time. The longer the period in which countries have adhered to the rules, the greater their credibility.

While each country might break the rules, some countries can ignore their commitments with much smaller impact than others. When small countries break the rules, they may be subject to sanctions imposed by the international institutions – effectively by the larger countries acting through the institution. The smaller countries accept the sanctions because of the continued benefit from their other relationships with the larger countries. The survival of the system of rules is not threatened if small countries fail to adhere to their commitments; uncertainty is not likely to be significantly affected. When large countries break the rules, however, they threaten the survivability of the system. Sanctions cannot be effectively imposed on the large countries by the international institutions, for the large countries can ignore the sanctions.

The effectiveness of the rules in reducing uncertainty depends on the confidence that various countries have in the willingness of the largest countries to abide by the rules. As the confidence declines, so does the value of the rules – even though the rules are maintained.

THE HIERARCHY OF RULES

Sets of monetary rules or agreements can be arranged in a hierarchy according to their comprehensiveness. The rules deal with three general issues – the rates of domestic money supply growth, exchange market intervention, and international credit transfers. The most comprehensive agreement would regulate national monetary policies, especially the rates of growth of the money supply in participating countries. One money supply rule is that changes in the money supply would be determined automatically under this rule by the country's international payments position; if a country had a payments surplus, its money supply would increase and conversely. The national authorities would lack discretion about the rate of growth of their money supplies. Alternatively, the rules might be somewhat less restrictive, and specify that the rate of money supply growth in each country be held within a specific range.

The rates of money supply growth in various countries might be made identical; this approach is consistent with the view that all countries should be treated in the same way. A subsidiary decision involves determining the appropriate rate of money supply growth; this choice determines the distribution of the countries which are likely to incur greater-than-average unemployment or more-rapid-than average inflation. Alternatively the rates for each country might be fixed, although not necessarily at the same levels. Identical rates of money supply growth or fixed, non-identical rates would not ensure that changes in exchange rates would be redundant.

The more extensive the constraints on national discretion in varying the rates of money supply growth, the less constraining the rules on exchange market intervention need be for a consistent system – one not likely to break down. In the extreme case, where the rates of money supply growth are determined automatically by payments surplus and deficit, the rule on exchange market intervention would stipulate that countries follow a fixed exchange rate.

The rules for exchange market intervention and those for international credit transfers are related. The ability of the deficit countries to finance their deficits depends on their ability to borrow, and the obligations of the surplus countries to lend. If the rules provide that the surplus countries must lend to the deficit countries, changes in exchange rates might be avoidable. Unless the rules provide for an unlimited credit transfers, changes in exchange rates are inevitable. The smaller the obligation of the surplus countries to extend credit to the deficit countries, the more likely that the deficit countries will take the initiative in changing the parities. Commitments about the required size of credit transfers have implications about where the initiative for changing the exchange rates is likely to arise.

The less ambitious the rules for constraining national rates of money supply growth, the more likely that payments imbalances will arise, and the greater need for changes in exchange rates; the greater the need for rules about exchange market intervention and credit transfers. Rules about credit transfers may be necessary to induce countries to follow particular exchange rate policies. The rules about exchange market intervention may be designed to reduce the frequency of exchange rate changes, or to speed such changes. In the context of floating rates, the rules may deal with the appropriateness of intervention in various situations. The rules might specify when intervention is appropriate, and when it is prohibited.

Whether rules about credit transfer policies should be 'generous' or 'tight' depends on the prospective economic scenarios – whether inflation or recession seems more likely. The greater the likelihood of inflation, the greater the need for exchange rate changes and the more restrictive the approach toward credit transfers.

Whether the more ambitious approach toward rules – in effect some form of currency unification – is preferable depends on the empirical conclusions on some of the optimum currency area arguments. Even if the data suggest that a move toward a unified currency area is preferable on economic criteria, the political leaders in various countries may not accept the argument because they believe their constituents will not share adequately in the gains. The loss of control over monetary policy may be expensive to national political ambitions. And the less ambitious approach may be more feasible even though less preferable. Even if the ambitious approach is deemed preferable, the problem of endowing the rules with credibility means that the move in this direction must be gradual.

RULES AND MONETARY SYSTEMS

The monetary rules of the three major international financial systems of the last century – the gold standard, the gold exchange standard, and the Bretton Woods system – differ. The characteristic of the gold standard was the interconvertibility of gold and domestic fiat monies. The system developed in response to the risk and return decisions of central banks in various countries. These institutions accepted the convertibility commitments in their own self-interest, and ceased such conversion when other objectives of national policy seemed overriding, as in the exchange crises on the outbreak of war. The system worked as long as countries were willing to follow the money supply rule that made convertibility feasible; the system broke down when they would no longer adhere to the rules. The decisions by various central banks to adhere to the gold standard commitments were made on a decentralised basis; any country could participate by imposing a convertibility requirement on its banks.

The key feature of the gold exchange standard was that various central banks would hold sterling assets and dollar assets part of their reserves, rather than gold. The system was based on the resolutions of several international conferences; no international treaty required countries to hold sterling assets as reserves. Whether the resolutions altered the reserve asset preferences of individual central banks or instead ratified these preferences must remain conjectural.

The key feature of the Articles of Agreement of the International Monetary Fund Bretton Woods was the set of restrictions on the exchange market intervention practices of central banks and their credit transfer commitments; the rules did not deal with the national rates of money supply growth. This agreement was comprehensive and universal, and based on an international treaty. As the Fund membership expanded, the new members accepted the obligations.

That the Fund had formalised voting procedures may give a misleading impression of the group decision process. Formally, the number of votes of each national member depended on its quota. The required majority varied according to the type of decision. However, votes were rarely if ever taken; there was an effective rule of unanimity. While any member could veto a proposed action, only the larger countries used their implicit veto.

The negotiations at Bretton Woods and the subsequent modifications of Fund structure indicate a central features of any international monetary arrangement: the largest economic power must assent to any proposed rules before they can be adopted. Moreover, the largest country is likely to be the source of many of the proposed rules, since it will wish to minimise the costs it anticipates from participating in the arrangement.

International monetary agreements are negotiated by nation-states. These agreements are not an end in themselves, but rather an input to the achievement of other objectives. Nation-states vie for power internationally, just as politicians compete for power in the domestic settings. Power is concerned with attention, fame and prestige, the right to decide, and the distribution of benefits and costs associated with various decisions. The success of politicians in the domestic context partly depends on their ability to satisfy the demands of their constituents for employment and economic rents.

Politicians have a growth cycle – an expanding set of constituencies. As the constituencies become larger, so does the apparent importance of the decisions to be made. While some politicians believe their constituency is more extensive than their country – some have a global following – ultimately the national constituency decides whether the politician will retain power.

These generalisations can be translated into the international monetary context. National leaders view participation in an international monetary agreement in cost-benefit terms. They are reluctant to accept international arrangements which constrain on their domestic policy choices; hence monetary reform negotiations virtually ignore rules limiting rates of money supply growth. The leaders favour arrangements which minimise their susceptibility to imported shocks. They prefer rules which enhances their country's power internationally; they are likely to be wary of extending power to international agencies and their civil servants.

The conflicts among nations that affect their security, commercial relations and fiscal relations also affect their monetary relations. Small countries inevitably want to assert their independence relative to larger nations. Larger countries are reluctant to accept rules which limit their choice of domestic policies.

Because of its economic size and wealth, the United States has been in a unique position throughout the post-war period. Initially, the United States provided both security and economic umbrellas for the recovery of Western Europe and Japan. The essential feature of the monetary rules was that other countries should not discriminate against US imports, although they might apply exchange controls on a generalised basis.

Credit transfers were available, both on a bilateral and multilateral basis. The burden of adjustment to payments imbalances was to be accepted by Western Europe and Japan in exchange for the US burden in carrying the umbrella. The umbrella metaphor became less appropriate in the late 1960s; Western Europe and Japan moved into payments surplus; they extended rather than received international credit. Hence they no longer were willing to carry the burden of adjustment. Whereas Western Europe and Japan felt the United States was exporting a much more severe shock, the United States perceived that the system imposed constraints on its actions that were not imposed on other countries. Paradoxically, the United States worried that it would not be able to devalue successfully whereas Western Europe and Japan sought to force the United States to adopt the exchange rate initiative.

The current environment for monetary reform differs sharply from that of the time of the Bretton Woods negotiations. Then the bargaining position of other countries was so weak that they had to accept the thrust of the US proposals. The United States is no longer in such a dominant position, although it retains effective veto over the proposals of other countries, simply by the decision not to participate. Inevitably the thrust of the rules will be to constrain the shocks that might originate in the United States; at the same time, the rules must offer sufficient advantage to the United States to justify any constraints.

SUMMARY

International monetary reform is concerned with establishing rules about behaviour of national monetary authorities, including money supply growth rates, exchange market intervention practices, and international credit transfers. The rules may constrain the authorities from taking actions they otherwise would take, and compel them to take measures they would not otherwise take. The benefit from the rules is the reduction in uncertainty that participating countries have about the monetary behaviour of other countries; the rules may also affect the distribution among countries of the costs both of payments imbalance and of the measures taken for adjustment to imbalance.

The thrust of rules is to reduce the economic shocks that countries might export to other countries. Thus rules, while not country-specific, are likely to have a much greater impact on the countries that generate substantial shocks than on smaller countries whose economic size limits the severity of shocks they can export. The success of the rules in reducing uncertainty depends on the confidence that participating countries develop in the willingness of other member countries to adhere to the rules when doing so may complicate the achievement of their domestic or other objectives. The more comprehensive the rules, in the sense of the greater the constraints on the national monetary authorities, the less likely the rules will be adhered to. Hence the rules are more likely to reduce small uncertainties than large uncertainties, since members will not adhere by the agreement if the perceived costs are high.

Initially the success of the rules in reducing uncertainty is likely to be small, until credibility is established in the willingness of countries to adhere to the rules. Rules are more likely to succeed when they formalise the accepted modes of monetary behaviour than when they require substantial changes in such behaviour.

Traditionally, rules have dealt with the consequences of differential rates of money supply growth by centring on exchange market intervention policies and international credit transfers; international rules have not been applied to money supply growth rates. Unless rules specify that money supply growth rates be determined by a formula, as under the gold standard, uncertainty is inevitable about whether the deficit or surplus countries should take the initiative in exchange rate adjustment.

Establishing an agreement about monetary arrangements may have significant ramifications about relationships among the participating countries. The rules will have a major impact on the United States as a potential supplier of shocks. The United States must determine the constraints that it will accept on its behaviour before rules are likely to become embodied in a treaty.

2 On the Political Economy of Monetary Integration: A Public Economics Approach

Koichi Hamada*

One of the fundamental problems of international monetary relations is how and to what extent national economies should be incorporated into monetary unions. A main concern of the countries belonging to the European Community is the process of their monetary integration. For the world as a whole, the basic question is whether a subset of countries—or all the nations —should unite into a single currency area with fixed exchange rates or each nation should remain as an independent currency area with floating exchange rates. [1]

There has been considerable research on the benefits and costs of monetary integration. [2] However, the research has been mostly concerned with the global advantages and disadvantages of monetary integration. The analysis of the impact of monetary integration on the incentives for the participating countries has been studied less frequently. Only a few studies have concerned the feasibility of monetary integration in the light of these advantages or disadvantages for each participating country. [3]

The purpose of this paper is to clarify the strategic positions of participating countries. This paper does not propose a plan for monetary union or a world monetary regime; instead, it presents a positive analysis of the political–economic process of monetary integration and the

* I am very much indebted to Professor Charles P. Kindleberger for his constructive suggestions. I am also grateful to Professors Robert Z. Aliber, John Greenwood, Takashi Inoguchi, Kinhide Mushakoji and Kanji Ishii for their helpful comments.

formation of a new world monetary regime.[4] We shall ask the following questions: What kind of monetary integration do the individual national actions based on national benefit and cost calculations lead to? Does the politically feasible monetary union tend to be larger or smaller than the optimal size of monetary union?

There are several reasons why these strategic or political aspects of international monetary relations have been neglected. First, traditional equilibrium theory is more powerful when an individual economic agent has negligible influence on the whole economy. This methodological limitation has probably led economists to avoid the strategic consideration of world monetary relations where large countries have substantial influence. Game theory and the theory of public goods are needed to recognise the strategic interdependence of the participating national economies.

Second, economists, if potentially representative of the interest of a particular country or a group, sound more persuasive when they advocate a programme that appears general, rather than one that speaks to the national interests.

Finally, and more seriously, it is often argued that since economists are laymen in political science, it is dangerous to be involved excessively in political considerations. Too great a concern with political feasibility mean ideal plans may be discarded.[5]

Recent developments in public economics, however, enabled economists to analyse the political economic aspects of economic conflicts. Progress in the application of price theory to institutional arrangements has made it possible to study the incentives to participate in joint actions. Olson developed an analysis of collective action; but the analysis is of limited significance to co-operation in monetary integration because it assumes a predetermined membership.[6] Buchanan developed an economic theory of clubs which allows variable size of membership.[7] Even though his analysis is mainly directed to the problem of efficiency rather than the political structure of conflict, it presents a useful tool to analyse a collective action. I have characterised international monetary relations as a two-stage game.[8] The first stage involves agreeing on a system or a rule, the second playing with economic policies under the given rule. The second stage is analogous to the prisoner's dilemma, while the first stage is analogous to the battle of the sexes. Most of my previous analysis concentrated on the second stage, the strategic interplay of monetary policies. This paper concerns the first stage of agreeing on rules for monetary integration.

The domestic monetary system in a single country rests on the national consensus. This system evolved through a long process in which the seigniorage rights to issue money gradually became concentrated in the hand of a nation state along with the development of banking systems. On the other hand, political power is only partly concentrated in the European Community or other monetary unions. Since no 'world government' exists, the world monetary regime rests directly and explicitly upon the consensus among the nations. This situation has an analogy in international law where the power relationship is still often explicit in resolving conflicts of interests, while in domestic law it is mostly behind the veil of rule and order.

This paper first summarises the discussion on the economic benefits and costs of monetary integration; the public nature of benefits and the individual nature of costs to participating countries are clarified. Then the calculus of participation, a new development in political science, is used to assess the political feasibility of reforms in the world monetary regime.

BENEFITS AND COSTS OF MONETARY INTEGRATION

'Monetary integration' or 'monetary unification' means various degrees of integration. The following components should be distinguished:

(1) The linking of national currencies with fixed parities accompanied by a narrowing or vanishing band, without common reserves and a common central bank: Corden's pseudo-exchange rate union.[9]

(2) The co-ordination of economic policies, in particular monetary policies, to prevent disequilibria in the balance of payments.

(3) Some clearing mechanism for the disequilibrium in the balance of payments using a common reserve asset. The choice asset may be that of a member country, or of a non-member (like the dollar for European Community unity, or a new accounting currency, the SDR's or gold).

(4) Convertibility between currencies for capital transactions as well as current transactions is established.

(5) The public confidence in the irrevocable nature of the fixity of exchange parities is established. This confidence normally emerges only after a substantial transition period during which there is successful maintenance of the *de facto* fixity of exchange parities, or only after some kind of political unification.

(6) Finally, a common currency issued by a single central bank circulates in the area of the monetary union. This leads to *the complete exchange rate union.*

At least one, and usually more than one of these components exists in any monetary union. Monetary integration proceeds by adding new components to those already realised.

Depending upon the degree of monetary integration, the benefits and costs from the monetary union differ. The main benefits from monetary integration include:[10]

(a) The reduction or even the disappearance of the uncertainty in the fluctuations of the exchange rates among national currencies of the members of the union: This benefit is promoted by component (1), but fully realised only after the emergence of component (4).

(*b*) The economy of foreign exchange reserves for the countries as a whole, derived mainly from component (3).

(*c*) The shock-absorbing function of international reserves stressed by Laffer and Mundell,[11] derived from component (1).

(*d*) The increase in prestige from the increased size of the monetary unit, either in the form of increased actual voting power in a monetary institution like the IMF[12] or in the form of increased satisfaction of the political leaders[13] in participating countries. This benefit is normally derived from the increased co-ordination of economic policies, component (2).[14]

(*e*) The saving of the cost of mutual conversion of currencies within the union for trade and travel, which occurs fully in the last stage of monetary integration.[15]

Most of these benefits share non-rivalry in consumption; enjoyment by a member does not reduce the enjoyment of other members. This jointness in consumption is one characteristic of public goods. On the other hand, these benefits accrue mostly to participating member countries, except for the spill-over effects, such as the reduced attention to the relative exchange rates among the member countries by those in non-member countries and the saving of the cost of currency exchange by tourists from non-member countries. Thus most of the benefits have the nature of non-rivalry, one characteristic of public goods, but they do not usually have the nature of non-exclusion, another characteristic of public goods.[16]

The most important of these benefits seem to be (*a*) and (*e*), which are closely associated with the functions of money as the unit of account, the medium of exchange and store of value. Thus more basically, their public goods nature stems from the nature of money. Money economises the cost of information required for transactions and secures a stable bundle of goods with less cost.[17] As the property of information in general, the use of money has intrinsic externality. Each individual chooses by himself whether to hold money and how much; the choice of an asset as money is a social choice. Once a monetary system is built, once an asset is chosen as its money by a society, or once a mutual confidence emerges in the use of a particular commodity or currency as the common money, then the benefit from this public (implicit) consensus becomes a public good.

One cost of joining a monetary union is that the monetary independence of national economies becomes limited, particularly when international capital mobility is high. Therefore, the attainment of the nationally desired level of unemployment and price levels is sacrificed. The floating exchange rate system gives national economies the opportunity to take a maxi–min strategy in the interplay of monetary policies.[18] By joining a monetary union, a country gives up this maxi–min position; it must rely on the outcome of mutual consensus of the policy co-ordination. Since countries differ in their position of the

Phillips curves, in their rates of productivity growth, and in their preferences in the choice between unemployment and inflation, policy co-ordination does not mean that most of the participating countries may not have to sacrifice attainment of their policy objectives.

In contrast to the benefits that are mostly collective and international, the costs of monetary integration are mostly national. The sacrifice made when a country joins a monetary union is mostly national. This contrast between benefits and costs of monetary integration is a crucial factor that makes it feasible to apply the calculus of participation to the problem of monetary integration.

The costs can be public if the non-linearity of the Phillips curve means the aggregate trade-off between inflation and unemployment is less favourable after a monetary union than before.[19] The size of this negative effect of monetary integration is an empirical question. The following analysis assumes that the public-goods nature dominates the negative effects.

The cost-benefit pay-off to a participating country changes over time. At first, the costs of the sacrifice of domestic economic objectives and an independent monetary policy are large. Capital market integration means that the financing of deficits becomes easier, so adjustment costs are smaller. In contrast, some of the common benefits can be enjoyed only at a later stage of monetary integration.

For example, the saving of the cost for conversion of different currencies occurs only after complete exchange rate union is attained. The benefit from the stability of the exchange rate occurs when confidence in the fixity of parities is established. Therefore the benefit can be attained only in the long run, and uncertainty remains whether the benefits will be realised while costs of sacrificing independent monetary policy actually take place.

The costs are concrete in the form of higher rates of inflation or unemployment while most of the benefits may seem vague and abstract. It is hard, at the same time, to neglect completely the benefit of a single currency in a well-integrated economy. Suppose the United States were divided into two regions, each with its own monetary authority. The post-transition disadvantages of two monetary systems express the upper limit of the possible advantages from a complete monetary union.

The openness of a participating country is an important element in deciding the magnitude of cost and benefits it receives from monetary integration. If a country is open, import and export flows are large relative to domestic transactions. Then the cost of adjusting its employment level to cope with the balance of payments is small.[20] If it is closed, the cost is large. Moreover, the benefit from common improvement in trade environment, from stability and predictability of exchange rates or the saving of costs of frequent currency conversion, is larger the more open a country. The degree of economic integration plays a crucial role; the more integrated are the international markets for goods and factors, the more open a country tends to be. Therefore the integration of the goods and factors market strengthens the feasibility of monetary integration by increasing benefits and decreasing costs.

THE CALCULUS OF PARTICIPATION

Recent developments in the theory of participation are an application of tools of public economics to political science. The tool of economic analysis enables political science to acquire the theoretical basis for associating group behaviour with individual rationality. The application of the tools developed in economics to politics requires careful evaluation. However, recent developments in political science can clarify the analysis of economic conflicts.

The unit of individual decision, namely the individual agent or player in the international conflict, should be specified. The nation state is the natural unit of decision-making, and can be regarded as the individual agent. To define the 'national interest' is hard. A country is indeed an economic as well as a political unit, and a unit of international negotiation. But individuals in the same nation do not necessarily share common benefits and costs. The interests of exporters and of importers differ, so do the interests of producers and of consumers, and of the rich and of the poor. Moreover, the interest of savers may conflict with that of exporters over the value of the exchange rate.

The rational theory of participation[21] indicates that an individual decision unit decides to participate in a collective action if the anticipated benefit is larger than the cost. The rational decision for a country contemplating membership in a monetary union is to join if the benefits from participation, such as the use of common currency, reduction in uncertainty and the increase in the bargaining power as a group, are larger than the costs, such as the sacrifice of independent monetary policy and the wider variation in the unemployment rate.

When there exists public good character in the collective benefit, however, the amount of collective action may be smaller than optimal, where optimality is judged by the Paretian standard. Olson developed the analogy of the theory of public goods to the collective action.[22] Suppose there is a single public good whose benefits are commonly shared by participating agents. The rational decision by an individual agent is to equate the marginal private benefit from the public good to the marginal cost of supplying a unit of public goods. However, the optimal social measure is to equate the marginal cost to the *social* benefit that is the sum of individual benefits. Thus the supply of public goods may be less than optimal because the individual decision unit does not take account of the external effect upon other decision units. Therefore even when there is a consensus on the objective of a collective action, the amount produced may be too small. The interesting testable hypothesis about the group behaviour is that the behaviour of a large group is different from that of a small group; the shortfall in supply is more likely, the larger the group, because the free-rider problem intrinsic in the supply of public goods without the possibility of exclusion is more acute if the members share the common benefit only to a small degree. A second hypothesis is that the decision unit that receives a relatively large portion of the benefit of public goods is likely to bear more than a proportional burden of the cost. In other words, if each participant behaves rationally according to the private benefit-cost calculation, the small decision unit can exploit the large one.[23]

One criticism of this theory of collective action is the neglect of the role of political entrepreneurship of leadership to integrate the individual benefits to a collective action.[24,25] If an agent with political entrepreneurship can persuade the group of the effectiveness of collective action in spite of the apparent excess of individual cost over individual benefit, then the proper amount of collective goods may be supplied and some leadership surplus is left to the agent.

The analysis assumes the passive behaviours of each participant, and accordingly neglects the leader – follower relationship.[26] If a participant picks the most profitable point on the opponent's reaction curve, then he behaves as a leader, so he can enjoy the leadership or the exploitation solution. To avoid complication due to the two meanings of the word 'leadership', this case is called 'exploitation', while leadership in the sense of political entrepreneurship is 'political entrepreneurship'.

Finally, the analysis is limited by the assumption that the size of a collective group is given and that the collective benefit is not exclusive. Under these assumptions, in a group with a given number of participants, the collective benefit is enjoyed by each participant regardless of his willingness to pay.

An economic theory of clubs with variable size of the group, and with possible exclusion of the collective benefits against the non-members, has been developed.[27] Collective goods are supplied optimally provided that appropriate charges are imposed on the use of the service, and the service of the collective goods can be exclusively supplied to the members of the group.

This approach has more relevance to monetary integration, since the benefit from integration is public in that its enjoyment by a particular member does not diminish the enjoyment of others. But, at the same time, most of the benefits are almost exclusively enjoyed by the countries participating in the monetary union.[28] There exists the non-rivalry in the consumption of the service of a monetary union, but not the non-exclusiveness. Another characteristic of participation is that the decision to join the monetary union is discrete. This decision is based on agreement concerning the process of the monetary integration, and the distribution of adjustment burdens. The process of agreeing on monetary integration can be modelled as follows.

The choice for the countries deciding whether to participate is determined by the comparison of the gains from joining in a union with the costs, an all-or-nothing choice as formulated in Appendix part II. The conclusion is straightforward; if there are externalities in increasing the size of membership, the national decision based on rational calculation may lead to a smaller currency area than optimal even if the participating country is fully aware of costs and benefits. The national decision depends on the private benefit-cost calculation, while the public benefit to the group as a whole includes the gains to the countries that are already joining the union.

MONETARY INTEGRATION IN HISTORICAL PERSPECTIVE

Several examples of monetary integration are evident in the formation of nation states. The developments of monetary and currency unification in Germany, Italy and Japan involved uniting monies issued by local provinces into single national currencies.[29] In Germany[30] economic unification had been in progress when the second Reich was founded in 1871. The Zollverein (customs union) led by Prussia was a significant step towards economic unification because commerce among the member states became free from custom barriers. Numerous currencies were issued by local authorities. Accordingly trade among states relied on the use of the foreign money. People had to convert currencies. Exchange rates changed frequently. Attempts were made to fix the parities among local monies. The southern states agreed to fix the parities among their currencies by the München Convention of 1837. This led to the Dresden Convention; a fixed relation was established between the thaler of northern states and the florin of southern states on the basis of the Cologne mark of fine silver. Prussia was the political entrepreneur in promoting monetary integration.

There was, however, no common currency. When Germany became a nation state in 1871, it was still divided into seven separate currency areas, based on silver. There were thirty-three banks of issue totally unconnected with each other and under different rules and regulations. When the new Reich was established, the states agreed on the relative values of their respective currencies. At the same time, the Reich established a unified currency on the gold standard. In 1871 the mark was adopted as a currency unit. Two years later, the gold standard was established by law; the use of silver was reduced to small coins. In 1875 the Prussian Bank, one of the thirty-three banks of issue, was reorganised as the Reichsbank. Not until 1935 was the right of issue concentrated in the Reichsbank.[31]

In Italy[32] the political unification led by the Kingdom of Sardinia came so suddenly that economic as well as monetary unification was not planned prior to 1861. Upon political unification, the tariffs of Sardinia were extended to the entire nation, creating a customs union. The monetary situation was chaotic; two different liras, that of Piedmont and of Tuscany, the Austrian florin, the ducat of the Sicilies, and the *scudo romano* of the Papal States circulated simultaneously. To unify the coinage the Piedmont lira, based on the decimal system, was chosen as the standard currency. Piedmont played the role of political entrepreneur. In 1865 when Italy joined the Latin Monetary Union, the ratio of silver to gold was fixed as $15\frac{1}{2}$ to one, although the existence of a large amount of irredeemable notes prevented Italy from completely joining the union.

The unification of paper currency was more difficult. Banks did not want to give up their seigniorage rights. The Sardinian National Bank grew far more rapidly than any other and absorbed two Tuscan banks of issue by merger to become the Bank of Italy in 1893. The Bank of Italy then became the *de facto* central bank; it became a central bank *de jure* in 1926.[33]

In the Edo period of Japan, before the Meiji Restoration of 1868, the central (Tokugawa) feudal government had almost fully concentrated political power. Agricultural labour was not movable from one local district (Han) to another. The trade of commodities by authorised merchants was free without customs barriers between local districts. The right to issue coins was concentrated in the central (Tokugawa) feudal government. The coinage system was on the bimetallic standard; three types of coin, gold, silver and copper (later occasionally substituted by iron) circulated, gold being currency by tail, silver currency by weight (later transformed to by tail) and copper for auxiliary use.

The right to issue notes for local circulation (*Hansatsu*) was left to feudal lords of local provinces, subject to the authorisation of the central government. In 1661 the first feudal note was issued. Local notes were issued, mostly to ease the financial difficulty of local feudal lords, Han (clans), and occasionally to provide a sufficient amount of medium of exchange during the periods when deflationary coinage policies were taken by the central government. In 1871, 244 provinces were issuing nearly 1700 kinds of local notes. This is probably the largest number of local issuing agents within a national border.[34] The outstanding local notes amounted to more than 90 million Ryo, as compared to the outstanding coinage of 130 million Ryo.

After the Meiji[35] restoration, the central government introduced the decimal system, and the yen became the new unit of currency. From 1872 to 1879, the new government redeemed these local notes. Newly established national banks were given the right to issue notes. After an inflationary period, due to the excessive issue of inconvertible bank notes and a subsequent deflation, the Bank of Japan was chartered as the sole issuing bank in 1882.

There were several attempts at monetary integration even across national borders in the nineteenth century. In 1857 Bruck was instrumental in forming the monetary union to fix parities between the north and the south states in the Zollverein, and between them and the Austrian monetary system (Vienna Convention). He tried to fix the exchange parity between the currencies of these areas, based upon the metric pound (Zollpfund), though not to create a single currency in all the Zollverein states and in the Habsburg Empire. This effort did not succeed, because the Austrian government did not follow the agreement of 1857 but retained its fluctuating paper money. Then the monetary union came to an end with the Seven Weeks War. The provisions, however, remained alive in the Zollverein, and paved the way for genuine currency unification in the new Reich.[36]

The Latin Monetary Union was the most notable attempt for monetary unification in the nineteenth century.[37] Belgium, Switzerland and Italy adopted the monetary system of France that had originated in 1803. Some joint circulation of currencies had already taken place before the Union was formalised. The discovery of gold in Australia and California caused a wide variation due to the changing legislation in different countries. Moreover, silver coins of lower quality minted in Italy and Switzerland flowed into Belgium and France. Therefore, in 1865 Belgium took the initiative to create a union on the franc standard.

The unit of denominations of currencies in the member countries in the Latin Monetary Union – France, Belgium, Switzerland and Italy – was adjusted to conform to the French franc. Each member could issue standard coins of 100, 50, 20, 10 and 5 francs in gold, and 5 francs in silver; these coins were to circulate freely throughout the union. In addition, each member could mint subsidiary coins in limited amounts. The public offices in the member countries were required to accept limited amounts of these coins in payment. The union was open to any country; only Greece joined. Other countries, including Austria, Spain, Sweden, the Papal states, and the Balkan states, introduced the franc standard without joining the union.

The Latin Monetary Union was formed under the dominating influence of France in an attempt to sustain the bimetallic standard. In the 1870s, however, the gold standard was a worldwide tide, accompanied by the rapid depreciation of silver. This was probably the reason why many countries refrained from joining the Union. The Union was forced to depart from its bimetallic policy because the free coinage of silver in France and Belgium induced a flood of silver inflows. The Union limited the coinage of silver in 1874, and discontinued it in 1878, thus transforming bimetallism into a 'limping gold standard'.

Another difficulty concerned the subsidiary currencies in Italy and Greece, both of which had irredeemable paper money, and coined Union token money. When the paper money depreciated, subsidiary currencies were exported. In 1878 the Italian small currency ceased to be legal tender in the other countries, and this provision was extended to Greek token money in 1908. On the outbreak of the First World War, member countries introduced a paper standard, leading to the actual breakdown of the Union. It was formally dissolved in 1925 when Belgium withdrew.

Another, and quite successful, monetary union was the Scandinavian Monetary Union. In addition to the growing sympathy among the Scandinavian nations, there had been actual joint circulation of currencies in several border regions. The union was established between Sweden and Denmark in 1873, and joined by Norway in 1875. The krone was the common unit. At first, joint circulation was virtually limited to coins; in 1894, however, the note banks of Norway and Sweden agreed to accept one another's notes at par, and in 1900 Denmark joined this agreement. The banks of the member countries opened accounts for each other. Cheques could be drawn on these accounts; but credit balances earned no interest. Monetary integration proceeded to the point that bank notes as well as token money circulated at par, cheques could be liquidated at par, and the quotation of exchange rates was discontinued.[38]

After 1905 joint circulation of drafts was modified so that the commissions were changed. However, joint circulation of bank notes was successfully carried out until the First World War. With the war the redemption of bank notes was suspended and the Union ended.[39]

One observation from these historical cases is that political integration preceded complete monetary integration, while economic integration sometimes preceded and sometimes followed political integration. In Germany customs union preceded political integration; in Italy political integration occurred before the free movements of goods and factors were attained. In Japan, free trade had been going on when the Meiji government completely centralised political power, but free movement of labour occurred only after the Meiji Restoration. In Germany, some attempts to fix the parities between local currencies were effective even without political integration, but they did not last long unless actual political integration consolidated the fixity of parities by the unification of currency.[40]

Monetary unions in the form of exchange rate unions across national borders did not last long because political integration did not consolidate them. These unions were effective at least in the short run, only if there was political leadership of a dominant country, only if members were few, and only if there was extensive economic integration.

The existence of a metal money, or metal monies, was instrumental in maintaining confidence in the exchange rate union. The irredeemable paper money in Italy and Greece created difficulty in the Latin Monetary Union. On the other hand, adherance to the gold standard helped the Scandinavian Monetary Union.

These findings can be related to the calculus of participation. The benefits from monetary integration are similar to those from public goods, while the costs are directly borne by individual participants. Moreover, the benefits can be enjoyed only when strong confidence is attained in the fixed parities or when a single currency is circulated. Therefore, metallic content of currencies was important to create confidence in the exchange rate union, and political integration was necessary to sustain the confidence for a long period.

These historical experiences suggest the difficulty in keeping two kinds of money circulating at the same time. Gresham's Law was always working; the currency with relatively higher quality was either hoarded or exported, leaving the currency with lower quality flooding in the union. Moreover, wherever there were two kinds of money, conflicts of interest often occurred. In the Latin Monetary Union France had a vested interest in using silver as a standard currency; in the Edo period of Japan, the conflict over the metallic content of gold and silver coins was created between merchants around Tokyo where gold was more popular and those around Osaka where silver more popular.

The cost conceived by participating members of a monetary union in the nineteenth century involved the sacrifice of seigniorage, not the cost of policy adjustments. The cost due to the underutilisation of resources in order to correct the disequilibrium in the balance of payments was hardly observed before the great depression.[41]

These historical experiences suggest that the relationship between economic and political factors depends on the performance of monetary unification.They remind us of the long debate on the state theory of money.[42] The chartal theory of money states that money circulates because it is a legal tender. This theory in its purest form should be refuted by the effectiveness of Gresham's Law. But at the same time, in such cases as Italy and the Zollverein, political leadership in the sense of entrepreneurship functioned as a catalyst in realising the public good character of money. It does not seem to be operationally meaningful to ask whether economic factors or political factors dominate the emergence of common money. But more analysis is needed to clarify the interaction of economic and political factors in the creation of a currency area.

CONCLUDING REMARKS

The political – economic analysis and historical sketches of monetary integration in the last century give several lessons for the current process of monetary integration in the European Community and more generally for the world monetary reform. It is difficult to achieve, and even more difficult to sustain, a monetary union without political unification. If the European Community moves forward to political integration, then the promotion of monetary integration can be an important step towards building the community.

The benefits from monetary integration have the nature of public goods, not so much because of their non-exclusiveness as because of their non-rivalry in consumption. On the other hand, most of the costs from monetary integration have the nature of private goods (or bads). That is, each nation bears the costs directly and individually.

Another important characteristic of monetary integration, particularly that of the European Community, is the difference in the time profile of benefits and costs. At present, and in the short run, the benefits seem mostly political: increased prestige and negotiating power by the enlarged scale of the decision unit of Europe as a whole. In other words, benefits are abstract and political (or psychological) rather than concrete and economic. In the short run, the costs from joining a (pseudo) exchange rate union are concrete and definite. They are mostly economic except for some political or psychological loss from giving up the monetary sovereignity. The loss to individual countries is mainly the sacrifice of the attainment of suitable employment and price levels.[43]

Economic benefits from participating in a monetary integration, if they exist, are realised only in the long run. They are attained only after the pseudo exchange rate union becomes, or comes close to a complete exchange rate union. Benefits of exchange stability are generated only after the public confidence in the irrevocable fixity of exchange rate emerges, and those of the saving of exchange transactions are realised eventually after a single currency circulates in the whole community. The maintenance of public confidence is hard without a metallic standard, and the attainment of the circulation of a single currency is even harder in the absence of political integration.

Thus many economists are dubious about the prospect of the monetary integration in the European Community. The immediate political effect from the increased prestige of Europe as a whole seems to be the main driving force for actual negotiators.

One analytical proposition we have obtained from the calculus of participation is that if the benefits from a joint action have the property of non-rivalry in consumption, then the isolated, individual, rational decision will make the realised size of the union smaller than optimal. This simple proposition, of course, needs several reservations, if it is applied to the actual process of monetary integration in Europe.

First, the conclusion is reversed if the public bads character of costs dominates the public goods character of benefits. In some situations, the inclusion of an additional member may hurt the common benefits of monetary integration due to the non-linearity of the Phillips curve.[44] At the outset of monetary union, this public bads effect could become significant. However, in the later stage of monetary integration as transaction and information costs are economised, the public goods character will dominate.

The different time patterns of benefits and costs should be recognised. The choice is not between actual costs and benefits, but between the expected and discounted value of the streams of future costs and benefits. The time preference, the attitude towards risk and the subjective evaluation by participating countries concerning the probability of the evolution of the union in the future plays a crucial role.

If some side payments are feasible – for example, in the form of a concession in agricultural policies in favour of a new member – then the mutual negotiation with the perfect understanding of benefits and costs may lead to the optimal configuration of the size of the union.

Finally, the calculus of participation is applicable only on the assumption that the participants have correct information on the benefits and the costs that accrue to them from joint action. The question of the relative size of an actual union to the optimal size can be answered only if this assumption is satisfied. There are two difficulties; one is whether politicians are fully aware of economic as well as political benefits-costs from monetary integration. The other difficulty is whether they represent some consensus of the preference of the public, namely, some weighted average of the interests of people.

The benefits of irrevocably fixed exchange rates, and all the more the benefits of a unified currency, are recognised. At the same time, however, we cannot neglect the fact that the benefits are attainable only in the long run, after public confidence is generated in the fixity of parities or after political integration progresses far enough to sustain a single currency. The recent difficulty in the European Community in keeping the same exchange rates with the dollar is a symptom of the substantial magnitude of immediate economic loss due to the sacrifice of a short-run domestic objectives.

Another important question concerns how monetary policies will be co-ordinated once an exchange rate union becomes effective. The strategic analysis developed in the context of two participants[45] can be generalised to a many-country case along the lines of the public goods analysis.[46] Suppose the international common price level depends on the weighted average of the rates of monetary expansion in excess of real growth by the participating countries, and the real gain or loss of a country, that is, the negative of the balance of payments, depends on the difference of the rate of (excess) monetary expansion and their weighted average,[47] then isolated, rational choices by participating countries will lead to the situation more inflationary than the Pareto optimal configuration. In other words, the Cournot solution, on the assumption that each country behaves passively given the other's behaviour constant, lies on the inflationary side of the contract surface.

The frame of reference developed in this chapter is applicable also in the international monetary reform. The gold standard before the First World War was a loose exchange rate union. The Tripartite agreement to the formation of the International Monetary Fund was an endeavour to create the service of public goods from the fixity of exchange rates. Recent breakdown of the Bretton Woods regime suggests that the exchange-rate union without a unified world political authority is rather difficult. Costs are immediate; benefits are uncertain and depend on such precarious factors as public confidence in the fixity of parities.

Suppose the world is united by an irrevocable currency union, or even by a uniform currency. The public gain is quite large; the cost of information in exchanges is smaller, people can travel without worrying about exchanges of different currencies. This gain, however, is realised only at the last moment, that is, only after people believe firmly in the fixity of exchange rates, or only after worldwide political unification proceeds so that a common currency can be circulated all over the world. Yet the costs are immediate and concrete; the number of participants are too large; many countries lack the openness large enough to reduce the cost of adjustments. The Bretton Woods regime collapsed because of the immediate costs of policy adjustments. The United States does not seem likely to recover in the near future the leadership that she had in the last two decades. Therefore, we regret to conclude that a single currency area for the whole world is still an ideal dream.

APPENDIX I

Analytical Formulation of the Calculus of Participation

I. Suppose there are N countries ($j = 1, 2, \ldots, N$). Let C_j and X be the contribution of j'th country and the supply of collective good. Let us assume that X is produced by the following production relationship:

$$X = F\left(\sum_{j=1}^{N} C_j\right) \qquad F' > 0, \quad F'' < 0.$$

The satisfaction level of j'th participant is

$$U^j(X, C_j), \qquad U_1^j > 0, \quad U_2^j < 0; \quad U_{11}^j < 0, \quad U_{22}^j < 0.$$

Then the analysis of Olson and Zeckhauser can be reformulated as follows:
The individual rational behaviour leads to

$$U_1^j F' + U_2^j \leqq 0, \qquad C_j = 0 \text{ if strict inequality holds.} \qquad (1)$$

On the other hand, in order to obtain the Pareto optimal configuration we have to maximise $\sum\limits_{j=1}^{N} \beta^j U^j(X, C_j)$, where β^js are the Lagrange multipliers indicating the weight of evaluation, leading to

$$\sum_{j=1}^{N} \beta^j U_1^j F' + \beta^j U_2^j \leqq 0, \qquad C_j = 0 \text{ if strict inequality holds.}$$

$$(2)$$

Multiplying (1) by β_j and summing with respect to j

$$\sum_{j=1}^{N} \beta^j U_1^j F' + \sum \beta^j U_2^j \leqq 0 \tag{3}$$

Since $U_{11}^j < 0$ $F'' < 0$, the level of public good X corresponding to (2) is larger than that corresponding to (3). Therefore, we can see that public good is produced short of the optimal, if each participant behaves according to individual rationality. It is also clear from (2) and (3) that the shortage of collective good is more serious in a group with many participants than in a group with few participants.

Moreover, if we assume in addition that the marginal rate of substitution between collective good and individual sacrifice, i.e. $-U_1^j / U_2^j$ is smaller for a country whose relative size is smaller, then we can deduce from (1) that a participant whose relative size is large shares the burden more than proportionately to her relative size. See Olson and Zeckhauser, 'An Economic Theory of Alliances', op. cit., and Olson, 'The Logic of Collective Action', loc. cit., pp. 23 ff.

II. In the above analysis the size of the group is predetermined as N. Here let us relax the assumption, so that a subgroup of countries creates a monetary union. Let I_j be the index of participation such that

$$I_j = 1 \qquad \text{if } j\text{th country is in the union}$$
$$= 0 \qquad \text{if } j\text{th country is not in the union.}$$

Also define the set of j already participating in the union as J^+ such that

$$J^+ = \{j/I_j = 1\}.$$

Let $\lambda_j \left(\sum\limits_{j=1}^{N} \lambda_j = 1 \right)$ be the relative size of country j. Assume that the collective benefit is the function of the relative size of the monetary union. Let C_j be the cost of joining the union to country j. Then the individual rational choice for country j outside the monetary union is given by the rule.

If $\qquad U^j(F(\sum\limits_{i \varepsilon \{J^+ + j\}} \lambda_i),\ C_j) > U^j(0, 0), \quad$ then join

$\qquad\qquad\qquad\qquad\qquad\quad < \qquad\qquad$, then not join.

However, for the international community as a whole, the criterion for country j to join the union is

$$\sum_{i\varepsilon J^+} \beta^i \left\{ U^i(F(\sum_{i\varepsilon\{J^++j\}} \lambda_i),\ C_i) - U^i(F(\sum_{i\varepsilon J^+}\lambda_i),\ C_i) \right\}$$

$$+ \beta^j \left[U^j(F(\sum_{i\varepsilon\{J^++j\}} \lambda_i),\ C_j) - U^j(0,0) \right] > 0.$$

There the term expressing the sum of braces is positive if there exist external economies in the monetary union. Therefore, if the common benefits of a monetary union increase with its size, then the individual rational choices tend to form a smaller monetary union than optimal.

NOTES

1. The terms monetary union or integration are used in a general sense to include both loose associations of national economies, connected by fixed exchange rates with or without co-ordination of monetary policies, as well as perfectly united national economies using a common currency.

2. The most recent include W. M. Corden, *Monetary Integration*, Essays in International Finance, no. 93, Princeton (1972); J. C. Ingram, *The Case for European Monetary Integration*, Essays in International Finance, no. 98, Princeton (1973), and H. G. Johnson and A. K. Swoboda (eds) *The Economics of Common Currencies*, Allen & Unwin, London (1973).

3. Among these exceptions are J. S. Nye, 'The Political Context', in Johnson and Swoboda (eds) *The Economics of Common Currencies*, H. G. Johnson, 'Political Economy: Aspects of International Monetary Reform', *Journal of International Economics*, vol. 2 (1972). Related topics are discussed in R. N. Cooper, *The Economics of Interdependence*, McGraw-Hill, New York (1968), C. K. Kindleberger, *Power and Money*, Basic Books, New York (1970) and R. Z. Aliber, *National Preferences and the Scope for International Monetary Reform*, Essays in International Finance, no. 101 (1973).

4. The political economy aspects of economic integration in general are discussed in R. N. Cooper, 'Worldwide vs Regional Integration: Is there an Optimal Size of the Integrated Area?', a paper presented at the 4th World Congress of the International Economic Association (Aug 1974).

5. See the concluding remark of L. B. Yeager, *International Monetary Mechanism*, Holt, Rinehart & Winston, New York (1968).

6. M. Olson Jr, 'The Logic of Collective Action: Public Goods and Theory of Groups', *Harvard Economic Studies*, vol. 124, Cambridge (1965).

7. J. M. Buchanan, 'An Economic Theory of Clubs', *Economica*, vol. 32.

8. K. Hamada, 'Alternative Exchange Rate Systems and the Interdependence of Monetary Policies', in R. Z. Aliber (ed.) *National Monetary Policies and the International Financial System*, University of Chicago Press (1974).

9. Corden, op. cit.

10. For the benefits and costs of monetary integration see Robert Z. Aliber, 'Uncertainty, Currency Areas and the Exchange Rate System' (Nov 1972) pp. 432–41. Also for

the costs, Corden, op. cit., and for some of the benefits, Ingram, *The Case for European Monetary Integration*, op. cit.

11. A. B. Laffer, 'Two Arguments for Fixed Rates', and R. A. Mundell, 'Uncommon Arguments for Common Currencies', in H. G. Johnson and A. K. Swoboda (eds) *The Economics of Common Currencies*, Allen & Unwin, London (1973). See also critical remarks by Bela Balassa.

12. The chance of becoming the pivot of decision measured by the Shapley value, or by power index, will definitely increase. For the discussion of the Shapley value and related power index, see W. H. Riker and P. S. Ordeshook, *An Introduction to Positive Political Theory*, Prentice-Hall, N.J. (1973) ch. 6.

13. The increased satisfaction of political leaders or central bankers does not necessarily mean the increased satisfaction of consumers.

14. If the world takes the system of fixed exchange rate then the bargaining position in the game consisting of the interplay of monetary policies increases. See Hamada, op. cit.

15. Early writers emphasised this benefit of monetary integration. See T. Guggenheim, 'Some Early Views on Monetary Integration', in Johnson and Swoboda (eds) *The Economics of Common Currencies*, op. cit.

16. There are two facets in the public nature of some benefits such as (*a*) and (*e*). For they have non-rivalry character not only between participating countries, but also between individuals belonging to these countries.

17. K. Burnner and A. H. Meltzer, 'The Use of Money: Money in the Theory of an Exchange Economy', *American Economic Review*, vol. 61 (1971) pp. 784–805.

18. Hamada, op. cit.

19. J. Marcus Fleming, 'On the Exchange Rate Unification', *Economic Journal*, vol. 81. (Sep 1971) pp. 467–88.

20. R. I. McKinnon, 'Optimal Currency Areas', *The American Economic Review* (Sep 1963) vol. 53, no. 4, pp. 717–25.

21. W. H. Riker and P. C. Ordeshook, *An Introduction to Positive Political Theory*, ch. 3.

22. M. Olson Jr, 'The Logic of Collective Action', loc. cit., and also Mancur Olson and Richard Zeckhauser, 'An Economic Theory of Alliances', *Review of Economics and Statistics*, vol. 43 (Aug 1966) pp. 266–79.

23. See Appendix part I.

24. R. E. Wagner, 'Pressure Groups and Political Entrepreneurs: A Review Article', *Papers on Non-Market Decision Making*, vol. 1 (1966) pp. 161–70.

25. N. Frohlich, J. A. Oppenheimer and O. R. Young, *Political Leadership and Collective Goods*, Princeton, N. J. (1971).

26. Hamada, op. cit.

27. J. M. Buchanan, 'An Economic Theory of Clubs', op. cit.

28. The spill-over effect upon non-members discussed above is an exception.

29. Similar approach was taken in H. R. Kramer, 'Experience with Historical Monetary Unions', in H. Giersch (ed.) *Integration durch Wahrungsunion*, Institute fur Weltwirtsschaft an der Universitat Kiel, Mohr, Tübingen (1971).

30. G. Stolper, *The German Economy: 1870 to the Present* (translated by T. Stolper), Harcourt, Brace & World (1967): W. O. Henderson, *The Zollverein*, Cambridge University Press (1939).

31. See Stolper, op. cit., pp. 14–19.

32. S. B. Clough, *The Economic History of Modern Italy*, Columbia University Press, N.Y. (1964).

33. Clough, op. cit., pp. 39–42.

34. Y. Sakudo, *Kinsei Nihon Kaheishi* (Monetary History of Modern Japan), Kobundo, Tokyo (1968).

35. K. Yamaguchi *Hansatsu Shi Kenkyu Josetsu* (Towards the History of Local Notes), Bank of Japan (1966).

36. Henderson, op. cit., pp. 246–52.

37. See, for details, H. P. Willis, *A History of the Latin Monetary Union: A Study of*

International Monetary Action, University of Chicago Press (1901): see also Krämer, op. cit., A. Nielsen, 'Monetary Union', *Encyclopedia of Social Science*, vol. X, New York (1933).
38. Nielsen, op. cit., p. 598; Krämer, op. cit.
39. Some provisions were still active after the First World War. See Nielsen, op. cit.
40. For a similar conclusion, see Kråmer, op. cit.
41. For the neglect of adjustment cost, and some exception to this see, T. Guggenheim, op. cit., p. 97.
42. H. S. Ellis, *German Monetary Theory* 1905–1933, Harvard University Press (1934) ch. 2.
43. The cost of aggregation of non-linear Phillips curves is also of the short-run character.
44. Marcus Fleming, op. cit.
45. Hamada, op. cit.
46. Olson, op. cit.
47. H. G. Johnson, 'The Monetary Approach to Balance of Payments Theory', *Journal of Financial and Quantitative Analysis* (Mar 1972). The statement in the text assumes the unitary elasticity of the demand for money. But it can be generalised easily to the case of non-unitary elasticity.

3 Current Account Targets and Managed Floating

Anne O. Krueger*

The dilemmas confronting policy-oriented economists are always difficult, especially when the policy deemed optimal is also judged politically infeasible. Such was the case in the 1960s: floating exchange rates were regarded as desirable but out of the question. Proposals for reform of the system therefore centred upon second-best approximations to flexible exchange rates, such as widened bands and crawling pegs, though the participants in the discussion were usually careful to acknowledge their commitment to flexible rates.

Because the exchange rate system adopted by most countries *was* a fixed rate system, detailed analysis of the workings of various aspects of the pegged rate system in practice was undertaken. By contrast, discussion of flexible rates was much more limited: most economists implicitly meant market-determined rates in a world in which governments were indifferent to the actual rate, so that exchange rates and payments positions would no longer be a policy concern.[1]

The events of the early 1970s, and the abandonment of fixed rates by major trading countries, were surprises for those who had long advocated flexible exchange rates. However, the same sort of careful analysis is required for the current system as was made of the earlier, fixed rate system.

This paper assesses the extent to which the managed floating rate system represents an improvement over the fixed-rate, discrete-alterations system of the 1960s. The current exchange rate system is not the neat, simple, supply-and-demand-determined system of the classroom. Governments are far from indifferent to the path of their exchange

* This paper benefited greatly from the comments of the participants at Wingspread. Needless to say, not all of them agree with the conclusions expressed herein.

rates and to the size and composition of their balance of payments. That they intervene in the foreign exchange market in an effort to attain particular targets gives rise to potential difficulties in a number of dimensions.

The first section provides an analysis of the 'adjustable-peg, dollar-standard' (APDS) system of the 1960s. The second section concerns reconciliation of conflicting targets under a floating rate system. The final section provides an assessment of the present, dirty-floating system contrasted with the earlier APDS system.

I

After the incredible number of pages of discussion and diagnosis of the maladies of the international monetary system pre-1971, it seems presumptuous to return for yet another look. However, the trouble with the diagnoses so far provided is that there were too many problems with the old system. There was the crisis problem, the liquidity problem, the adjustment problem, the key-currency problem, the problem of the American balance of payments, the gold problem, and so on. One could take any one of these problems as a central theme, and show the difficulties the APDS was likely to encounter.

On superficial examination, it might appear that the abandonment of APDS has solved the particular problems of the international monetary system. Yet, in a sense, that verdict overlooks the fact that the APDS permitted unprecedented liberalisation and expansion of world trade and payments, at least among developed countries. There is an apparent paradox: how could a system that performed so well have had so many fatal flaws?

One way of interpreting the experience within a unifying framework is to think of a stable international monetary system as one in which two conditions are satisfied: (1) within a neighbourhood of the equilibrium of domestic real output levels, price levels, exchange rates, and balance of payments positions, a small improvement in the balance of payments position of any country at given exchange rates will result in expansionary monetary and/or fiscal policy to reattain a preferred point in terms of its price level, output and employment (and exchange rate?) preferences, while conversely, a small deterioration will result in contractionary monetary and fiscal policy; (2) an increase in the world price level, in terms of the numéraire commodity, does not lead to a proportional, or more than proportional increase in world liquidity, and conversely.

The necessity of the first condition can be seen by considering a case in which balance of payments improvement results in contractionary policy shifts. Those shifts result in further improvement in payments positions for the affected country and deterioration for the rest of the world – clearly an unstable situation, with no equilibrium position. The second condition is necessary because otherwise a small departure from equilibrium – if indeed an equilibrium existed – would result in continuing world inflation or deflation.

Under the APDS system, these two conditions were met as long as all countries but the United States were free to set their balance of payments targets while the United States determined the world price level, with the US dollar as the numeraire of the system. Other countries then accepted the world price level as determined by US domestic considerations, while the US accepted the payments position determined by other countries. That the United States' balance of payments position was a residual determined by the behaviour of other countries ensured against the possibility of inconsistent targets. As long as arrangements were mutually satisfactory, the system worked.[2]

However, the system had certain features that led to increasing unwillingness on the part of the rest of the world to accept the US determined price level, and even more unwillingness on the part of the United States to accept the payments position determined by other countries. So the system became unworkable. It was stable for a considerable period. Built-in tendencies led to its abandonment.

The particular feature that led to reduced acceptability of the US determination of the world price level and passive payments position was the asymmetry[3] of the fixed exchange rate system. A country with a payments deficit of x per period of time was likely to alter its exchange rate sooner than a country with a surplus of the same size, the deficit country was likely to devalue by enough to eliminate a high fraction, possibly even in excess of one, of the deficit, while the surplus country was likely to appreciate by a much smaller fraction.

This asymmetry was often noted, but its consequences were, perhaps, not fully appreciated. Asymmetry had both benefits and costs. On the benefit side, asymmetry enabled countries to reconcile their current account and payments position targets with their internal goals, as long as the United States would let other countries determine the US payments position. Thus, mutually inconsistent targets were not possible. On the cost side, however, asymmetry had some dynamic effects that led to the abandonment of the system: it resulted in overvaluation of the US dollar in the price sense, which in turn resulted in increasingly large American deficits, greater world liquidity, and a more rapidly rising world price level. The Vietnam war, and the associated inflationary pressures, may have speeded up the process a little, but did not alter it fundamentally.[4]

A notion of the underlying mechanism and its consequences can be gained from a very simple model.[5] Assume a world in which inflation rates differ from country to country, but factor endowments, individual preferences, production functions and other underlying parameters of the real system do not change over time. Deficit countries devalue when their reserves reach certain critical minimum levels, and by enough so that they can expect to restore their lost reserves before going into deficit again. Surplus countries may or may not revalue. If they do, they do so only after their reserves are above their 'desired level' by some multiple of the amount by which deficit countries' minimum levels are below 'desired' levels, and they do not aim at appreciating enough to lose their past reserve accumulations. The dollar is the only international currency and claims to dollars can be obtained only by incurring a surplus.

These assumptions provide a good prototype model for understanding the motion of the system. Where factors other than price level changes may have altered equilibrium exchange rates and caused payments imbalances, the cause of imbalances is not central. Similarly, gold and sterling, as well as dollars, provided international liquidity, but the amount of new monetary gold was small and the US dollar was the principal and residual source of liquidity.

To see why a tendency for dollar overvaluation is systematic, consider first the behaviour of the system over time from an initial position of zero deficit when the American inflation rate is equal to the world average. Countries with inflation rates above the average will initially incur deficits, but then devalue; rapid inflation then forces them into deficit again and further devaluation. Over time, however, the deficit countries will lose on average only a small amount of reserves; after the initial devaluation there is no further net reserve loss. By contrast, countries with slower than average inflation rates initially accumulate reserves. At the point when deficit countries as a group devalue to restore their reserve position, surplus countries are still ahead: their source of net reserve accumulation must, at that point, be the US deficit. Over time, surplus countries continue to add to reserves, although their rate of accumulation is occasionally slowed as they appreciate.

Systematic overvaluation of the dollar results because countries with faster inflation devalue enough to restore equilibrium whereas surplus countries do not revalue. As the dollar is numéraire of the system, the dollar becomes, on average, overvalued. To state the same proposition another way, deficit countries devalue 'too much' against the dollar and 'not enough' against the surplus countries. Had Germany, for example, appreciated sufficiently to be in equilibrium in 1967, the British devaluation against the dollar would have been far smaller for the same payments position that was in fact achieved: German maintenance of a surplus implied an American deficit *and* overvaluation of the dollar *vis-à-vis* both Germany and Britain.

If the United States tried to remove the tendency toward overvaluation by reducing her rate of inflation, more countries would have felt pressures to devalue sooner. The initial round of devaluations would therefore come a little sooner, and the same mechanism would operate as described above. Conversely, if the US rate of inflation were faster, other countries would devalue more slowly and surplus countries would appreciate sooner.

The US rate of inflation determines the world price level, but not the US payments position except for short-term lags. In fact, except for time lags and external additions to world liquidity such as gold and SDRs, the US deficit must equal the other countries' surpluses, as long as deficit countries cannot incur deficits. The US dollar became overvalued to provide the liquidity demanded by the rest of the world and, as long as surplus countries wished to increase their reserve holdings, the overvaluation of the dollar had to increase over time.

Despite the simplicity of Henderson's model, it describes the salient characteristics of the behaviour of the APDS over time remarkably well. Casual inspection of prices over the 1953–70 period suggests support for the model. The index of world export prices expressed in dollars (1958 = 100) as reported by the IMF stood at 99 for industrial countries in 1951, was 100 in 1962, and 105 in 1965, rising to 109 in 1969. Thus, the world price level did not increase more than about 9 per cent in 18 years, less than half the rate of inflation in any major trading country. If one compares the behaviour of the world export price index with US prices, the world inflation rate is about 2 per cent below the American inflation rate – both before and after 1965. The US inflation in the late 1960s did not result in the deteriorating payments position: world inflation increased in proportion to US inflation.

Under the APDS, therefore, the American payments position was not – with the exception of lags in adjustment – a function of the US inflation rate. The opposite, however, may not have been true, as the deteriorating trade balance resulting from overvaluation led to pressures for expansionary monetary and fiscal policy. Of course, as the dollar became increasingly overvalued in the price sense, American deficits would have in any event increased. The excess demand associated with the Vietnam War led to a more rapid increase in the deficits and speculative capital flows finished the system quickly. None the less, the underlying asymmetry in adjustment, US dollar overvaluation, and more rapid devaluation than appreciation would have operated anyway, although perhaps more slowly. The anomaly that the very feature that provided the stability of the system – the American dollar's role as key currency, the US role in determining the world price level, with a passive American balance of payments – led to the dissolution of the APDS.

II

After 15 August 1971 the American government was unwilling, if not unable, to continue the passive role taken earlier. The US proposal for reform of the system – the Shultz – Volcker plan – involved the use of international diplomacy to provide future stability of the system and enable the US to abandon its passive rule. Thus, countries were to negotiate 'target reserve levels' and thereafter be subject to sanctions if they failed to stay within a specified (and symmetric) range of the target. Sanctions were to apply with equal force to surplus and deficit countries, so that exchange rate adjustment would be frequent and symmetric.

While the Shultz – Volcker plan was under discussion, two related objections were voiced, both of which are relevant to the current international monetary situation. The first pertained to the feasibility of negotiation of targets and the second related to means of enforcement.

Concern over negotiations of target reserve levels centred around the belief that countries would all claim targets which, when summed over all countries, would result in a highly inflationary level and rate of growth of world liquidity. In effect, the view was that countries would always aspire to increases in reserves to enable payments surpluses.

It was never clear how the problem would be resolved: If reserve levels were scaled across-the-board, then countries would have an incentive for overstating initial target aspirations. Target reserve levels could have been defined in terms of objective criteria, but the conflicting claims of reserve centre nations, international bankers, international investors, primary product exporters, and other nations would have been so great that the formula approach was not feasible. Casual consideration led to the conclusion that targets could be set, if at all, only through that most unquantifiable of processes – international consultation and negotiation.

Closely related to the determination of country targets was a second problem: how to prevent countries from 'cheating' as levels of their reserves deviated from the target. Two forms of cheating could be anticipated: (1) countries accumulating reserves might alter their regulations on capital account to 'hide' their reserve accumulation; and (2) if countries were really concerned about their current account balances rather than their overall payments balances, they could intervene on capital account to attain their current account targets.

The first problem relates to the degree to which 'cheating' might enable countries to avoid taking action with respect to their payments situations. If surplus countries did not wish to adjust, they could purchase foreign securities, alter regulations on private purchases of foreign assets, induce their banks to lend abroad, or otherwise prevent the reserve accumulation and need for action. The ability to delay action on the part of surplus countries would have placed a greater share of the burden of adjustment on deficit countries and thus have left some asymmetry in the system. To the extent that asymmetry was operative, either the system would have remained comparable to the APDS, with the dollar's tendency toward greater overvaluation, or it would have broken down as countries would have been unwilling to accept further dollar assets.

The problem of current account targets was the more serious and fundamental. Under the Shultz – Volcker plan the major means by which it was hoped to prevent difficulties was by proscribing interventions in various capital account markets. Such proscriptions would have been extremely difficult to monitor or enforce. However, because capital account intervention would not alter the current account automatically under pegged exchange rates, it was hoped that agreement on changes in capital account regulations would prevent the problem from arising. In general, countries would have had to alter their reserve levels outside of the target range to change the value of their currency and their current account target. In view of the reluctance of countries to alter their exchange rates, it did not appear that intervention to enable exchange rate changes to adjust current account balances would be a preferred course of action.

The Shultz – Volcker plan became academic with the abandonment of fixed exchange rates in 1973. However, some of the concerns voiced about the Shultz – Volcker plan apply to the system of 'dirty floating'. The problem of current account targets becomes central: intervention in the foreign exchange market can have significant repercussions on the current account balance. While speculative behaviour might prevent currency appreciation or depreciation, nothing in principle determines the current account (capital account) balance independently of the country's own policies and rate of growth: at different interest rates (and monetary-fiscal policies), different current account balances would be expected.

As a first approximation, therefore, it is apparently within the power of any central bank to intervene in the foreign exchange market to achieve a target current account balance (or perhaps a target exchange rate) if the bank has sufficient information about the behaviour of the private sector with regard to capital flows. The word 'apparently' is, however, the word of critical importance, because it is clear that current account targets, summed over all countries, may well be inconsistent. To that extent, the power is apparent rather than real.

Hence, the stability problem reappears: a mechanism is needed to reconcile inconsistent targets. There are three possibilities: (1) the United States can, as before, allow its current account (and overall payments balance) to adjust passively; (2) countries can agree on current account targets through international negotiations, as under an approximate version of the Shultz – Volcker plan; or (3) the system can be inherently unstable and perhaps degenerate into competitive devaluations, as in the 1930s.

It might be argued that countries do not attach much importance to their current account targets. Then targets may be sufficiently consistent just by chance (or lack of concern) so that stability is not an issue. This view may be correct much of the time. Thus, in the summer of 1973, the inconsistencies among independently arrived-at targets were sufficiently modest so that small exchange rate changes could reconcile divergences, and prospects were favourable that that situation might continue. The huge increase in the price of oil in the fall of 1973, however, eliminated the possibility that the oil-importing countries would accept the same cumulative current account deficit that the oil-exporting countries wished as current account surpluses. Moreover, the current account deficit had to be allocated among the oil-importing countries.

There was widespread recognition that there would not be a net 'balance of payments problem' for the oil importers as a result of the oil price increase. That part of the oil revenues which was not spent on purchases of current goods and services would automatically result in asset accumulation by the oil exporters. The problem involved the division of the current account deficit among the oil importers. The January 1974 announcement that the French franc would float separately from the other EEC currencies signalled the French determination to finance part of the increased oil import bill through additional exports. Comparison of the French announcements at the time of the devaluation with the subsequent behaviour of the franc suggests that diplomatic manoeuvres were the mechanism by which consistency was reattained in that particular instance.

There were, and are, only three resolutions. The United States can run a current account deficit large enough to enable the oil exporters to increase their holdings of foreign assets by the desired amount. The alternatives are negotiations to reconcile differences or competitive devaluations, trade war, and a return to protectionism because the system is unstable.

Consider the absence of agreement on current account targets if negotiations are not successful. Suppose that Western Europe and Japan wish to increase their exports and reduce their imports to cover their prospective current account deficits. Their currencies would depreciate. The rest of the world consists of the developing countries, themselves in deficit, and the United States and a few related dollar-area countries. The United States will not absorb such current account deficits, and would intervene in the foreign exchange market to keep the dollar from appreciating.[6]

III

Given the potential dangers of the current system, the question remains: how much better is the current system than the old APDS? The answer has three parts. The current system is really a continuation of the former system: countries have not abandoned their policy concerns with respect to the exchange rate and the size and composition of their balance of payments. What has changed has been the size of dollar holdings by foreigners and the consequent ability of central banks to withstand private speculative flows. The likely direction of movement of an exchange rate is no longer a one-sided bet, and private funds are less able to force changes in rates.

Second, the fact that rates are not pegged implies that it requires a conscious decision to intervene in the foreign exchange market. As such, market forces can absorb a much higher fraction of the burden of adjustment than under the APDS system. To the extent that governments were previously forced to take painful decisions before allowing markets to operate, the removal of that pressure is an improvement. Further, the burden of proof is now upon those wishing to intervene, again a step in the right direction.

Thus, in day-to-day operations, the current system represents a distinct improvement over the old APDS. Indeed, it is possible, and perhaps even probable, that market forces can absorb any inconsistencies in targets. However, the possibility of inconsistencies leads to the third part of the answer: the need for international consultation and negotiation is not as apparent as it was under the APDS. Under the old system, mounting dollar balances in European central banks and/or private speculative capital flows signalled the need for international co-operation; it was painfully evident that an alternative to a co-operative solution was a breakdown of the system. Under the current system, it is not obvious that a signal as readily interpretable as huge capital flows will be visible and that the need for negotiations to reconcile divergent interests will be apparent.

The danger, therefore, is that inconsistent targets can lead to mutually contradictory interventions with consequent instability for the system. The way out must be through an agreement upon a mechanism for designation of target current accounts (including, possibily, levels of transfer of resources to the developing countries). There are three alternatives: (1) rules or criteria and/or intervention can be agreed upon; (2) intervention can be totally eschewed; and (3) continuing diplomacy can monitor current developments as they occur.

Clean floating would be preferable, in that it would approximate the neat flexible-exchange-rates world of the blackboard; but it would require extensive consultation on what does or does not constitute currency intervention. The objections to the Shultz – Volcker plan about incentives to 'cheat' would apply to a clean float. The impossibility of setting down rules for currency intervention is also apparent: all the objections about 'cheating' still apply.

That leaves the task to central bankers, finance ministers, and foreign ministers. There is considerable evidence that consultations are already proceeding: agreements that the OECD countries would refrain from imposing additional barriers to imports for one year, and on other matters, have already been announced. In a sense, academic inputs to the discussion will be much more difficult with dirty floating than they were under the APDS system. Government and central bank decisions were clearly visible in that balance of payments figures generally indicated the extent to which market forces were being bucked, while international swap agreements, devaluations and other consultations were fully reported.

Under the new system, international economic interdependence is as great as ever, but the decisions made will be less visible and less easily assessed by those outside government. Evaluation of those decisions will be more difficult as the whole range of issues pertaining to relative bargaining power, *quid pro quos* unrelated to the payments balance, and other non-visible aspects of diplomatic stances will become relevant to a judgement of the efficacy of policy. Sensible academic discussion must surely start with the recognition that the present dirty floating is not the nice classroom abstraction of flexible exchange rates, and that international co-operation and consultation are vital to the stability of the system. Whether academic economists can contribute further remains to be seen.

NOTES

1. The Canadian experience generated some exceptions to the above statement, notably in the discussion initiated by Fleming and Mundell on the behaviour of monetary and fiscal policies under fixed and floating rates.
2. An interesting question, but one not explored here, is how the decreasing *relative* size of the United States affected her ability to be the passive country.
3. The word 'asymmetry' has been used in a number of other senses, including the 'asymmetry' of pressures on surplus and deficit countries, and the different constraints facing the United States and other countries with respect to their payments and liquidity positions.
4. It might have been possible that exogenous shifts could have occurred to offset the progressive overvaluation of the dollar; that may have happened to some extent in the early 1960s. The argument here is that there was systematic pressure toward overvaluation which exogenous shifts (unrelated to American prices) would have had to offset.
5. A careful statement of the proposition sketched in this section is contained in James M. Henderson, 'Asymmetry in Quasi-Fixed Exchange-Rate Systems', *Journal of International Economics*, 1975. The model, simple as it is, has no analytical solution. Henderson's paper contains the results of simulations of the world economy with asymmetric adjustment rules, as well as formal development of the model.
6. The US motive in removing capital controls at the end of 1973 and early 1974 may have reflected in part the fact that dollar appreciation was generally regarded as 'too much'. According to the *New York Times* of 18 July 1974 the net increase in bank lending abroad in the first half of 1974 was $8.5 billion; the depreciation of the US dollar dates from about the same time.

4 Beyond Fixed Parities: The Analytics of International Monetary Agreements

Ronald I. McKinnon

The breakdown of fixed exchange rates within the European Monetary Union – with the separate floats of Britain, Italy and France – has coincided over the 1971–4 period with the broader collapse of the Bretton Woods and Smithsonian agreements, which were designed to keep exchange rates within more or less narrowly defined bands. Fortunately, the floating of exchange rates has so far prevented inconvertibility among major currencies. Yet these floating rates have also been associated with high international inflation, continued large changes in relative currency values, and erosion in the confidence that individuals had in fiat money whatever its national origin.

This paper lays down a *minimum* set of guidelines for national central banks if an international monetary agreement is to be successful. 'Success' is defined to be the stabilisation of relative convertible currency values of the participating countries together with the maintenance of stable prices for the group as a whole. The political or economic desirability of a successful fixed exchange rate system – whether it be regional or worldwide in scope – is not in question. Instead, the analysis is confined to the necessary technical economic underpinnings of monetary agreements themselves.

A maximum sufficient condition for success is, of course, to establish a single central bank issuing a single currency over a domain consisting of all the countries party to the agreement. Yet this condition is terribly strong in its implications for political and economic sovereignty, and is likely only feasible in imperial regimes.

At the other extreme, one has what W. M. Corden (1972, p. 3) has called a 'pseudo exchange-rate union' in which 'member countries agree no doubt solemnly – to maintain fixed exchange-rate relationships within the union but there is no explicit integration of economic policy, no common pool of foreign-exchange reserves, and no single central bank'. More specifically for our purposes, a pseudo exchange rate union is one where there are no effective international restraints on open-market operations, discounting, or forward exchange operations by national central banks. Only pseudo exchange rate unions have been legally concluded in the post-war period, although *de facto* harmonisation of national monetary policies has been achieved in certain sub-periods under Bretton Woods.

Yet the minimum conditions for success are not so difficult to spell out as is commonly supposed, and are much less stringent than the requirement of a single international currency. Nevertheless, monetary guidelines for a successful agreement are stronger than those prevailing in the pseudo unions to which we have become accustomed.

The division of the supply of money from domestic sources among the members of the fledging union must be the centre-piece of any successful agreement. Controlling the money supply involves understanding the appropriate assignment of functions between 'automatic' and discretionary' monetary policies (say discounting versus open-market operations) by each national central bank. In turn, this assignment of the domestic instruments of monetary policy is influenced strongly by intervention in the markets for foreign exchange. The objective of this paper is to clarify the exact nature of preferred relationships governing the money supplies of member countries.

SECULAR GROWTH IN THE MONEY SUPPLY AND THE PRICES OF TRADEABLE GOODS

Monetary authorities seldom distinguish secular growth in the monetary base from transactions designed to influence the money supply on a day-to-day basis. However, a 'long-run' monetary policy can be defined for each member of a proposed monetary union, and particular instruments of national policy are best assigned more or less exclusively to this end. What should the secular monetary policy be?

Suppose initially that the partners in a proposed monetary agreement wish to stabilise relative exchange rates *without* direct offical intervention in the markets for foreign exchange. (Later we shall examine the circumstances under which direct intervention may be warranted.) They want relative rates of national monetary growth consistent with exchange rates showing no net upward or downward movements although not officially pegged. A second equally important objective is to control the growth in the aggregate money supply of the union as a whole in order to avoid general 'inflation', defined more precisely below.

To simplify further, assume that the problem of long-run control is one of managing each national monetary base – narrowly defined to be commercial bank reserves held with the central bank plus coin and currency held by the public. That is, secular growth in the monetary base is strongly positively correlated with long-run growth in other monetary aggregates, such as currency, demand or time deposits. (This assumption may be violated if there are major regulatory changes in reserve requirements or effective interest ceilings, or significant growth in unregulated financial intermediaries.) With no direct official intervention in the foreign-exchange markets, each national monetary base expands *pari passu* with expansion in domestic credit from its central bank. How fast then should central bank credit expand in each participating country? What should be the target for the price level?

For closed economies, the merits and demerits of alternative monetary standards have been widely discussed (Keynes, 1930; Friedman, 1969). A wage standard fixes average nominal wages in money terms while commodity prices fall smoothly in the face of general technical progress. A commodity standard is one where the average money price of a typical basket of commodities is stabilised, with money wages rising secularly. A general commodity standard necessitates choosing among the consumer price index (CPI), wholesale price index (WPI) or possible GNP deflators as the targets of monetary policy.

For open economies striving for exchange stability, however, one price index naturally suggests itself. The maintenance of fixed exchange rates implies that the prices of goods that enter foreign trade (exportables or importables) are tied together across countries. Although some short-term variation is possible, no one member of a union of fairly diversified industrial countries can inflate its domestic prices of tradeable goods in the long run at a rate faster or slower than the mean for the union. Furthermore, a zero rate of price inflation is the long-run target about which private expectations can coalesce most easily – particularly regarding long-term contractual arrangements between debtors and creditors. Thus, adherence to a goal of zero inflation in a price index for tradeable goods seems best suited for reconciling the need for exchange rate stability among partner countries on the one hand, and stability in the aggregate price level on the other.

Unfortunately, broad indices of tradeable goods prices are not now directly compiled by individual countries. Yet many countries have separate price indices for exports and/or imports fairly narrowly defined. A more general index of tradeable good prices would not seem difficult to construct. In the interim, wholesale price indices – including importables and exportables but excluding non-tradeable services – may approximate secular movements in a purer index of tradeable goods prices. If one wants to examine the historical experiences of member countries, in controlling the prices of tradeable goods, the WPI is likely to be the best single index currently available.

Although the prices of tradeable goods would be bound together across countries within the union, national indices of consumer prices need not move in unison. Indeed, countries experiencing the most rapid productivity growth, in which some tradeable goods industries are almost invariably the leading sectors, will find real wages and the prices of non-tradeable services rising more rapidly.[1] Hence consumer price indices, including non-tradeable services, may rise substantially faster than wholesale price indices from which non-tradeable services are excluded. In Japan, a very high growth economy, the WPI rose 14 per cent from 1953 to 1970 while the CPI *doubled* (McKinnon, 1971). Slower growing countries maintaining fixed exchange rates with Japan would experience less upward movement in their consumer price indices.

Thus the choice of a suitable price index to be stabilised can make a big difference to the conduct of secular monetary policy in each participating country. Growth in the nominal money supply in Japan in the post-war period would have been much slower if Japanese authorities had concentrated on stabilising the CPI. However, members of a potential monetary agreement have a vested interest in focusing on tradeable goods prices – while allowing residual movements in the prices of non-tradeable services to reflect differential productivity growth.

Once zero growth in an index of tradeable goods prices (TGPI) is established as a mutual target of long-run monetary policy, the appropriate rate of domestic credit expansion by each national central bank can be calculated. One procedure would be for each member country to project (based on historical experience) average real GNP growth for a year or more into the future. For a mature economy not experiencing major changes in financial regulation or inflationary pressure, a fairly constant ratio of money to GNP may also be projected. The required growth in the monetary base could then be calculated as real GNP growth plus a small allowance for the differential movement between a general GNP price deflator and a broad index of tradeable goods prices. Since the TGPI is to be perfectly stable, one would expect a GNP price deflator to rise slightly in the course of the year because of the increase in price of non-tradeable services – which may be substantial in rapidly growing economies. Algebraically, one can project the long-run growth in the monetary base to be

$$\Delta DC = \Delta Y + \Delta X \qquad (1)$$

ΔDC is the percentage change in domestic credit from the central bank

ΔY is projected percentage change in real GNP

ΔX is projected percentage change in GNP deflator assuming TGPI constant.

A key to successful international monetary agreement is, therefore, for each member country to expand central bank credit smoothly as described by (1) to ensure that relative exchange rates do not move persistently in one direction or another. Speculators (foreign exchange traders) would then have full information on how central banks were obligated to behave. Once the biggest single uncertainty in the system, i.e. the behaviour of central banks, is reduced, private intervention in the foreign exchange markets would become of a more 'stabilising' character.

In addition, the price level (TGPI) for the union as a whole would be anchored. Indeed, one can imagine a monetary agreement with strong transnational implications, but with no mutually supporting official intervention in the foreign-exchange markets! I emphasise this possibility because most monetary agreements focus on official intervention to fix exchange rates, rather than stress the importance of precisely targeting domestic rates of monetary expansion. A successful agreement may be able to do without the former, but it must have the latter.

OPEN-MARKET OPERATIONS AND SECULAR GROWTH

What instrument of domestic monetary policy is best suited to maintain smooth secular growth in the national monetary base as calculated in equation (1) above?

Again, let us provisionally assume that national central banks do not intervene directly in the foreign exchanges. Then, each national monetary base changes either through open-market operations – say, purchases of government securities in some market that broadly influences all domestic financial institutions – or rediscount of eligible securities with the central bank by particular institutions such as commercial banks or some central savings bank. (Changes in reserve requirements cannot be an instrument of long-run expansion in the effective monetary base.)

For those countries with broadly based markets in government securities, open-market operations are the preferred instrument because they occur at the discretion of the central bank, can be executed 'smoothly', and need not particularly influence one sector of the economy or another. This last characteristic is important if the monetary union is also a common market, where governments are supposed to behave neutrally with respect to individual industries or sources of finance.

On the other hand, with a completely 'open' discount window, where the discount rate of interest is equal to prevailing market rates, monetary expansion depends on the volition (discretion) of individual eligible borrowers. Smooth secular growth overall is then difficult to achieve by continually manipulating 'the' discount rate. Moreover, open-market operations may be confounded by an open discount window because the purchase of government securities is offset by a reduction in the outstanding volume of rediscounts. The trade-off between the two modes of creating money may generate substantial uncertainty.

A 'controlled' discount window is one where at least some discount rates are kept below market levels so that there is excess demand for loans. For secular growth, the central bank must continually allocate new loan tranches to particular borrowers while preserving penalty rates or arbitrary rationing for others. Again, this has non-neutral financial implications which are best avoided. Yet, in the absence of convenient open markets in government securities, the discount window may have to be so used. For example, most secular growth in the Japanese monetary base from 1950–67 was achieved through increased rediscount tranches (Patrick, 1972) to favoured institutions, unlike the United States and Great Britain that relied on open-market operations.

Since open-market operations are best assigned to smooth long-run growth in the monetary base, they should not be used for other objectives – such as pegging interest rates on government securities. Indeed, price support operations are best outlawed by the international monetary agreement so that member countries can have confidence in each others policies. Both Great Britain and the United States have engaged in operations designed to fix interest rates on certain classes of government securities, with unfortunate losses of control over their respective monetary bases.

To summarise, an 'ideal' control mechanism would assign open-market operations exclusively to increasing smoothly the monetary base over the long run and would limit discounting to short-term and temporary borrowing. For example, each commercial bank would work towards eliminating any net indebtedness to the central bank as was the case during the classical Bank of England regime prior to the First World War. But the system envisaged here differs from the gold standard because secular monetary growth is provided by domestic open-market operations.

OFFICIAL INTERVENTION IN MARKETS FOR FOREIGN EXCHANGE

The assumption of no official intervention in the foreign exchanges focuses on the core of any successful monetary agreement: the harmonisation of secular growth in domestic credit by each national central bank. Agreements that omit this core consideration, while sanctioning the direct official pegging of exchange rates, may ultimately undermine economic integration. The constellation of fixed exchange rates can easily become inconsistent with secular monetary expansion in each participating country. Governments then feel impelled to place direct restraints on trade or capital flows before the exchange rates themselves are forcibly altered by speculative pressure.

In the analysis to follow, therefore, participating countries are assumed to strive to harmonise secular growth in domestic bank credit. Is then further direct intervention to fix exchange rates not redundant? Or, are there circumstances that warrant official purchases and sales of member countries' currencies to maintain exchange parities?

If two countries experience exchange rate stability in the absence of formal exchange parities, the above analysis implies similar historical patterns of domestic monetary growth. The Canadian – US experience is an example. During periods without formal parities, the Canadian – US dollar exchange rate moved little. Even over the whole *melange* of fixed and floating intervals in the post-war period, there seems to be no net secular trend in the exchange rate.

Without exploring the reasons for this implicit but close co-ordination of national monetary policies, a formal Canadian – US exchange parity seems unnecessary for securing exchange stability. Although the Canadian government has often intervened, private speculative activity must have been broadly stabilising. The Canadian – US exchange rate has moved very little in the face of sharp cyclical oscillations in 1973 in their rates of exchange with third countries.

Most potential members of a monetary union, however, have not had the same implicit co-ordination of national monetary policies as Canada and the United States. On the contrary, France, Britain and Italy have had more rapid net secular monetary expansion than other members of the European Monetary Union – principally Germany. Alternatively, if one contemplates the re-establishment of a truly international monetary standard resting on the world's three major trading countries – Germany, Japan and the United States (McKinnon, 1974) – then domestic credit expansion by the Federal Reserve seems excessive in recent years relative to the Bundesbank or the Bank of Japan. Given this long-run incompatibility, unco-ordinated short-run changes in national monetary policies have become more frequent.

Little wonder that foreign exchange traders have been at sea regarding 'equilibrium' exchange rates over the past three years! Since official policies are an unknown but ultimately controlling factor, private expectations of future exchange rate movements simply cannot coalesce. Bandwagon effects, large day-by-day and quarter-to-quarter movements in exchange rates have become commonplace. These cyclical fluctuations have led many 'expert' banking and non-financial corporations to take sizeable losses on foreign exchange transactions in a manner that Friedman's (1953) classical analysis of speculative behaviour would not have predicted.

In conclusion, when private suspicions of official monetary actions are acute and unsettling, a case can be made for fixed foreign exchange parities to complement restraints on domestic credit expansion. While an 'equilibrium' constellation of official exchange parities is difficult to establish, foreign-exchange traders may find it invaluable as an indicator of official intentions. The information contained in official parities is only believable, however, if the parity system is credible. To achieve credibility, official purchases and sales of foreign exchange in each country must be made *consistent* with the monetary and price-level targets outlined in the preceding sections.

THE NON-STERILISATION RULE AND SHORT-RUN MONETARY MANAGEMENT IN EACH COUNTRY

Dropping the provisional ban on official foreign-exchange transactions, let us assume now that, wisely or unwisely, member countries commit themselves to a regime of fixed foreign-exchange parities. To keep matters simple, suppose the initial constellation of rates is an 'equilibrium' set in that a common bundle of tradeable goods costs more or less the same in each country at the parity rates of exchange.[2] What rules then must be imposed on official foreign-exchange transactions to ensure consistency between these formal exchange parities and the mutually established paths of domestic credit expansion by each national central bank?

A parity commitment – even in the form of a modest band within which exchange rates can move – may entail official trading in the spot foreign-exchange markets on a day-to-day basis. An 'official-settlements' deficit in the balance of payments will contract the monetary base because the central bank must sell foreign exchange and hence withdraw domestic high-powered money from circulation to maintain the official parity. These foreign transactions can be expected to dominate short-run monetary policy (changes in the supply of money) if open-market operations are assigned to smooth secular purchases of domestic securities. Indeed, 'consistent' behaviour requires that this secular growth rule in *domestic* central bank credit not be disrupted by swings in the balance of international payments. In other words, a short-run monetary contraction due to a deficit should not be sterilised, and such a *non-sterilisation rule* needs to be built into the monetary agreement.

What is the basic rationale for the non-sterilisation of short-run deficits or surpluses in the balance of payments? Suppose the long-run demand for money (the monetary base) in the economy is correctly approximated by equation (1) above, and thus is met by the expansion of domestic credit by each national central bank. One might still expect substantial short-run variation in the excess demand for (or supply of) domestic money in any one country. Under a fixed exchange rate regime, excess domestic demand for money would show up as a surplus in the balance of payments, whereas excess supply would show up as a deficit.

For example, if domestic nationals attempted to sell goods or bonds (securities) to satisfy their excess demand for money, this would cause a trade surplus or, more likely, a short-term capital inflow, as impressively demonstrated empirically by Kouri and Porter (1974). 'Correct' monetary policy would then allow the surplus in the balance of payments to clear the excess domestic demand for money by expanding the monetary base. In other words, no discretionary short-run policy by the monetary authorities in any one country is necessary to meet short-run fillips in the demand for and supply of domestic money.

On the other side of the coin, a non-sterilisation rule assures foreign-exchange traders that the fixed parity is invulnerable. If a deficit itself clears a temporary excess supply of domestic money as official reserves are drawn down, everyone knows that the excess money supply and the deficit will soon be eliminated. They will be self-liquidating if secular monetary expansion from domestic sources is restrained. Hence, the foreign exchange authority would never be in the role of an unsuccessful 'speculator' because the domestic monetary base would always change in the short run to support official intervention at the parity rate.

THE SYMMETRY RULE AND THE AGGREGATE MONETARY BASE

So far, only domestic monetary management in a hypothetical member country has been related to official foreign-exchange transactions. Yet, short-run monetary policy must be coherent for the proposed union as a whole. Whatever the system of official intervention, a rough symmetry should prevail by having deficit countries contract their monetary base by quantitatively the same amount as surplus countries expand – as least from the initial impact of the international payments imbalance. In this way the overall monetary base of the union is stabilised, and assurance is given that partner countries share the adjustment 'burden'[3] fairly.

Since there are several possible systems of intervention to maintain official parities (McKinnon, 1973), the appropriate symmetrical clearing arrangements across central banks for building up and drawing down of foreign-exchange reserves depends on the particular intervention system chosen. Although not considered carefully in Europe and elsewhere, currency pyramiding within the union is not difficult to prevent and should be an important part of any agreement allowing substantial official intervention in the foreign exchanges. For example, if the monetary authority in the surplus country intervenes by selling its own currency and acquiring the currency of the deficit country, these foreign claims should be impounded – perhaps in a special account in the deficit country's central bank. Otherwise, the monetary authority in the surplus country might hold claims only on commercial banks in the deficit country – so that an unfortunate asymmetry existed: the supply of high-powered money in the surplus country expanded whereas only low-powered money was withdrawn from domestic nationals in the deficit country.

The obvious implication of foreclosing short-run variation in the aggregate supply of money (remembering that secular monetary growth has been predetermined) is that the union as a whole would not engage in discretionary short-run monetary policy. This limitation is consistent with the absence of a single international central bank running its own currency. Fortunately, this loss of discretionary monetary authority may be as much an advantage as a disadvantage. National central banks will be more tightly constrained from using the monetary system to support the prices of government or other securities.

In a sense, a short-run monetary disturbance in any one country – say, an excess demand for money – will be smoothed by having funds drawn from all other members of the union. Moreover, a surplus in the balance of payments will accurately reflect that private individuals in the country in question have an excess supply of goods or securities. As long as all such disturbances are not highly correlated across member countries, the statistical law of large numbers should have a rather favourable smoothing effect. Only in the case of a general liquidity crisis, which greatly increased the demand for high-powered money in the union as a whole, need the presumption of short-run invariance in the aggregate supply of base money be suspended.

ON FLEXING THE SYSTEM

Many readers will balk at what seems to be excessive rigidity in, and the overly simplistic nature of this model of monetary union. Long-term secular growth in the domestic credit portion of each country's monetary base is projected on a once-and-for-all basis at the beginning of each year. Then only foreign-exchange transactions can move each national monetary base significantly above or below this secular trend – and only for short periods of time. Yet the potential flexibility of such a monetary union is greater than it may first seem.

First, symmetrical international adjustment is consonant with a wide variety of regulatory systems whereby each national central bank controls its commercial banks. Reserve requirements do not have to be identical, and differing national classifications of commercial banks, savings banks, merchant banks and so on need not be altered. National interest-rate restrictions or usury laws that force money-market yields below international levels will lead to unwarranted capital flight, but this would be true whenever a formal monetary union exists. In short, as long as each central bank controls the domestic credit portion of its national monetary base,[4] and the monetary base overall is firmly related to money holdings of individuals, a successful union would not require the same regulatory modes in each participating country.

Second, the apparent harshness of short-run adjustment to imbalances in international payments can be ameliorated through two channels: (1) the free international flow of portfolio capital that responds quickly to small interest-rate differentials; and (2) short-term 'automatic' rediscounting by commercial banks that are losing reserves with their national central banks.

Consider a deficit in the balance of trade or in long-term capital flows in one participating country, whose direct impact is to reduce the domestic monetary base on a dollar-for-dollar basis following the non-sterilisation rule. The loss of reserves causes short-term interest rates to rise in the domestic money market generally, and on the liabilities of commercial banks in particular. Hence, domestic financial institutions facing a short-term liquidity squeeze borrow on the international money market, replenish their reserves, and so quickly dampen the international deficit of the country in question. Since the maintenance of official parities is guaranteed, small interest-differentials should attract 'stabilising' flows of short-term capital from abroad in the classical manner – as described by Ingram (1962) for the case of Puerto Rico and the United States. The pressure on the deficit country is eased further by our symmetry rule that requires mirror-image adjustment in surplus countries, from which portfolio capital is expelled.

If international markets in financial instruments are not well developed within the union, a carefully designed form of 'automatic' discounting by commercial banks with their respective national central banks can, in part, replace short-term foreign borrowing. Suppose, again, that a deficit in international payments causes commercial banks in one country to lose reserves. With limitations on borrowing abroad, they are driven to the discount window of their central bank. The central bank then discounts freely but at a penalty rate – a rate of interest that is kept slightly above the market and perhaps automatically raised when an unusual demand for loans appears. A serious liquidity squeeze on the commercial banks is thus avoided, but their reserve positions are not completely restored because the penalty rate of interest (or an upward sloping supply curve for central bank finance) makes it unprofitable to do so. A lesser, but perhaps smoother, domestic monetary contraction remains to ensure the elimination of the deficit in international payments. Indeed, Michaely (1971) provides evidence that such automatic 'partial sterilisation' was common practice in Europe and Japan during the fixed-rate regime from 1950 to 1966.

This 'automaticity' of the discounting process, where discretionary short-run action by the national central bank is avoided, nicely complements and smooths the adjustment set in motion by deficits and surpluses in the balance of payments. Indeed, the authorities are unlikely, *ex ante*, to be able to identify the character of the monetary disturbance responsible for the deficit. For example, if there is an excess supply of domestic low-powered money that individuals dishoard to acquire foreign assets, then commercial banks will discount with the central bank to prevent the high-powered money base from contracting on a dollar-for-dollar basis. Nevertheless, the stock of low-powered money will diminish. If the source of the deficit is an excess supply of domestic high-powered money – say, excess commercial-bank reserves, these will be drained off directly by the balance of payments deficit and no commercial bank will feel pressed to appear at the discount window.[5]

Hence the authorities do not have to identify the precise nature of the disturbances causing deficits or surpluses in international payments to provide accommodating finance at the discount window; whereas open-market operations – which are necessarily discretionary – require such identification. Again open-market operations are best exclusively assigned to smooth secular expansion in the monetary base, while 'passive' discounting can be an important adjunct of short-term monetary policy governed mainly by the balance of payments. Most monetary unions may rely on some combination of short-term capital flows and 'temporary' discounting as automatic stabilisers, which nevertheless permit eventful full adjustment to international deficits and surpluses.

Discretionary monetary policies, designed to isolate altogether the domestic monetary base from incipient international payments imbalances, should be outlawed in the monetary agreement. As an example, official intervention in the forward foreign-exchange markets to, say, raise the covered interest-rate differential in favour of the home country, may possibly avoid a domestic monetary contraction this month at the expense of acquiring a forward foreign-exchange commitment that has to be unwound in three months. A prime concern of a successful monetary union is that central banks do not volitionally engage in operations whose monetary and exchange rate consequences are unknown and possibly inconsistent with mutual monetary adjustment. Hence, central banks would be prohibited from significant forward trading in foreign-exchange markets or engaging in equivalent forward swaps with their commercial banks. Official discretion is not the better part of monetary valour.

Finally, how rigid and accurate need be the rule that governs the long-run expansion in domestic central bank credit? If the domestic demand for money in one country rises faster secularly than money GNP, the demand for high-powered money will likely exceed domestic open-market purchases as proscribed by equation (1). This secular excess demand will be 'cleared' through the foreign-exchange markets by a persistent tendency towards surplus in the balance of payments. Correspondingly, all other members of the union will experience a persistent deficit on current or capital account. If the tradeable goods prices (TGPI) are also stable overall, we know that the monetary base of the union as a whole is tracking accurately. Hence adjustment simply requires that domestic credit expansion by the central bank in the surplus country be adjusted upward a percentage point or two, while other members of the union adjust downward their credit expansion by a commensurate amount. If tradeable goods prices have been falling slightly, perhaps only the former adjustment would be necessary.

Such rough 'tailoring' can occur annually under international auspices without significant upheaval in the foreign-exchange markets or in domestic monetary policies. The parameter estimates of long-run demand functions for money would simply be updated every year or so. Indeed meetings and tailorings should be infrequent to avoid the ever present temptation to direct the secular instruments of monetary policy towards short-term national goals, thus undermining the 'full-information' character of the union.

An example of a national policy that is clearly inconsistent with the secular growth rule outlined above is that of post-war Germany. In part because the German monetary reform of 1948–9 eliminated (froze) all government open-market securities leaving the Bundesbank without a convenient vehicle for conducting open-market operations, and in part measure because Germany aimed for a lower rate of inflation than that prevailing elsewhere, most of the secular growth in the German monetary base can be explained by official intervention to acquire foreign exchange which was then either kept as reserves or disposed of through official channels. (Mathieson, 1971). Clearly, this secular strategy puts continual upward speculative pressure on any official parity for the German exchange rate. To become a well-behaved member of a negotiated monetary union, Germany would have to expand domestic open-market operations until no further net accumulation of foreign exchange occurred. This would only be satisfactory to Germany if partner countries limited their domestic credit expansion so as to stabilise international prices at an agreed-on level.

CONCLUDING NOTE

The main theme of the foregoing analysis can be summarised thus:

(1) The long-run target for price 'stability' should be precisely defined by an index of tradeable goods prices for the union as a whole, rather than by a consumer price index or GNP deflator for each individual country.

(2) A Friedman-like rule specifying the rate of secular growth in domestic central bank credit can be applied to each country in a manner consistent with the overall price-level target.

(3) No country should allow official foreign-exchange transactions either to expand or to contract its monetary base on a secular basis, but all members would allow deficits or surpluses to dominate short-run changes in their domestic money supplies.

If these conditions are met, relative exchange rates among member countries can be stabilised because unpredictable behaviour by central banks is eliminated. Moreover, despite the apparent rigidity of rules (1) to (3) above, the operation of each member country's monetary system remains surprisingly flexible.

NOTES

1. Although formal price indices seem to indicate slower secular productivity growth (higher price inflation) in service activities, this could conceivably be a statistical illusion resulting from our inability to measure technical change in service sectors. If anything, however, this statistical difficulty strengthens the argument for constructing a more reliable index of tradeable goods prices as the target for monetary policy.

2. Whether or not a single intervention currency is designated to maintain the parity system, or whether there is multiple currency intervention with multiple reserve holdings, is an important issue not addressed here because it depends on the special character and purposes of the proposed monetary union. There is no universally 'best' system. Whereas the restraints on expansion of domestic central bank-credit outlined in this paper are generally necessary whatever specific system of foreign-exchange intervention is used.

3. While commonly used, the phrase 'burden of adjustment' has an unfortunate semantic connotation. In the present context, adjusting to the balance of payments need not be a 'burden' at all when deficits or surpluses clear domestic excess demands or supplies of money and so enhance monetary stability.

4. The Bank of England somehow contrived in the British monetary reforms of 1971 to lose control over the monetary base by allowing treasury bills and some short-term commercial paper to be included in the reserves of the commercial banks.

5. This distinction between different kinds of monetary imbalance is analysed in more depth in McKinnon (1973).

REFERENCES

Corden, W. M., 'Monetary Integration', *Essays in International Finance*, no. 93 Princeton University (Apr 1972).

Friedman, M., *The Optimum Quantity of Money* (Aldine, 1969).

— 'The Case for Flexible Exchange Rates', pp. 157–203, in M. Friedman, *Essays in Positive Economics* (University of Chicago Press, 1953).

Ingram, J., *Regional Payments Mechanisms: The Case of Puerto Rico* (Chapel Hill, University of North Carolina Press, 1962).

Keynes, J. M., *A Treatise on Money* (Macmillan, 1930).

Kouri, P. and M. Porter, 'International Capital Flows and Portfolio Equilibrium', *Journal of Political Economy* (May/June 1974) pp. 443–67.

McKinnon, R. I., 'Monetary Theory and Controlled Flexibility in the Foreign Exchanges', Essays in International Finance, no. 71, Princeton University, (Apr 1971).

— 'On Securing a Common Monetary Policy in Europe', *Banca Nazionale del Lavoro Quarterly Review* (Mar 1973) pp. 3–20.

— 'A New Tripartite Agreement or a Limping Dollar Standard?', *Essays in International Finance*, Princeton University, No. 106, October, 1974.

Mathieson, D., 'Portfolio Balance and International Finance', Ph.D., dissertation, (Stanford University, 1971).

Michaely, M., *The Responsiveness of Demand Policies to Balance of*

Payments: Postwar Patterns, NBER (Columbia University Press, 1971).

Patrick, H., 'Finance, Capital Markets, and Economic Growth in Japan', pp. 109–39 in Arnold Sametz (ed.) *Financial Development and Economic Growth* (New York University Press, 1972).

Part II

MONETARY INTERDEPENDENCE AND MONETARY POLICY

5 Stability and Exchange Rate Systems in a Monetarist Model of the Balance of Payments

Stanley Fischer*

INTRODUCTION

The fixed versus floating exchange rates debate appears destined for as long a life as any of the standing controversies in economics. The standard arguments are outlined by Johnson (1969) and Kindleberger (1969). This paper focuses on the effects of the exchange rate system on economic stability. We construct a simple model in which real disturbances affect the level of output each period and nominal disturbances affect the demand for money, and examine the resultant variability of the rate of consumption and the price level in a single country and in a two-country world under regimes of fixed and of floating exchange rates.

The formal examination of the effects of exchange rate systems on stability is not new: Mundell (1960), Stein (1963) and Tower and Courtney (1974) are among the contributors.[1] The impetus for the present paper, however, comes more directly from papers by Argy and Kouri (1974) and McKinnon (1974). In particular, one of the aims of the analysis is to study McKinnon's suggestion that adoption of a set of 'rules of the game' in a fixed exchange rate system could lead to better performance for each country individually than would result if each country pursued apparently stabilising policies on its own.

The stability of the price level and consumption in a single small country under floating and under fixed rates in response to monetary and real disturbances are examined in Sections I.A and I.B. An active monetary

* I am grateful to Rudiger Dornbusch for extremely helpful discussions.

policy for the small country under fixed rates is examined in Section I.C. The analysis of Sections I.A–C is paralleled in Sections II.A–C for a two-country world. Conclusions and comments are presented in Section III.

I   A SINGLE SMALL COUNTRY

The simplest monetarist model, due to Dornbusch (1973) is:

$$L_t = kP_tY_t \tag{1}$$

$$P_t = P_t^*e_t \tag{2}$$

$$B_t = M_t - M_{t-1} \tag{3}$$

$$M_t - M_{t-1} = \alpha(L_t - M_{t-1}) \qquad 0 < \alpha < 1 \tag{4}$$

$$C_t = P_tY_t - B_t \tag{5}$$

where L is the demand for money, P the domestic price level, Y domestic real income and output, P^* the foreign price level, e the exchange rate, B the balance of payments, α an adjustment coefficient, and C consumption.

The major shortcoming of this simple model from the viewpoint of this paper is that capital flows are ignored. Domestic output is initially assumed to be manna; later a Phillips curve is added. For analytical convenience in examining stability, the average rates of inflation at home and abroad are assumed to be the same and equal to zero. Thus, one of the major causes leading to the adoption of floating rates is not considered. However, there would be little difficulty in extending the analysis of the floating exchange rate system to situations in which rates of inflation between the two countries differ.

The object of enquiry is the steady-state behaviour, in particular the variances, of prices and consumption when the economy is subject to repeated shocks. Disturbances in the demand for money, the foreign price level, and real income and the resultant steady state variances of prices and particularly consumption are considered.[2] A passive monetary policy is assumed initially.

I.A   MONEY DEMAND AND FOREIGN PRICE LEVEL DISTURBANCES

Let the demand for money be represented by

$$L_t = kP_tY_t + \varepsilon_t \tag{6}$$

where ε_t is a random variable with mean zero, variance σ_ε^2 and serially uncorrelated. Let $P_t^* = P^*$ and $Y_t = Y$ for all t.

(i)   Floating Rate

Under floating rates with passive monetary policy,

$$M_t = M \qquad \text{for all } t. \tag{7}$$

Then the balance of payments is always zero, consumption has zero variance, and since

$$M = kP_tY + \varepsilon_{t'}$$

$$P_t = \frac{M - \varepsilon_t}{kY}. \tag{8}$$

Thus

$$\sigma_P^2 = \frac{\sigma_\varepsilon^2}{k^2Y^2} \tag{9}$$

is the variance of prices. The corresponding variance of the exchange rate is easily calculated from equation (2).

(ii) Fixed Rate

Under floating rates, all adjustment is in prices and none in quantities. Under a fixed rate, the adjustment is entirely in quantities and none in prices. Specifically, from equation (4), in steady state, the variance of the nominal money stock is

$$\sigma_M^2 = \frac{\alpha^2\sigma_\varepsilon^2}{1 - (1 - \alpha)^2} \tag{10}$$

Then, using equations (3) and (5), the variance of real consumption is:

$$\sigma_{c/p}^2 = \frac{2\alpha^3\sigma_\varepsilon^2}{P^2(1 - (1 - \alpha)^2)}. \tag{11}$$

Similar qualitative results emerge with foreign price level disturbances: under floating rates, changes in the foreign price level affect only the exchange rate while the domestic price level and consumption do not vary; under fixed rates, disturbances in the foreign price level produce disturbances in both the domestic price level and domestic consumption.

I.B REAL DISTURBANCES

The most interesting comparison between the responses of the two systems to disturbances occurs when the disturbance is in domestic income and output.
Let

$$Y_t = Y + u_t \tag{12}$$

where u_t has zero mean, variance σ_u^2 and is serially uncorrelated. Once again, $P_t^* = P^*$ for all t.

(i) Floating Rate

Under floating rates, with passive monetary policy, we have

$$\sigma_{c/p}^2 = \sigma_u^2 \tag{13}$$

and

$$P_t = \frac{M}{k(Y+u_t)}. \tag{14}$$

Without specifying the distribution of u_t, it is not in general possible to write down the mean and variance of the price level. It is, however, clear that the price level has non-zero variance.

(ii)   Fixed Rate
From (4) we have:

$$M_t = (1-\alpha)M_{t-1} + \alpha k P(Y+u_t). \tag{15}$$

Accordingly, the steady-state variance of the nominal money stock is

$$\sigma^2_{M} = \frac{\alpha^2 k^2 P^3 \sigma^2_u}{1-(1-\alpha)^2}. \tag{16}$$

Now rewriting the consumption function (5) and using (4):

$$\frac{C_t}{P} = Y_t(1-\alpha k) + \frac{\alpha M_{t-1}}{P}. \tag{17}$$

It is natural to assume $(1-\alpha k) > 0$ so that the propensity to consume from current income is positive. From equation (17) there are two sources of disturbance in consumption: there are changes in current income, which are smoothed through the balance of payments (via the $-\alpha k$ term), but also, past disturbances in the money stock affect current consumption as consumers try to restore money balance equilibrium. The variance of real consumption is:

$$\sigma^2_{c/p} = (1-\alpha k)^2 \sigma^2_u + \frac{\alpha^4 k^2 \sigma^2_u}{1-(1-\alpha)^2} \tag{18}$$

Now the variance of consumption under the two exchange rate regimes as given by (13) and (18) are compared. Consider the inequality:

$$1 > (1-\alpha k)^2 + \frac{\alpha^4 k^2}{1-(1-\alpha)^2}$$

With some manipulation this is equivalent to

$$(1-\alpha k) + (1-\alpha) > 0 \tag{19}$$

which is ensured by the assumptions on α and αk. Accordingly, the variance of consumption in the fixed rate regime is less than that in the floating rate regime. This result reflects the shock-absorber role of the balance of payments under fixed rates. Since there is also no variance of prices under fixed rates, fixed rates are preferable if disturbances are real.

I.C ACTIVE MONETARY POLICY

Thus far the monetary authority in the small country has been purely passive. Would more active policies change the conclusions? The model should be thought of as one in which there is very little for the monetary authority to do. The assumption is that the current disturbance does not affect current monetary policy – i.e. that there is at least a one-period recognition and decision lag for the monetary authority.[3] Accordingly there is nothing the monetary authority can do to stabilise the price level under floating rates where all adjustments to a particular disturbance are completed within the period the disturbance occurs.

Under fixed exchange rates, however, private adjustments to a given disturbance are not completed within a single period since the restoration of money balances takes place with a distributed lag. There is thus scope for some stabilising action by the government. Specifically, suppose that money can be freely manufactured (destroyed) and distributed (collected) by the monetary authority. Let ΔMG_t be the government-created money stock in each period. The balance of payments is no longer given by equation (3) but rather by

$$B_t = M_t - (M_{t-1} + \Delta MG_t) \tag{20}$$

The optimal monetary rule under fixed rates with stabilisation of consumption as the target is the certainty equivalence rule:[4]

$$\Delta MG_t = \alpha(kPY - M_{t-1}) \tag{21}$$

Thus, the monetary authority provides that amount of money which would put consumption at its mean leavel if there were no disturbance in the current period – i.e. the authority compensates for past disturbances.

(i) Money Demand Disturbances

Using equations (4), (6), (20) and (21), we obtain

$$\begin{aligned} B_t &= \alpha(L_t - M_{t-1}) - \alpha(kPY - M_{t-1}) \\ &= \alpha(kPY + \varepsilon_t - kPY) \\ &= \alpha\varepsilon_t \end{aligned} \tag{22}$$

Substituting into (5), we obtain

$$\sigma^2_{c/p} = \frac{\alpha^2 \sigma^2_\varepsilon}{P^2} \tag{23}$$

which is less than the corresponding variance in equation (11) with passive monetary policy.

(ii) Real Disturbances

It was noted, following equation (17), that there are two sources of variation in consumption with real disturbances under fixed rates: the variation arising from the current disturbance and that arising from lagged adjustment of the money stock. The latter source of variation is removed by the use of an active monetary policy.

Combining (4), (12), (20) and (21), we obtain

$$
\begin{aligned}
B_t &= \alpha(L_t - M_{t-1}) - \alpha(kPY - M_{t-1}) \\
&= \alpha(kP(Y + u_t) - kPY) \\
&= \alpha kPu_t
\end{aligned}
\tag{24}
$$

The variance of real consumption is then

$$
\sigma^2_{c/p} = (1 - \alpha k)^2 \sigma^2_u
\tag{25}
$$

which is less than the corresponding expression in (18) with passive monetary policy and is *a fortiori* less than the variance of consumption under floating rates.

It should be noted that although the stabilisation instrument above has been the money stock, there is no reason why fiscal policy could not be used with the same result. Monetary policy might operate through lump-sum taxes and transfers, so that monetary and fiscal policy become indistinguishable. Alternatively, one could think of a commodity stabilisation scheme to smooth consumption.

I.D   PRICE VERSUS QUANTITY CHANGES

If disturbances are real, then a fixed exchange rate system provides less variance of both consumption and prices than a floating rate system. With money demand disturbances, however, fixed rates provide a stable price level and variable consumption while floating rates yield variable prices and stable consumption. The question arises of how the variability of prices is to be compared with the variability of consumption in assessing the alternative exchange rate systems.

Concavity of utility functions expressed as a function of consumption justifies concern with the stability of consumption but it is not obvious that price variability is, of itself, undesirable. Indeed, for a while it was popular to argue that price variability is desirable.[5] In the context of this model, two possible costs of price level instability are suggested: first, price level changes could lead to output changes through Phillips-curve type phenomena referred to by Lucas (1973) in which entrepreneurs mistake absolute price level changes for relative price changes, or alternatively, because nominal wages adjust at a different rate than prices; second, it is sometimes argued that price variability reduces the quality of money. The second argument has attractive poetic qualities though the first is more plausible.

Consider now adding to the basic model represented by equations (1)–(5) the Phillips curve equation:

$$
Y_t - \mu_Y = \beta(P_t - E_{t-1}(P_t)) + u_t \qquad \beta > 0
\tag{26}
$$

where μ_Y is the mean level of output and $E_{t-1}(P_t)$ is the expectation of P_t conditional on information available up to and including period $t-1$. The addition of (26) complicates the model considerably and requires more precise specification of the distributions of the stochastic terms (as in Section II.B below) for the calculation of the relevant means and variances. Since qualitative conclusions on stability of consumption with the Phillips curve (26) in the model depend on the values of the parameters β, α and k it does not appear useful to develop the analysis here. The obvious is, however, worth stating: the greater is β – the more sensitive is output to absolute price level changes – the more likely is it that consumption is more stable under fixed than flexible rates, even in response to monetary disturbances.

II A TWO-COUNTRY WORLD

The extension of the results for a single country to a two-country world is obvious and straightforward for a floating exchange rate regime in which there is no Phillips curve. The simplest model is used in this section. Most equations of the two country model are the same as those of the one-country model, (1)–(5). Corresponding to (1), (3), (4) and (5) are identical equations for the foreign country, but with all variables asterisked. In addition, with inactive monetary policies, under floating rates we have

$$M_t = M \qquad (27)$$
$$M_t^* = M^* \qquad (28)$$
$$M_t + eM_t^* = \overline{M} \qquad (29)$$

where $\overline{M}$ is the world money supply. The countries are assumed to be identical – in size and behavioural parameters – except for stochastic components of the functions, and under fixed exchange rates the exchange rate is set at unity.

II.A MONEY DEMAND DISTURBANCES
In the two countries, let

$$L_t = kP_tY_t + \varepsilon_t \qquad (30)$$

and

$$L_t^* = kP_t^*Y_t^* + \varepsilon_t^* \qquad (31)$$

respectively. Assume that ε_t and ε_t^* have means zero, variances σ_ε^2 and $\sigma_{\varepsilon*}^2$ and each is serially uncorrelated; the correlation between ε_t and ε_t^* is specified below.

(i) Floating Rates
Under floating rates the money demand disturbances work themselves out entirely in price changes. If the disturbances are perfectly positively correlated and have the same variance, then the exchange rate remains

constant; otherwise it too varies. The rate of consumption is constant through time in each country. Thus, the single country conclusions carry over directly although the actual variance of prices is the same for the two cases only if the disturbances are perfectly correlated.

(ii)   Fixed Rates

Under fixed rates the qualitative conclusions of Section I apply. In general there is variability in both prices and consumption in the two countries. In particular

(a)   If the disturbances are perfectly negatively correlated with $\varepsilon_t = -\varepsilon_t^*$ then the price level in each country is constant and the variance of consumption in each country is given by the same formula, (11) as it is for the single country of Section I. To see this, use (29), (4), (30) and (31): then

$$\overline{M} = (1-\alpha)M_{t-1} + \alpha(kP_tY + \varepsilon_t) + (1-\alpha)M_{t-1}^* + \alpha(kP_tY^* + \varepsilon_t^*)$$

So, using (29) and (2):

$$P_t = \frac{\overline{M} - (\varepsilon_t + \varepsilon_t^*)}{k(Y+Y^*)} \tag{32}$$

With $\varepsilon_t = -\varepsilon_t^*$ then $P_t = \dfrac{\overline{M}}{k(Y+Y^*)}$ for all t.

The remainder of the analysis proceeds as in Section I.

(b)   If the disturbances in the two countries are perfectly positively correlated with $\varepsilon_t = \varepsilon_t^*$ then, from (32)

$$P_t = \frac{\overline{M} - 2\varepsilon_t}{k(Y+Y^*)}$$

Then using (4) to compute the asymptotic variance of the money supply in the home country:

$$\sigma_M^2 = (1-\alpha)^2\sigma_M^2 + \alpha^2(k^2Y^2\sigma_p^2 + 2kY \text{ cov } (P_t\varepsilon_t) + \sigma_\varepsilon^2) \tag{33}$$

$$= (1-\alpha)^2\sigma_M^2 + \alpha^2\sigma_\varepsilon^2\left(\frac{4Y^2}{(Y+Y^*)^2} - \frac{4Y}{(Y+Y^*)} + 1\right)$$

Since $Y = Y^*$ by assumption

$$\sigma_M^2 = 0. \tag{34}$$

Thus with perfect positive correlation of the disturbances the money supply in each country remains fixed, consumption is equal to output in each country, and behaviour is the same as under floating rates.[6]

(c)   In other cases – i.e. when the correlation coefficient is less than unity in absolute value – the variance of prices is greater than it is for the single country under fixed rates and the variance of consumption is less than it is for the single country under fixed rates.

II.B REAL DISTURBANCES

This case is analysed in greater detail than the case of money demand disturbances. Accordingly, it is necessary to make strong assumptions about the distributions of the levels of income in each country. Income is assumed to have the gamma distribution,[7] with parameters $n > 2$ and $\lambda > 0$ in each country. For $n > 1$, the distribution is hump-shaped and skewed to the right. The mean and variance of Y_t are given by

$$E(Y_t) = \frac{n}{\lambda} = \mu_Y \quad E\left(\left(Y_t - \frac{n}{\lambda}\right)^2\right) = \frac{n}{\lambda^2} = \sigma_Y^2 \tag{35}$$

and similarly for Y^*. Given the assumptions on the distributions, the behaviour of the system under the two exchange rate regimes can be examined.

(i) Floating Rates

Under floating rates both prices and consumption are variable. The variance of real consumption is given by

$$\sigma_{c/p}^2 = \sigma_Y^2 = \frac{n}{\lambda^2} \tag{36}$$

The price level is determined by

$$P_t = \frac{M}{kY_t} \tag{37}$$

with resultant variance of prices

$$\sigma_P^2 = \frac{\lambda^2 M^2}{k^2 (n-1)^2 (n-2)} \tag{38}$$

(ii) Fixed Rates

(a) With perfectly negatively correlated disturbances, the analysis of section II.A (ii) (a) applies almost exactly. The price level in each country stays constant but there is variability of consumption for each country, equal to

$$\sigma_{c/p}^2 = \sigma_Y^2 \left((1 - \alpha k)^2 + \frac{\alpha^4 k^2}{1 - (1 - \alpha)^2} \right)$$

$$= \frac{n}{\lambda^2} \left((1 - \alpha k)^2 + \frac{\alpha^4 k^2}{1 - (1 - \alpha)^2} \right) \tag{39}$$

This variance of consumption is less than that under floating rates.

Surprisingly, although world output is constant, consumption in each country is not constant. Thus smoothing through the balance of payments is not complete. There would be more – though probably not complete – smoothing of consumption in the presence of capital movements.

(b) If the disturbances are perfectly positively correlated, then $Y_t \equiv Y_t^*$ and the system behaves exactly like the floating exchange rate system, with the same variances of prices and consumption in each country.

(c) With zero correlation of the disturbances, we have

$$P_t = \frac{\overline{M}}{k(Y_t + Y_t^*)} \tag{40}$$

with

$$\sigma_p^2 = \frac{\overline{M}^2 \lambda^2}{k^2 (2n-1)^2 (2n-2)} \tag{41}$$

Comparing (38) with (41), assuming $2M = \overline{M}$, the price level for the individual country is more stable under fixed than floating rates on the assumption $n > 2$, which is required for the variance to exist for the single country.

To calculate the variance of consumption, it is first necessary to obtain the variance of the money stock, using (4), (29) and (40).

$$M_t = (1-\alpha)M_{t-1} + \alpha \overline{M} \frac{Y_t}{Y_t + Y_t^*} \tag{42}$$

yielding[8]

$$E(M_t) = \frac{\overline{M}}{2} \text{ and } \sigma_M^2 = \frac{\overline{M}^2}{4(2-\alpha)(2n+1)} \tag{43}$$

Then, from (3), (4) and (5),

$$\frac{C_t}{P_t} = Y_t(1-\alpha k) + \frac{\alpha M_{t-1}}{P_t} = Y_t(1-\alpha k) + \frac{\alpha k M_{t-1}}{\overline{M}}(Y_t + Y_t^*)$$

It follows that

$$E\left(\frac{C_t}{P_t}\right) = \frac{n}{\lambda} \tag{44}$$

and[9]

$$\sigma_{c/p}^2 = \frac{n}{\lambda^2}\left((1-\alpha k) + \frac{\alpha^3 k^2}{1-(1-\alpha)^2}\right) \tag{45}$$

This variance is smaller than the variance of consumption under floating rates but larger than the corresponding variance when incomes in the two countries are perfectly negatively correlated.

Thus, as one would expect, with real disturbances, consumption is more stable under fixed than floating rates, and is more stable under fixed rates, the smaller (algebraically) the correlation between the disturbances in the two countries.

II.C ACTIVE MONETARY POLICY

Under fixed exchange rates there is room for stabilising monetary policy by one or both countries: the effects of one country's stabilising actions on the other depend critically on the correlation of disturbances in the two countries.

At one extreme, where total world income and output are constant (perfect negative correlation of disturbances), stabilisation of consumption by one country is automatically stabilising for the other country. At the other extreme of perfect correlation, stabilisation by one country is automatically destabilising for the other.[10]

With zero correlation of disturbances, there is room for the adoption of the same monetary rule in each country, such that the rule is mutually stabilising and more stabilising than the adoption of the rule by one country alone.

Let ΔMG_t and ΔMG_t^* be the policy induced changes in period t in the money supply domestically and in the foreign country respectively. Let $\overline{M}_t$ be the world money supply in period t. Then it can be shown that

$$P_t = \frac{\alpha \overline{M}_{t-1} + \Delta MG_t + \Delta MG_t^*}{\alpha k(Y_t + Y_t^*)} \tag{46}$$

and

$$\frac{C_t}{P_t} = Y_t(1 - \alpha k) + \frac{\alpha M_{t-1} + \Delta MG_t}{P_t}$$

$$= Y_t(1 - \alpha k) + \frac{\alpha M_{t-1} + \Delta MG_t}{\alpha \overline{M}_{t-1} + \Delta MG_t + \Delta MG_t^*} \alpha k(Y_t + Y_t^*)$$

$$= Y_t(1 - \alpha k) + \phi(\quad) \alpha k(Y_t + Y_t^*) \tag{47}$$

Consider now the potential for agreement on rules of the game. From the viewpoint of each country, and conditional on the assumption that ΔMG_t and ΔMG_t^* are functions only of lagged variables, the optimal policy is to keep the function $\phi(\quad)$ in (47) and the corresponding $\phi^*(\quad)$ function constant. If one country – say the foreign country – uses a purely passive policy, it appears at first that the domestic country can manipulate ΔMG_t to keep $\phi(\quad)$ constant, even though ϕ^* will then be stochastic. However, that implies that the asymptotic variance of the price level is infinite[11] – i.e. that adoption of a stabilising rule for domestic consumption by the domestic monetary authority creates price level instability for the world.

On the other hand, both countries acting together can stabilise consumption in each country and maintain world price stability.[12] In particular, subject to each country's using the same rule, an optimal rule for stabilising consumption is the policy rule (21) where kPY is now $kE(P_tY_t)$. Then, for the home country,

$$\frac{C_t}{P_t} = Y_t(1 - \alpha k) + \frac{\alpha k}{2}(Y_t + Y_t^*) \tag{48}$$

yielding

$$\sigma_{c/p}^2 = \frac{n}{\lambda^2}\left(1 - \alpha k + \frac{\alpha^2 k^2}{2}\right), \tag{49}$$

a variance which is less than that obtained under passive policy in (45). In addition, the variance of the price level is finite.[13] If the domestic country alone followed the rule, the variance of its consumption would exceed that in (49).

III CONCLUSIONS

The paper had two basic aims: first, to study the responses of an economy to various repeated disturbances under systems of floating and fixed exchange rates; and second, to consider potential rules of the game for monetary policy under fixed rates.

The conclusions with regard to the first point are simple: if disturbances are monetary, then under floating rates, price level changes absorb the shocks completely while the shocks are transmitted to consumption under fixed rates. If disturbances are real, then floating rates prevent the transmission of shocks abroad and result in greater instability of consumption – even for both countries in a two-country world – than occurs under fixed rates. The results in the small country case are equivalent to those in the two-country world with perfect negative correlation of disturbances. The conclusions on the superiority of floating rates in the face of monetary shocks depends on the assumption that price level instability, *per se*, has no real effects. If price level instability produces real instability through a Phillips curve or some other mechanism, then the superiority of floating rates in the face of monetary shocks becomes less certain. Despite their simplicity, the conclusions differ from those of Mundell (1960), who argues that, with capital immobility, stability is always greater under floating than under fixed rates.

Given the structure of the model in which money balances are restored to equilibrium with a distributed lag, there is room for a stabilising active monetary policy under fixed rates with real disturbances. The extent to which one country's stabilisation policy with regard to consumption is stabilising for the other country depends on the correlation of the disturbances in the two countries. If the disturbances are perfectly positively correlated, then one country can stabilise only by destabilising the consumption of the other country. If the disturbances are perfectly negatively correlated, then any stabilisation by one country is automatically stabilising for the other country. In the case of zero correlation of disturbances, a simple monetary rule is derived which stabilises consumption for both countries if used by each.

It is appropriate to comment on certain features of the analysis and to consider extensions. First, it should be noted that the assumption of a one-period lag by the authorities in adjusting the money supply is very strong: in this model some private sector adjustments are made before the authorities can react. In particular, under floating rates, price level adjustments in response to monetary disturbances occur within one period and absorb the entire shock. Under fixed rates, the monetary authorities are not given an opportunity to react to the monetary disturbance until the next period. The more usual assumption may be that the authorities respond faster than the private sector; evidence on this issue is hard to find. Second, it should be noted that it has been assumed that mean rates of output are independent of the exchange rate system and also, for most of the analysis, that output is exogenous. Third, and most important, the analysis will be extended to include capital movements which would presumably smooth consumption and permit the modification of the very tight link between consumption and money stock behaviour of the present model.

NOTES

1. References to other literature are provided by Tower and Courtney.
2. Baumol (1961) has emphasised the distinction between the transient response of a system to a single disturbance and its behaviour under repeated shocks.
3. See, however, the discussion in Section III.
4. This is for the cases of disturbances in money demand and income; the rule for disturbances in the foreign price level is different.
5. For references to this literature, and for the resolution of the debate, see Hanoch (1974).
6. It will be recalled that with perfect positive correlation of the disturbances under floating rates, the exchange rate remained constant.
7. See Mood, Graybill and Boes (1974, p. 112) for details on the gamma distribution. The chi-square distribution belongs to the gamma family.
8. The reason for using the gamma distribution should now be clear. The sum of independent gamma-distributed variables with the same λ is gamma-distributed; the ratio of gamma-distributed variables with the same λ has the beta distribution. Thus $(Y_t + Y_t^*)$ is

gamma-distributed with parameters $2n$ and λ; the ratio in (42) is beta distributed with parameters n and $2n$. See Mood, Graybill and Boes (1974, p. 115) for the beta distribution.

9. The derivation of (45) is fairly lengthy and will be supplied on request.

10. Accordingly, as Jacob Frenkel has pointed out, the potential for conflict with regard to policy depends on the correlations of disturbances.

11. At issue is the root of the difference equation for M_t^* since for $\phi(\ ) \equiv \theta$,

$$P_t = \frac{M_{t-1}^*}{(1-\theta)k(Y_t + Y_t^*)}.$$

The relevant difference equation is $M_t^* = \left(1 - \alpha + \dfrac{\alpha Y_t^*}{(1-\theta)(Y_t + Y_t^*)}\right)M_{t-1}^*$.

Now, for the expected price level not to have a trend, it is necessary to set $\theta = 1/2$. But then the asymptotic variance of the price level is infinite.

12. In the sense that price level variance is finite.

13. The rule (21) is not the only rule which yields the variance (49) – hence the reference to it as 'an' optimal rule. However, it is probably the only one of those rules which also keeps the price level stable.

REFERENCES

Argy, Victor and Kouri, Pentti J. K., 'Sterilisation Policies and the Volatility in International Reserves', Robert Z. Aliber (ed.) *National Monetary Policies and the International Monetary System* (University of Chicago Press, 1974).

Baumol, William J., 'Pitfalls in Contracyclical Policies; Some Tools and Results', *Review of Economics and Statistics* (Feb 1961) 21–6.

Dornbusch, Rudiger, 'Devaluation, Money, and Nontraded Goods', *American Economic Review* (Dec 1973) 871–80.

Hanoch, Giora, 'Desirability of Price Stabilisation or Destabilisation', Harvard Institute of Economic Research, Discussion Paper Number 351 (Mar 1974).

Johnson, Harry G., 'The Case for Flexible Exchange Rates, 1969', *Federal Reserve Bank of St. Louis Review* (June 1969) 12–24.

Kindleberger, Charles P., 'The Case for Fixed Exchange Rates, 1969', in the Federal Reserve Bank of Boston Conference Series No. 2, *The International Adjustment Mechanism* (Oct 1969) 93–108.

Laffer, Arthur B., 'Two Arguments for Fixed Rates', in H. G. Johnson and A. K. Swoboda (eds) *The Economics of Common Currencies* (London: Allen & Unwin, 1973) 25–34.

Lucas, Robert E., Jr, 'Some International Evidence on Output – Inflation Tradeoffs', *American Economic Review* (June 1973) 326–34.

McKinnon, Ronald I., 'Sterilisation in Three Dimensions: Major Trading Countries, Euro-currencies, and the United States', forthcoming in Robert Z. Aliber, (ed.) *National Monetary Policies and the International Monetary System* (University of Chicago Press, 1974).

Mood, Alexander M., Graybill, Franklin A., and Boes, Duane C., *Introduction to the Theory of Statistics*, third edition (New York: Macmillan, 1974).

Mundell, Robert A., 'The Monetary Dynamics of International Adjustment under Fixed and Flexible Exchange Rates', *Quarterly Journal of Economics* (May 1960) 227–57.

Stein, Jerome L., 'The Optimum Foreign Exchange Market', *American Economic Review* (June 1963) 384–402.

Tower, Edward and Courtney, Mark M., 'Exchange Rate Flexibility and Macro-Economic Stability', *Review of Economics and Statistics* (May 1974) 215–24.

6 International Investment and Interest Rate Linkages under Flexible Exchange Rates*

Pentti J. K. Kouri

I INTRODUCTION

One of the main arguments against the Bretton Woods system of pegged exchange rates was that it seriously limited the freedom of Central Banks, with the exception of that of the United States, to use monetary policy for domestic stabilisation. With the growth of the Eurocurrency markets and other channels of international investment interest rates in different countries tended to be equalised by arbitrage, except at times of speculation when substantial margins developed in an anticipation of an exchange rate change. The other side of the same phenomena was the problem of 'offsetting capital flows'. An independent tightening (or easing) of monetary policy in some country would induce an inflow (outflow) of capital that would offset, at least partially, the intended effect of the policy on the monetary base. The other two manifestations of this lack of monetary independence were the transmission of external business cycles and in particular the problem of imported inflation. In principle the first problem could have been taken care of by the assignment of fiscal policy to domestic stabilisation but in none of the

* This is a revised version of a paper given at the Wingspread Conference on the Political Economy of Monetary Reform, July 1974. I have benefited from comments of and discussions with several people in addition to the participants of the conference. In particular I would like to thank S. Fischer, C. P. Kindleberger and F. Modigliani. They are not responsible for whatever errors the paper may contain.

major industrial countries could fiscal policy be flexibly used for this purpose. The result was the recurrence of situations of conflict between external and domestic objectives of monetary policy, bound to arise when one instrument is used to achieve two targets.

The problem of 'imported inflation' or more generally of divergent inflationary tendencies became serious from the late 1960s and in the end contributed to the collapse of the Bretton Woods system. One of the consequences of the persistent conflict between external and domestic objectives of monetary policy was the use of restrictions on international capital movements even in countries that traditionally favoured maximum freedom of such transactions.

Against this background the system of flexible rates is in theory supposed to take care of all of these problems at the same time. In the words of H. G. Johnson:

> The fundamental argument for flexible exchange rates is that they allow countries autonomy with respect to their use of monetary, fiscal, and other policy instruments, consistent with the maintenance of whatever degree of freedom in international transactions they choose to allow their citizens.[1]

In addition to the simultaneous achievement of national autonomy with free trade in goods and capital the third argument for flexible exchange rates is that stabilising speculation evens out short-term disturbances while it permits long-term shifts in supply and demand conditions to have an effect on the exchange rate and thus takes care of the required balance of payments adjustment automatically.

This paper investigates the interdependence of national financial markets under the regime of flexible exchange rates in the framework of a general equilibrium model of the international capital markets. It is assumed that all financial assets except money are traded in the international financial markets in which transactions costs and other impediments to trade are small enough to be ignored. Money is used only in the country in which it is issued. There is no international money in the narrow sense of a medium of exchange, nor are different monies substitutable in domestic transactions. It is implicitly assumed that international transactions are largely settled by credit amongst trading partners so that the net demand for transactions balances in international trade is insignificant. This assumption also assumes away the potentially important problem of Gresham's law – the problem of coexistence of more than one money. This problem is deep enough to warrant a separate investigation. Investors are, however, free to borrow and lend in any currency of their choice—the holdings of foreign assets thus reflect portfolio motives rather than transactions demand for international reserves.

The model assumes that the exchange rates between currencies satisfy the purchasing power parity equation. The relative prices of commodities are assumed to be fixed.[2] Underlying this is the assumption of full employment and flexible prices.

It is further assumed that there is one country – the centre country – that has settled on a fully anticipated path of inflation. The real rate of interest in that country is assumed exogenous. International arbitrage ensures that the same real rate on riskless assets will prevail in all countries – in this respect there is no autonomy despite flexibility of exchange rates. The interest rates on bonds denominated in different currencies may, however, differ because of differences in inflation rates. If inflation rates were deterministic the nominal interest rates on bonds denominated in different currencies could differ only by the expected change in the exchange rate (with transactions costs there would be a neutral band of interest rates within which no arbitrage opportunities would arise). These interest rate parity equations no longer hold with uncertainty and risk aversion. It is shown in this paper that in addition to the expected change in the exchange rate the interest rate of a periphery country differs from that of the centre country by a variance term and a currency premium that is a compensation for the systematic inflation risk of the currency of that country. It is shown that this currency premium can be changed by monetary policy and by changes in the distribution of wealth between countries. Furthermore if the rates of inflation are correlated with the real returns on equity the difference in interest rates will also depend on the average real return on capital assets. These implications of the analysis demonstrate that changes in nominal interest rates between countries in excess of changes in exchange rate expectations are not in any way inconsistent with complete integration of the financial markets. It is also shown that unless the demand for money is completely interest inelastic interest rate differentials will not completely adjust to changes in the expected rate of inflation.

Forward markets in currencies are not introduced explicitly – there is no need to do so since there are bond markets in every currency. As Kindleberger (1975, appendix F to ch. 17) has emphasised, the forward market is related to the spot market by arbitrage once the interest rates are given; except for transactions costs or other risks the forward premium and the interest rate differential must be equal.[3] The results of the analysis can be directly applied to some questions discussed in connection with forward markets – for instance that the forward premium is not related in any simple way to the expected change in the exchange rate.

Another important implication of the analysis is that if there is no correlation between inflation rates and real equity returns the control of nominal interest rates does not enable the periphery countries to have any effect on the required real returns on risky capital (the cost of capital) which only depend on the exogenous real interest rate and on the real returns on other capital assets.

The plan of the paper is as follows. The next section develops the underlying model of portfolio selection and money demand by using the approach developed by Merton (1969, 1971, 1973) and applied to international capital markets by Solnik (1973, 1974). The only novelty there is the explicit introduction of money in a manner suggested by Sidrauski (1967) amongst others in a deterministic context. A reader who is not interested in techniques can go directly to section III that derives the equilibrium interest rate relationships. Section IV analyses the effects of monetary policy and other shifts in more detail in a two-country version of the model. The concluding section discusses the limitations of the model and suggests directions for further research. Whilst no empirical testing is undertaken in this paper there are a number of testable implications and the results do resolve some puzzles observed by other researchers.

II THE MODEL

The world economy consists of n countries each with its own currency. Currency is used only in the country in which it is issued – it is thus a non-traded asset. The implicit assumption is that international transactions are settled by credit amongst the trading partners – a feature not much unlike actual practice.[4] Each investor is, however, able to lend and borrow in any currency of his choice. In line with the standard assumptions of the models of capital market equilibrium I shall assume away transactions costs or other causes of differences in borrowing and lending rates; I shall also assume away the problem of default. These assumptions imply that the only attribute that distinguishes one bond from another is its currency denomination. An example that approximates this assumption might be the deposits and loans in the Eurocurrency markets. In addition to bonds investors may buy and sell equity in every country. For convenience but with no loss of generality it is assumed that there is only one equity in each country. Short sales in equity are allowed. Equity can be interpreted quite broadly in the analysis – for instance it can be thought of as holdings of gold or inventories of primary commodities.

There are altogether $3n$ assets that are traded in the financial markets and $3n - 1$ relative prices that are determined by the conditions of asset market equilibrium, namely n interest rates, n equity prices and $n - 1$ exchange rates between currencies. It is assumed that the asset markets are always in equilibrium.

The only novel feature in the analysis of investor behaviour is the introduction of money, although admittedly in a rather crude way. It is clear that it does not make much sense to talk about exchange rates in a model in which money does not appear, since the exchange rate is a relative price of one money with respect to another. It is assumed that investors derive utility from the stock of real balances they hold as well as from consumption. The approach is the same as that used in a deterministic context by Sidrauski (1967) and in a stochastic model by Dixit and Goldman (1970). The aim of each investor is to maximise the expected value of discounted utility over an infinite time horizon subject to the wealth constraint and stochastic returns to be specified below.

II.1   PRICE AND EXCHANGE RATE DYNAMICS

It is assumed that the centre country, taken as the nth country, has a certain rate of inflation (Π_n) fully anticipated by everybody. The reason why Π_n is assumed to be deterministic is to have one asset with a known real rate of return. This assumption simplifies the analysis although it is not critical for the main results.

The assumption implies that the price level (P_n) in the nth country behaves according to

$$\frac{dP_n}{P_n} = \Pi_n dt. \tag{1}$$

The other countries can maintain an inflation rate different from Π_n by allowing their exchange rate *vis-a-vis* the currency of the nth country to change. Ignoring the problems that arise from changes in relative prices, in particular between tradeable and non-tradeable goods, we assume that the price level in country i, (P_i), is determined by the purchasing power parity equation:

$$P_i = E_{ni} \cdot P_n. \tag{2}$$

The dynamics of the exchange rate is given by

$$\frac{dE_{ni}}{E_{ni}} = e_i dt + \sigma_i du_i, \quad i = 1, \ldots, n-1 \tag{3}$$

where du_i is a Wiener process or Brownian motion. The meaning of continuous stochastic processes like (3), known as Ito processes, in the context of portfolio theory is discussed in Merton (1971) and Fischer (1974). Briefly (3) implies that over a short time interval the proportionate change in the exchange rate is normal with mean $e_i dt$ and variance $\sigma_i^2 dt$. Also (3) implies that the exchange rate follows a random walk and is log-normally distributed.[5] Furthermore the stochastic component of (3) is serially uncorrelated no matter how short the time interval.

Using Ito's Lemma[6] we can obtain the dynamics of inflation in country i:

$$\frac{dP_i}{P_i} = (\Pi_n + e_i)dt + \sigma_i du_i, \quad i = 1, \ldots, n. \tag{4}$$

The economic rationale of these equations is the following. Each country has settled on some rate of inflation, which varies stochastically around its mean. The market participants have learnt the mean rate of inflation as well as its variance. They are right on an average although they may be in error in any given period. These assumptions correspond to what McKinnon (1971) calls the Fisherian model. The exchange rate adjusts continuously to enable the countries to maintain divergent rates of inflation.

II.2 ASSET RETURN DYNAMICS

The nominal return on bonds is known with certainty. It is assumed that market participants expect the nominal interest rate to remain constant – otherwise we would have to deal with the difficult problem of term structure of interest rates. Let B_j^i be the nominal value of bonds of country j held by an investor in country i. The real value of this investment is B_j^i multiplied by the exchange rate (E_{ji}) and divided by the price level in country $i(P_i)$. By the purchasing power parity equation this is simply B_j^i divided by the price level in country $j(P_j)$. Thus the real return on a bond denominated in currency j is the same for all investors; it is the nominal return plus the expected change in the price of money (inverse of the price level) in country j. In addition there is a stochastic component reflecting unanticipated inflation in country j. More formally if $\overline{B}_j$ is the real value of bonds denominated in currency j it changes stochastically according to

$$d\overline{B}_j/\overline{B}_j = (R_j - \Pi_j + \sigma_j^2)dt - \sigma_j du_j, \quad j = 1, \ldots, n. \tag{5}$$

Since there is no unanticipated inflation in the nth country σ_n is equal to zero.

Money differs from bonds only in that its nominal return is equal to zero. Therefore the real value of money of country $j(\overline{M}_j)$ changes stochastically according to

$$d\overline{M}_j/\overline{M}_j = (-\Pi_j + \sigma_j^2)dt - \sigma_j du_j, \quad j - 1, \ldots, n. \tag{6}$$

The similarity between (5) and (6) will prove useful below.

It is assumed that the return to equity accrues in the form of capital gains or losses. A detailed discussion of this approach is given in Merton (1973); it amounts to assuming that the firms distribute dividends by buying back their shares. The real price of equity, q_i , $i = 1, \ldots, n$, is assumed to change according to:

$$dq_i/q_i = \alpha_i dt + s_i dz_i, \quad i = 1, \ldots, n. \tag{7}$$

II.3 THE BUDGET EQUATION

At each moment an investor in country i is constrained by the wealth constraint:

$$W^i \equiv M^i/P_i + \Sigma B^i_j/P_j + \Sigma K^i_j q_j, \tag{8}$$

where W^i is the real stock of wealth and M^i is the nominal stock of money, and all other variables are as defined above. At each instant the investor chooses the composition of his portfolio and the rate of consumption. Once these decisions are made the stock of wealth changes stochastically according to:

$$dW^i = M^i d(1/P_i) + \Sigma B^i_j d(1/P_j) + \Sigma B^i_j R_j dt + \Sigma K^i_j dq_j - C^i dt. \tag{9}$$

A detailed derivation of this equation is left out, since its interpretation is obvious. The first part on the right-hand side represents income accruing to wealth; that income takes the form of capital gains and interest payments on bonds. The difference between income and consumption is saving which is exactly what the equation says.

Substituting from above we may write equation (9) in the more convenient form:

$$d\,W^i = [(M^i/P_i)(-\Pi_j + \sigma^2_i - r_n) + \Sigma(B^i_j/P_j)(r_j - r_n)$$

$$+ \Sigma K^i_j(\alpha_j - r_n) + W^i r_n] dt - C^i dt - (M^i/P_i)\sigma_i du_i$$

$$- \Sigma(B^i_j/P_j)\sigma_j du_j + \Sigma K^i_j s_j dz_j, \tag{10}$$

where $r_j = R_j - \Pi_j + \sigma^2_j$ $(j = 1, \ldots, n-1)$ and $r_n = R_n - \Pi_n$.

II.4 THE INVESTOR'S CHOICE PROBLEM

It is assumed that each investor chooses that consumption and portfolio strategy that maximises the expected value of utility from the programme over an infinite time horizon. The instantaneous utility is assumed to be a strictly concave function of consumption and the stock of real balances. The choice problem for a typical investor in country i is thus:

$$\mathrm{Max} E_t \int^\infty_t U(C^i, M^i/P_i)e^{-\rho\tau}d\tau \tag{11}$$

subject to the budget constraint (9).

The problem is solved by the technique of stochastic dynamic programming. Define

$$J(W^i, t) \equiv \mathrm{Max} E_t \int^\infty_t U(C^i, M^i/P_i)e^{-\rho\tau}d\tau \tag{12}$$

subject to the same constraint as above. The detailed derivation of the fundamental equation of optimality is left out. After some manipulations it can be written in the form (the subscripts and superscripts are left out for clarity):

$$0 \equiv \mathrm{Max} \{U[C, M/P]e^{-\rho\tau} + J_t + J_w W[-mR_i + b'r + k'\alpha + r_n]$$

$$- J_w C + 1/2 J_{ww} W^2 [b'\Omega b + k'Sk + 2b'\Gamma k]\} \tag{13}$$

where m = proportion of wealth invested in money $((M/P)/W)$.

             b = column vector whose ith component is $b_i + m_i$ and other components b_j, the proportion of wealth invested in jth bond, $j = 1, \ldots, n-1$.

             k = column vector whose typical element is k_j; proportion of wealth invested in jth equity, $j = 1, \ldots, n$.

             r = column vector of excess returns on bonds whose typical element is $R_j - \Pi_j + \sigma_j^2 - R_n + \Pi_n$.

             α = column vector of excess returns on equity whose typical element is $\alpha_j - R_n + \Pi_n$.

             Ω = $(n-1) \times (n-1)$ variance–covariance matrix of inflation rates.

             S = $n \times n$ variance–covariance matrix of equity returns.

             Γ = $(n-1) \times n$ variance–covariance matrix of inflation rates and equity returns.

This is now a standard optimisation problem which is unconstrained because the safe asset has been eliminated by the wealth constraint.

The first-order conditions are:

$$U_C = J_w. \tag{14.1}$$
$$U_M = R_i J_w. \tag{14.2}$$
$$J_w W r + J_{ww} W^2 [\Omega b + \Gamma k] = 0. \tag{14.3}$$
$$J_w W r + J_{ww} W^2 [S k + \Gamma' b] = 0. \tag{14.4}$$

These conditions are also sufficient because of the assumed strict concavity of $U(C, M/P)$.

II.5 THE OPTIMAL PORTFOLIO

From 14.1 to 14.2 we obtain immediately the result

$$U_C = (1/R_i) U_M. \tag{15}$$

This equation simply says that the marginal rate of substitution between money services and consumption (U_M/U_C) should equal the relative price, namely the rate of interest. Thus the demand for money can be written as a function of *only the desired consumption and the nominal rate of return on short-term bonds*. The intuitive reason for this result is that money and bonds have identical risk characteristics. The result does not depend on the assumption that there is no (unanticipated) inflation. In particular if we assume that $U(C, M/P)$ is a homogeneous function of C and M/P the demand for money function can be written in the familiar liquidity preference form:

$$M_i/P_i = v(R_i)C. \tag{16}$$

Consider first the case in which equity returns are not correlated with the rates of inflation. In that case the equilibrium portfolio proportions are given by:

$$b = a\Omega^{-1}r \qquad (17.1)$$
$$k = aS^{-1}\alpha, \qquad (17.2)$$

where $a = -J_W/WJ_{WW}$ is the Arrow–Pratt measure of relative risk aversion. The noticeable feature of these results is that the proportion of wealth invested in equity does not depend on exchange rate (inflation) risk.[7] Similarly the composition of the bond portfolio only depends on the real returns and risk attributes of bonds. Also the usual separation theorem holds – the composition of the portfolio of risky assets is the same for all investors who have homogeneous expectations. The other interesting feature of these results is that for investors of country i money and bonds can be aggregated into a single asset the demand for which depends on the same variables as that for any other asset. This means that domestic residents always 'hedge' their holdings of money balances by borrowing an equal amount in local currency. Complete hedging is possible because money and bonds have identical risk characteristics.[8] This result would not obtain – nor would equation (15) above – if there were no short-term asset with a riskless nominal return.

II.6 THE CONSUMPTION FUNCTION AND THE DEMAND FOR MONEY FUNCTION

A complete solution to the choice problem is obtained by specifying the utility function and solving for the consumption and demand for money functions. Whilst this can be done in more general cases I shall assume that the utility function is of the form:

$$U(C, M) = \alpha \log C + (1 - \alpha)\log(M/P). \qquad (18)$$

Using this and the first-order conditions one can rewrite (14) as a partial differential equation in J which can be easily solved.[9] Using the first-order condition (14.1) and equations (15) and (18) one obtains the simple and familiar result that consumption is a constant proportion of wealth:

$$C = cW, \qquad (19)$$

where $c = \alpha\rho$.

The consumption propensity depends only on the rate of time preference and parameter α. The economic meaning of α is the following. At any given instant total consumption is the sum of the consumption of commodities and the consumption of 'money services', which is assumed to be proportional to the stock of money (there is no harm in making that proportion equal one). Total consumption expenditure is then $C + R\dfrac{M}{P}$. The proportion of the consumption of commodities is $C/(C + R\dfrac{M}{P}) = C/\dfrac{1}{\alpha}C = \alpha$. Thus equation (19) also implies that the total consumption propensity is equal to the rate of time preference.

From (15) and (19) we get the demand for money function:

$$M_i^d/P_i = m(R_i)W = (1/R_i)cW. \tag{20}$$

The demand for money depends on permanent income or wealth rather than current income, the reason for this being that consumption depends on wealth rather than income.

III THE EQUILIBRIUM YIELD RELATIONSHIPS AMONGST ASSETS

III.1 EQUILIBRIUM RETURNS ON EQUITY

Assuming that investors have identical expectations we can now derive the equilibrium relationship between expected returns on equity in different countries. The total demand for equity for country i is given by:

$$K_i^d = (\sum k_i^h W^h)\sum_j S_{ij}^{-1}(\alpha_j - R_n - \Pi_n) = K_i q_i, \tag{21}$$

where $K_i q_i$ is the market value in real terms of the existing supply of equity. Let V be the market value of all stocks and let v_i be defined by $K_i q_i = v_i V$. Substituting this above we obtain:

$$\alpha_i - R_n - \Pi_n = KA\sum_j w_j S_{ij} = K_i A s_{iK}, \tag{22}$$

where $\quad A = 1/(\sum k_i^h W^h)$.

s_{iK} is the covariance of the return on the ith security with the return on a portfolio consisting of all stocks with the share of each security corresponding to its share of the total market value (the so-called market portfolio). Multiplying both sides of equation (22) by v_i and adding up we get:

$$\alpha_M - R_n - \Pi_n = K A s_K^2, \tag{23}$$

where s_K^2 is the variance of the return on the market portfolio. Combining these two equations we obtain:

$$\alpha_i - r_n = \frac{s_{iK}}{s_K^2}(\alpha_M - r_n) = \beta_i(\alpha_M - r_n), \tag{24}$$

where $\quad r_n = R_n - \Pi_n$.

This is the standard security market line equation which states that investors are compensated in terms of expected return for bearing systematic (market) risk. $(\alpha_M - r_n)/s_K^2$ is often called the market price of risk and accordingly s_{iK} is defined as the systematic risk of security i. The important implication of this result from the viewpoint of the theory of flexible exchange rates is that as long as the purchasing power parity holds and there is no systematic relationship between inflation rates and equity returns the flexibility of the exchange rates in no way alters the equilibrium relationships between returns on risky capital. In this sense, there is no more monetary autonomy under flexible exchange rates than there is under fixed exchange rates under similar circumstances.

In particular, a small economy that is extensively integrated into the world commodity and capital markets (for instance a state in the United States) cannot insulate itself by simply having its own money. The relative prices of commodities continue to be determined in the world market. Similarly, the real interest rate and the required rates of returns on risky capital are given exogenously.

If there is a systematic relationship between equity returns and the rates of inflation, the effect of changes in nominal interest rates on equity returns can be of either sign depending on the signs and magnitudes of the covariance terms. For example, it is quite possible that domestic bonds and equity are complements rather than substitutes in the portfolio of investors.[10]

III.2   EQUILIBRIUM RELATIONSHIPS BETWEEN INTEREST RATES

Flexibility of exchange rates permits, however, differences in nominal interest rates between various countries. A common hypothesis about interest rate differentials is that the interest rate differential can be attributed to the expected percentage change in the exchange rate. There is one case in the model developed above in which the expectations hypothesis is (almost) correct. This is when there is no net outside supply of bonds in any currency. To demonstrate this consider the total demand for bonds denominated in currency i:

$$B_i^d/P_i = (\sum a^h W^h)\sum \Omega_{ij}^{-1} r_j - M_i^d/P_i = B_i^s/P_i, \quad i = 1, \ldots, n-1. \tag{25}$$

The right-hand side is the net supply of bonds to the private sector. It is equal to the outstanding stock of government debt (B_i^G) less the amount held by the central bank. Assuming that the central bank changes the money supply by open-market operations in bonds that is equal to the nominal supply of money. We can therefore rewrite (25) in the form:

$$B_i^d/P_i = (\sum a^h W^h)\sum_j \Omega_{ij}^{-1} r_j = B_i^G/P_i, \quad i = 1, \ldots, n-1. \tag{26}$$

An immediate implication of this is that if the supply of government debt is zero, or if the government chooses the composition of its debt according to the same criterion as the private sector, the expectations hypothesis is valid. In other words:

$$R_i - R_n = \Pi_i - \Pi_n - \sigma_i^2 = e_i - \sigma_i^2, \quad i = 1, \ldots, n-1. \tag{27}$$

The difference in interest rates between countries i and n is equal to the expected change in the exchange rate corrected for the variance term. The reason why the variance term appears in equation (27) is that the expected change in the purchasing power of money (inverse of the price level) is not the same as minus the rate of inflation. As an illustration consider the following example.[11] The price level today is equal to one, and it is 1.6 with probability 0.5 and 0.4 with probability 0.5 tomorrow. The expected rate of inflation is obviously zero (the expected price level being $1.6 \times 0.5 + 0.4 \times 0.5 = 1$). However the expected real return on money is the expected value of $1/P_2 - 1$ where P_2 is the price level in the second period. That is equal to $1/0.64 - 1 = 56\%$. There is no expected inflation but yet money has a large expected positive return. It turns out that in the continuous time case the difference between the mean rate of inflation and the mean rate of change in the purchasing power of money is equal to minus the variance of inflation.

In general, however, the expectations hypothesis does not hold. If there exist net supplies of bonds exogenously given to the private sector interest rates on assets will contain a premium (or discount) in compensation for the systematic risk that the holders of these bonds must bear. This currency can be interpreted as a 'habitat' effect on interest rates in that there are some market participants who have a 'strong preference' for particular currencies, e.g. governments who issue debt in their own currency. The exogenous supply could also be interpreted as the net supply (demand) of bonds by investors who only hold a few assets and do not operate in the international capital market in the same way as the rational investor described in the model.

In the same way as in the previous section we can derive the required compensation in terms of expected return for investors to hold the existing supply of bonds denominated in various currencies:

$$r_i - r_n = b_i(r_M - r_n) = (\sigma_{iB}/\sigma_B^2)(r_M - r_n), \quad i = 1, \ldots, n-1, \quad (28)$$

where r_i is the expected real return on bonds denominated in the ith currency, r_M is the weighted average real return on all bonds (each bond yield weighted by the market share; in the standard terminology r_M is the expected real return on a market portfolio of bonds). As before σ_{iB} is the covariance between the expected return on the ith bond and that on the market portfolio of bonds, and σ_B^2 is the variance of the return on the market portfolio of bonds.

The difference in nominal interest rates is accordingly:

$$R_i - R_n = e_i - \sigma_i^2 + b_i(r_M - r_n), \quad i = 1, \ldots, n-1. \quad (29)$$

In addition to the expectations term the interest rate differential contains a premium for the systematic inflation risk. This premium is neglected in the traditional interest rate parity calculations.[12] Since the forward premium on the ith currency is equal to the difference in nominal interest rates in the absence of transactions costs equation (29) provides yet another demonstration that the forward premium is not an unbiased predictor of the change in the exchange rate.[13] Equation (29) also implies the possibility that a country with a depreciating exchange rate will have a lower interest rate than that in the centre country – this happens when the inflation rate in country i is negatively correlated with the average inflation rate in the world (which implies that b_i is negative).

IV   MONETARY POLICY, EXPECTED INFLATION AND THE RATE OF INTEREST

This section analyses the effects of monetary policy and exchange rate expectations in more detail. Since equation (33) obtains in general the effect of monetary policy is to change the 'currency premium' via changes in the b coefficient and the average return on the market portfolio of bonds. For simplicity it is assumed that there are only two countries – a centre country (denoted by asterisk) and a 'periphery' country. The real rate of interest in the centre country is exogenously given as before.

There are three assets in the periphery-money, bonds and capital, the latter two of which are internationally traded. The first equilibrium condition is that the demand for and the supply of money are equal:

$$M^d/P = m(R)W = M/P. \tag{30}$$

The second is that the net demand for government debt equals the outstanding stock:

$$B^d/P = d(R - R^* - \Pi + \sigma^2, \sigma^2)(W + W^*) = B^G/P, \tag{31}$$

where $d(R - R^* - \Pi + \sigma^2, \sigma^2) = \dfrac{1}{\sigma^2}(R - R^* - \Pi + \sigma^2).$

It is assumed for simplicity that the rate of inflation in the centre country is equal to zero. The demand functions can be aggregated since in the framework of the model the portfolio proportions are the same for investors in the two countries. This implies that the distribution of wealth between the two countries does not depend on current asset values although it may change over time if the saving propensies differ between the two countries. The underlying assumptions are that investors have identical expectations and the same degree of risk aversion, namely one. In general the distribution of wealth will obviously be endogenous, and a complete macroeconomic model is required to establish the determination of the aggregate stock of wealth and its distribution. The following analysis would still apply except that the distribution of wealth must be interpreted as an endogenous variable. Let then w be the proportion of world wealth owned by investors of the periphery:

$$W = w(W + W^*). \tag{32}$$

We can combine equations (30) to (32) to yield:

$$m(R) = w\phi d(R - R^* - \Pi + \sigma^2, \sigma^2) \qquad (33)$$

where ϕ is the ratio of the money stock to the total supply of government debt. It is the variable that the central bank of the periphery country controls by open-market operations. The left-hand side gives the desired ratio of the money stock to wealth as a function of the rate of interest. The right-hand side gives the ratio of the money stock to wealth that is consistent with equilibrium in the bond market. The two loci are depicted in Figure 1 (MM and BB schedules respectively).

Consider now the effect of an increase in the supply of money relative to the supply of government debt. The BB schedule will shift to the right while the MM schedule will remain unchanged. Assuming that there is no change in the expected rate of inflation the nominal interest rate will decline from R to R' and the proportion of wealth in the form of money will increase from m to m'.

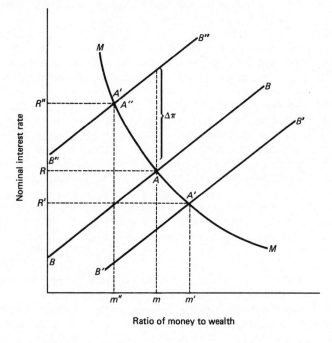

Figure 1

Of particular interest is the effect of an increase in the expected rate of inflation. It is often implied in the literature that this should increase the difference in nominal interest rates by the same amount. It is clear from Figure 1 that unless the demand for money is completely interest inelastic this is not the case. The shift of the *BB* schedule to the left results in a higher interest rate and a lower proportion of wealth held in the form of money. The magnitude of the decline in the real return on domestic bonds depends on the interest elasticity of the demand for money. This failure of the Fisher parity is well known in the domestic monetary theory literature (see, for example, Mundell (1971) ch. 2).

An increase in the variance of inflation leaves the *MM* schedule unchanged but shifts the *BB* schedule upwards. Therefore both the nominal and the real interest rate on the bonds of the periphery country will rise.

To complete the analysis we need to consider the determination of the price level in the periphery country. With the nominal interest rate given by equation (32) the price of money has to adjust to equilibrate the demand for and the supply of money in equation (30). Because the domestic stock of wealth is proportional to the world stock of wealth it is not affected by changes in the periphery country's monetary policy.

We can therefore easily establish the effects of the three shifts considered above on the price level (exchange rate) by considering equation (30). An open-market operation will increase the price level but not in proportion because the nominal interest rate and hence the velocity of circulation will change. This case of non-neutrality is, of course, well known in the literature (see, for example, Tobin (1972) p. 861).[14] An increase in the expected rate of inflation will raise the nominal interest rate and hence the velocity of circulation resulting in a jump in the price level. An increase in the variance of inflation will have the same effect since it increases the nominal rate of interest.

All of these disturbances leave the relative price of capital and hence the rate of investment unchanged. Furthermore the trade account will also remain unchanged since it is the difference between domestic consumption and the domestic supply of consumer goods, both of which are unaffected by the shifts considered above.

In summary a country that is integrated into the world commodity and capital markets and is not large enough to affect relative prices in these markets (in particular the real rate of interest) will not increase its autonomy by allowing the exchange rate to fluctuate except in terms of nominal magnitudes. Regarding these we have shown that various neutrality postulates do not in general hold: open-market operations do not change the exchange rate and hence the price level in proportion, an increase in expected inflation will lower the real interest rate on domestic bonds. In addition we have, in this section and in the previous sections, identified the variances and covariances of inflation rates, the distribution of wealth and the composition of government debt as important determinants of differences in interest rates.

It is also of interest to note that the above analysis can be applied almost without alteration to the problem of indexation if the real interest rate in the centre country is interpreted as the return on indexed bonds. In terms of that problem the analysis extends the work of Fischer (1974) by incorporating money in an explicit way and also has a bearing on the issue raised by Tobin (1971, ch. 21, sec. 4). Tobin points out that open-market operations in indexed bonds have a much more powerful effect since real bonds are much closer substitutes to real capital assets. In the above analysis open-market operations in nominal bonds – which are close substitutes to money – have no effect on the prices of real capital assets. If the central bank of a periphery country would carry out open-market operations in indexed bonds there would be complete offsetting in the same way as under the regime of fixed exchange rates with open-market operations in nominal bonds. The reason for this offsetting is the fact that the periphery country is not large enough to affect the world interest rate. In this sense there is a complete symmetry between fixed and flexible exchange rates.

V   CONCLUDING REMARKS

V.1   LIMITATIONS OF THE MODEL

The analysis of this paper was built on a set of simplifying assumptions which one obviously has to modify when analysing the actual behaviour of international financial markets. The assumption of a given real rate of interest in the centre country is one of these. A complete general equilibrium analysis would allow for the endogenous determination of the real interest rate. Another problem arises if there is no riskless asset. In that case the analysis of the paper, suitably modified, would still apply. As is shown by Black (1972) and Merton (1972) the equilibrium relationships between expected real returns would be modified only in that the real rate of interest would be replaced by the expected return on a portfolio of all risky assets constructed in such a way that its rate of return is uncorrelated with the average market rate of return.

The effects of taxes on foreign investments could be incorporated into the analysis along the lines suggested by Black (1974). If some financial assets were non-traded internationally again the analysis could be suitably modified. In that case the asset demand functions of investors in different countries would obviously be different. Completely non-tradeable assets – such as human capital – could also be incorporated into the model as is shown in a different context by Fischer (1974). Mayers (1972) analyses the case of non-marketable assets in the context of the standard mean variance model.

Aliber (1973, 1974a) has emphasised the political risk as an important attribute of assets traded in the international financial markets. The risk of default because of bankruptcy is another obvious factor explaining differences in interest rates.

Merton (1973) has shown how stochastic changes in the interest rate and in the expected returns on assets can be handled in the framework of the type of model and in this paper. The term structure of interest rates and its relationship to the term structure of exchange rate expectations is obviously an important area of research. Porter (1971) develops a model of the term structure of interest rates in an open economy that is based on the expectations hypothesis.

In this context one might also want to replace the random walk hypothesis with alternative assumptions. For instance a more reasonable assumption about exchange rates might be that there is some level or path around which the exchange rate fluctuates. A treatment of portfolio problems with regressive and adaptive expectations is given in Merton (1971, sec. 9) and a general discussion of the nature of speculative price processes is given in Samuelson (1972, especially sec. 8).

Rather than assume given stochastic processes for exchange rates and asset prices it would be desirable to derive these from the stochastic processes of the exogenous variables – such as money supply, productivity growth and so forth. For instance one might start by specifying some rules for monetary policy and then examine the effects of these rules on the stochastic behaviour of exchange rates assuming that expectations are rational.

Transactions costs have been introduced as an explanation of deviations from the interest rate parity by Branson (1969), Prachowny (1970), Frenkel (1973) and Frenkel and Levich (1974). Transactions costs between countries introduce a 'neutral band' within which interest rate differentials do not give rise to arbitrage. The available evidence suggests however that these transaction costs are not very large in the foreign exchange markets or in the short-term money markets. Aliber (1974) provides evidence that these costs have risen recently with the increased variability in exchange rates.

The assumptions of full employment, flexible prices and the purchasing power parity need to be changed when analysing short-run movements in exchange rates. When the purchasing power parity does not hold or when there are changes in relative prices and consumption patterns differ between countries the same asset will yield different real returns to investors in different countries. There would be thus exchange risk in addition to inflation risk.[15]

V.2   SUMMARY OF THE ANALYSIS

This paper has identified the various determinants of differences in interest rates between countries under flexible exchange rates. It has shown how these differences depend on the expected rates of inflation and on the variances and covariances of inflation rates. It has also shown that the expectations hypothesis is not in general valid. Interest rate differentials contain a currency premium which depends on the composition of asset supplies and may therefore be changed by monetary policy.

The model was constructed in such a way that the central banks of small economies had little freedom except with regard to nominal magnitudes. Further research can proceed along two lines. One is to recognise the various limitations discussed in the previous section and to explore the implications of departures from the 'perfect markets' assumptions for the interdependence of financial markets. Another line of research is to pursue further the theme of integration of this paper by allowing for the substitutability of monies. A complete substitutability of monies would mean, of course, that the central banks would not even have the freedom of pursuing different rates of inflation – the Gresham's law would obtain and monies of inferior quality would completely lose their value.

NOTES

1. H. G. Johnson (1969) page 12.

2. For a discussion of the purchasing power parity (PPP) doctrine see Yeager (1958), Balassa (1964), Samuelson (1964), Gaillot (1970) and Holmes (1967). Holmes gives a favourable interpretation of Cassel's pioneering work on the purchasing power parity. The empirical evidence on the PPP is mixed. It certainly does not hold in the short run except in the trivial sense that prices of standardised traded commodities in different currencies obey the PPP (in a competitive market). Gaillot concludes from his empirical study that PPP is a good approximation when explaining long-run movements in the exchange rate.

3. In practice the forward premium (or discount) does not quite equal the interest rate differential. One reason for the observed differences is the cost of arbitrage: Frenkel and Levich (1974) show that most observations on forward premiums fall in the neutral band introduced by transactions costs. Another reason is the fact that the supply of arbitrage funds may be constrained by restrictions on borrowing. Also if bonds of different countries have different risk characteristics apart from the currency risk one would not expect the interest parity equation to hold (e.g. Aliber (1974)). A detailed discussion of the interest parity equation is provided in Officer and Willet (1970) and Stoll (1972).

4. It has been commonly assumed that the US dollar has served as an international medium of exchange in the post-war period. This view has been challenged by S. Grassman (1973) who provides empirical evidence that in the case of Sweden, Denmark and more tentatively of the Federal Republic Germany, 'most transactions are settled *in the seller's or the purchaser's currency*' (Grassman (1973) p. 106).

5. More precisely, the mean and variance of the logarithmic change in the exchange rate are given by:

$$E_0 \log \left(\frac{E_{ni}(t)}{E_{ni}(0)} \right) = (e_i - 1/2\sigma_i^2)t, \text{ and}$$

$$E_0 \left[\left(\log \left(\frac{E_{ni}(t)}{E(0)} \right) - E_0 \log \left(\frac{E_{ni}(t)}{E_{ni}(0)} \right) \right)^2 \right] = \sigma_i^2 t, \text{ respectively.}$$

6. Ito's lemma is sometimes called the Fundamental Theorem of Stochastic Calculus. Let $Y = F(P_t, \ldots, P_n t)$ be twice continuously differentiable, defined on $R^n x[0, \infty]$ where P_is satisfy the stochastic process:

$$\frac{dP_i}{P_i} = \alpha_i dt + \sigma_i dz_i, \quad i = 1, \ldots, n. \tag{1}$$

Ito's lemma states that the stochastic differential of Y is given by

$$dY \equiv \sum_1^n \frac{\partial F}{\partial P_i} dP_i + \frac{\partial F}{\partial t} dt + 1/2 \sum_i \sum_j \frac{\partial^2 F}{\partial P_i \partial P_j} dP_i dP_j. \tag{2}$$

The product $dP_i dP_j$ is defined by

$$dz_i dz_j = \rho ij dt, \quad i, j = 1, \ldots, n \tag{3.1}$$

$$dz_i dz_j = 0, \quad i = 1, \ldots, n \tag{3.2}$$

where ρ_{ij} is the correlation coefficient between the Wiener processes dz_i and dz_j. A further discussion of Ito's lemma is given in Merton (1971).

7. The general solution is

$$\begin{bmatrix} b \\ k \end{bmatrix} = a\Sigma^{-1} \begin{bmatrix} \Gamma \\ \alpha \end{bmatrix}, \quad \text{where } \Sigma = \begin{bmatrix} \Omega & \Gamma \\ \Gamma & S \end{bmatrix}.$$

Since Σ_{ij} can be of any sign domestic bonds and equity, for instance, can be either complements or substitutes.

8. Notice that this property is quite different from that usually assumed in macroeconomic models of the *IS–LM* variety that aggregate bonds with equity. If the short term interest rate moved randomly in the model then the return to long term bonds would be stochastic, and they should be included in the aggregate of risky capital assets.

9. See Merton (1969, 1971) for a detailed derivation of the optimal consumption-portfolio policy.

10. If the rates of inflation are correlated with the real returns on equity the required expected return on equity depends also on the returns to bonds. In that case equation (24) is replaced by 24[1]:

$$\alpha_i - r_n = \beta_i'(\alpha_M - r_n) + \gamma_i(r_M - r_n), \quad i = 1, \ldots, n,$$

where r_M is the expected real return on the market portfolio of bonds. The β_i' and γ_i coefficients are defined by:

$$\beta_i' = \frac{1}{1-\rho^2} \frac{s_{iK}}{s_K^2} - \frac{\rho^2}{1-\rho^2} \frac{s_{iB}}{\sigma_{BK}}, \text{ and}$$

$$\gamma_i = \frac{1}{1-\rho^2} \frac{s_{iB}}{\gamma_B^2} - \frac{\rho^2}{1-\rho^2} \frac{s_{iK}}{\sigma_{BK}},$$

where ρ = correlation coefficient between the real return on the market portfolio of equity and bonds.

σ_{BK} = covariance between the same.

s_K^2 = variance of the real return on the market portfolio of equity.

σ_B^2 = variance of the real return on the market portfolio of (risky) bonds.

s_{iK} = covariance between the real return on equity i and the market portfolio of equity.

s_{iB} = covariance between the real return on equity i and the market portfolio of bonds.

If s_{iB} and ρ are equal to zero, 24^1 reduces to equation 24.

If there is no safe asset the safe return r_n in equations (24) and (24^1) is replaced by the real return on a portfolio that has zero correlation with the market portfolio of all assets (say r^*), the so-called 'zero-beta' portfolio (see Black (1972) and Merton (1972)).

Solnik's equation for equity returns (Solnik, 1973, p. 32), differs from equation (25) in that in his model the domestic bond is a safe asset for domestic investors while it is not safe for foreign investors. This is because Solnik assumes that there is no unanticipated inflation despite the unanticipated movements in the exchange rate. A result of this assumption is that r_n is replaced by r_i on the left-hand side of equation (24) and by r_M on the right-hand side.

11. I am indebted to S. Fischer for suggesting this illustration.

12. If the rates of inflation are correlated with equity returns equation (28) must be replaced by:

$$r_i - r_n = b_i'(r_M - r_n) + c_i(\alpha_M - r_n), \quad i = 1, \ldots, n-1. \tag{28^1}$$

Coefficients b_i' and c_i are defined by:

$$b_i' = \frac{1}{1-\rho^2} \frac{\sigma_{iB}}{\sigma_B^2} - \frac{\rho^2}{1-\rho^2} \frac{\sigma_{iK}}{\sigma_{BK}},$$

$$c_i = \frac{1}{1-\rho^2} \frac{\sigma_{iK}}{s_K^2} - \frac{\rho^2}{1-\rho^2} \frac{\sigma_{iB}}{\sigma_{BK}},$$

where ρ, σ_B^2, σ_{BK} and s_K^2 are as defined in note 10 above and

σ_{iK} = covariance of the real return on bond i with the real return on a market portfolio of equity;

σ_{iB} = covariance of the real return on bond i with the real return on the market portfolio of (risky) bonds.

(28) collapses to (28^1) if σ_{iK} and p are equal to zero. If there is no riskless asset r_n is replaced by r^* as defined in note 10 above. In that case equation 28^1 (or 28) applies to the centre country as well.

Solnik's equation (25) (Solnik 1973, p. 37) appears similar to equation (28) in our model in that it also contains 'a currency premium' term. In his model the currency premium has to do with the hedging of equity investments by borrowing in the currency in which the equity is denominated rather than with the hedging of the purchasing power risk of bonds.

13. Aliber (1974[a]) provides evidence that the forward premium is not an unbiased estimate of the change in the exchange rate. He interprets the difference as a measure of 'currency preference'. Aliber's data seems to indicate that the departure from the Fisher parity is greatest for currencies with the most variable exchange rate. Irving Fisher (1930, ch. xix) also analyses the differences in interest rates on bonds of different currency denomination. It would be interesting to re-examine Fisher's long time series data on the basis of our model.

14. See also Foley and Sidrauski (1971) for a more detailed analysis.

15. Solnik's (1973, 1974) model contains no inflation risk, although the exchange rate moves stochastically. This is strictly speaking acceptable only if the investors only consume domestic goods the prices of which change in a foreseen way. In our model all goods are traded and hence a domestic currency bond is not necessarily any safer than a foreign currency bond.

REFERENCES

Aliber, Robert Z., 'The Interest Parity Theorem: A Reinterpretation', *Journal of Political Economy*, 81, no. 8 (Nov/Dec 1973) 1451–9.

—'Attributes of National Monies and the Independence of National Monetary Policies', in Aliber, Robert A. (ed.) *National Monetary Policies and the International Financial System*, Chicago: University of Chicago Press, 1974 (a).

Balassa, B., 'The Purchasing Power Parity Doctrine: A Reappraisal', *Journal of Political Economy*, 72, no. 6 (Dec 1964) 584–96.

Black, F., 'Capital Market Equilibrium with Restricted Borrowing', *Journal of Business*, 45 (July 1972) 444–55.

—'International Capital Market Equilibrium with Investment Barriers', unpublished manuscript (Sep 1974).

Branson, William H., 'The Minimum Covered Interest Differential Needed for International Arbitrage Activity', *Journal of Political Economy*, 77, no. 6 (Nov/Dec 1969) 1028–35.

Dixit, A. K. and S. M. Goldman, 'Uncertainty and the Demand for Liquid Assets', *Journal of Economic Theory*, 2, no. 4 (Dec 1970) 368–82.

Fischer, S., 'The Demand for Index Bonds', working paper no. 132, M.I.T. (May 1974).

Fisher, Irving, *The Theory of Interest*, New York: Macmillan Co., 1930.

Foley, D. and M. Sidrauski, *Monetary and Fiscal Policy in a Growing Economy*, New York: Macmillan Co., 1971.

Frenkel, Jacob A., 'Elasticities and the Interest Parity Theory', *Journal of Political Economy*, 81, no. 3 (May/June 1973): 741–7.

Frenkel, Jacob A. and Levich, Richard M., 'Covered Interest Arbitrage: Unexploited Profits?', unpublished manuscript, 1974.

Gailliot, H. J., 'Purchasing Power Parity as an Explanation of Long Term Changes in Exchange Rates', *Journal of Money, Credit and Banking*, II, no. 3, (Aug 1970) 348–57.

Grassman, S., 'A Fundamental Symmetry in International Payments Patterns', *Journal of International Economics*, 3 (1973) 105–16.

Hodgson, J. S., 'An Analysis of Floating Exchange Rates: The Dollar-Sterling Rate, 1919–25', *Southern Economic Journal*, XXXIX, no. 2 (Oct 1972) 249–57.

Holmes, J. M., 'The Purchasing Power Parity Theory: In Defense of Gustav Canel as a Modern Theorist', *Journal of Political Economy*, 75, no. 5 (Oct 1967) 686–95.

Jensen, M. C., 'Capital Markets: Theory and Evidence', *Bell Journal of Economics and Management Science*, 3 (Autumn 1972) 357–98.

Johnson, Harry G., 'The Case for Flexible Exchange Rates, 1969', *Federal Reserve Bank of St Louis Review* (June 1970) 12–24.

Kindleberger, C. P., 'The Benefits of International Money', *Journal of International Economics*, 2 (1972) 425–42.

—*International Economics*, 5th edition, Homewood, Illinois: Richard D. Irwin Inc., 1973.

McKinnon, Ronald I., 'Monetary Theory and Controlled Flexibility in the Foreign Exchanges', *Princeton Essays in International Finance*, no. 84, International Finance Section, Princeton University, June 1969.

Makin, J. S., 'Equilibrium Interest Rate or Special Drawing Rights', *Southern Economic Journal*, 41, no. 2 (Oct 1974) 171–81.

Mayers, D., 'Nonmarketable Assets and Capital Market Equilibrium under Uncertainty', in M. C. Jensen (ed.) *Studies in the Theory of Capital Markets*, New York: Praeger Publishers, 1972, 223–48.

Merton, Robert C., 'Lifetime Portfolio Selection under Uncertainty: The Continuous Time Case', *Review of Economics and Statistics* (Aug 1969) 247–57.

Merton, Robert C., 'Optimum Consumption and Portfolio Rules in a Continuous-Time Model', *Journal of Economic Theory*, 3 (Dec 1971) 373–413.

Merton, Robert, C., 'An Analytic Derivation of the Efficient Portfolio Frontier', *Journal of Financial and Quantitative Analysis*, VII, no. 4 (Sep 1972) 1851–72.

Merton, Robert, C., 'An Intertemporal Capital Asset Pricing Model', *Econometrica*, 41, no. 5 (Sep 1973) 867–87.

Mundell, R. A., *Monetary Theory: Inflation, Interest and Growth in the World Economy*, Pacific Palisades, California: Goodyear Publishing Co. Inc., 1971.

Officer, L. H. and J. D. Willet, 'The Covered-Arbitrage Schedule: A Critical Survey of Recent Developments', *Journal of Money Credit and Banking*, II, no. 2 (May 1970) 247–57.

Pippenger, J., 'Spat Rates, Forward Rates, and Interest Rate Differentials', *Journal of Money, Credit and Banking*, III, no. 2 (May 1972).

Porter, M., 'A Theoretical and Empirical Framework for Analysing the Term Structure of Exchange Rate Expectations', *IMF Staff Papers*, XVIII (1971) 613–45.

Prachowny, Martin F., 'A Note on Interest Parity and the Supply of Arbitrage Funds', *Journal of Political Economy*, 78, no. 3 (May/June 1970) 540–45.

Samuelson, P. A., 'Theoretical Notes on Trade Problems', *Review of Economics and Statistics*, XLVI, no. 2 (May 1964) 145–54. Reprinted in J. E. Stiglitz (ed.) *The Collected Scientific Papers of Paul A. Samuelson*, vol. II, Cambridge, Mass. : M. I. T. Press, 1966. ch. 65, pp. 821–30.

Samuelson, P. A., 'The Mathematics of Speculative Price', *Mathematical Topics in Economic Theory and Computation*, Society for Industrial and Applied Mathematics, 1972 1–42.

Sidrauski, M., 'Rational Choice and Patterns of Growth in a Monetary Economy', *American Economic Review*, LVII, no. 2 (May 1967) 534–44.

Solnik, Bruno H., *European Capital Markets*, Lexington, Mass. : Lexington Books, 1973.

Solnik, B. H., 'An Equilibrium Model of the International Capital

Market', *Journal of Economic Theory*, 8, no. 4 (Aug 1974) 500–24.

Stall, H. R., 'Causes of Deviations from Interest Rate Parity', *Journal of Money, Credit and Banking*, IV , no. 1 (Feb 1972) 113–17.

Tobin, J., *Essays in Economics*, volume 1, *Macroeconomics*, Chicago: Markham Publishing Co., 1971.

Tobin, J., 'Friedman's Theoretical Framework', *Journal of Political Economy*, 80, no. 5 (Sep/Oct 1972) 852–63.

7 New Cambridge Macroeconomics, Assignment Rules and Interdependence

John Spraos

A new theory of macroeconomic management has been evolving in Cambridge, England in the last several years. A central implication of this theory is that fiscal policy should be directed at the balance of payments target and the exchange rate at the employment target.[1] This theory overturns the conventional wisdom. It has generated considerable excitement, even though there is no fully articulated exposition of the new theory.[2] The excitement has become greater since the change of government in Britain in March 1974, because it is believed that the exponents of the new theory now hold the ear of the Chancellor of the Exchequer. This paper examines the theory in the context of the 'assignment' problem and then looks at the implications for the political economy of international relations.

AMBIGUOUS ASSIGNMENT IMPLICATIONS OF CONVENTIONAL MODEL

The conventional view, which takes for granted that the fiscal policy should be assigned to the domestic balance and the exchange rate to the external balance, does not rest on very solid foundations. In the familiar diagram of Figure 1 (p. 105), one axis measures government expenditure (revenue being held constant) and the other exchange rate (units of home currency per unit of the foreign currency). NN is the locus of points of domestic balance and XX of external balance.[3] Points A and B lie in region I where excess aggregate demand and a surplus in the balance of payments coincide. A movement to the south-west is required to move from point *A* to point *E* where domestic and external balance are attained simultaneously. Under the conventional assignment (exchange rate to external balance and fiscal policy to domestic balance) the exchange rate appreciates (moves toward the south) and government expenditure declines (moves toward the west). Both instruments will be pushing in the right direction.

Under the new Cambridge assignment the exchange rate appreciates and government expenditure increases. The second instrument pushes east – plainly in the wrong direction. However, starting from point *B*, both instruments push in the right direction under the Cambridge assignment, whereas one pushes in the wrong direction under the conventional assignment. It is true that under the conventional assignment an economy starting at *B* is pushed into region IV; as soon as this happens, both instruments push in the right direction again. But it is equally true that, starting at *A*, as soon as the economy is pushed into region II under the Cambridge assignment, both instruments push in the right direction. (In other words, a groping process will be stable under both assignments.) There is thus complete symmetry between the two assignments and no reason, at this level of generality, to prefer one.[4]

THE CAMBRIDGE MODEL

Restrictions stemming from additional hypotheses are required before one can opt for one assignment rather than the other. At the most extreme, the new Cambridge theory hypothesises that the private sector spends on goods and services (including capital goods) what it earns.[5] Time lags blur the picture but in the long run (which, according to the evidence adduced, is not so long as to render the proposition useless for demand management) the private sector does not give rise either to unabsorbed output to generate a trade surplus or to excess absorption to create a trade deficit. The planned budget surplus/deficit (which is shorthand for the net planned lending or borrowing of the public sector as a whole, including publicly owned enterprises) is thus the only source of systematic discrepancy between output and absorption and hence the only source of trade imbalance. Changes in the exchange rate can only have a transient effect on the trade balance. If initially a depreciation expands exports and contracts imports, the increase of employment ultimately increases imports to match the increase in exports, since a propensity to spend of unity means that no unabsorbed output will be generated.

The diagrammatic consequences of the new Cambridge theory are shown in Figure 2 (p. 105). The *XX* locus rises vertically from that point of government expenditure which equals a predetermined government revenue;[6] its vertical slope reflects the fact that no change in the exchange rate can offset the balance of trade implications of an unbalanced budget.

The *NN* locus has the usual slope since both the exchange rate and government expenditure have employment effects (only bigger, since under the new Cambridge hypothesis the only leakage is via imports) and there may be expected to be some change in one instrument which exactly offsets the employment effects of a given change in the other.

Unlike the earlier diagram, from any point in region I of Figure 2, which again combines excess aggregate demand and trade surplus, both instruments push in the direction of equilibrium if the Cambridge assignment is followed – the exchange rate appreciates to counter inflationary pressure and government expenditure expands to eliminate the trade surplus. The solid arrows represent the direction in which the instruments push under the Cambridge assignment. Both instruments push in the right direction, except in regions II *B* and IV *B*, where one instrument pushes in the wrong direction. In contrast under the conventional assignment (see dotted arrows), one instrument pushes in the wrong direction in regions I, II *A*, III and IV *A*.

The addition of the hypothesis that the private sector spends what it earns makes it possible to choose between the two assignment rules; the Cambridge assignment is preferable.

The importance of not making the wrong choice depends on the size of the various regions for a particular economy and the proneness of that economy to find itself in some regions more than others. If the import and export demand elasticities are very high, the *NN* curve will be nearly horizontal, in which event regions II *B* and IV *B* (where the conventional assignment works well and the Cambridge does not) will be nearly obliterated and the choice of the conventional assignment will be unambiguously wrong. If on the other hand the sum of the import and export demand elasticities just exceeds unity, the *NN* curve will be nearly vertical and the regions in which both instruments push in the required direction under the conventional assignment will nearly match area-wise the regions in which both do so under the Cambridge assignment. (In such a case, however, neither assignment would work well because the exchange rate would be inefficient as an instrument whether assigned to the domestic or external balance target.)

The Cambridge theory implies that a floating exchange rate free of central bank intervention would be highly inefficient. Not only would it respond to deviations from external balance when efficiency requires that it be assigned to the domestic balance, but it would respond wastefully to transient disturbances while the long-run balance of trade would be determined independently of the exchange rate by the budget surplus or deficit.

In its extreme version, the new Cambridge theory is too implausible to be acceptable. However, other new ideas in Economics have been launched by emphasising limiting cases. The sharp lines and clear focus of the limiting case make it attractive to the author(s) and marketable to the profession. Beyond the limiting case, the picture becomes blurred at the edges. But at the same time the most glaring implausibilities recede and the message, though weakened, is not fundamentally compromised. If the XX curve moves off the vertical but remains steeply sloped, the basic conclusion that the Cambridge assignment is superior to the conventional one remains though the superiority is less pronounced. A steeply sloped XX curve may be inconsistent with the facts; this question can be left open. But even then, the provocative ideas emanating from Cambridge focus attention on the empirical issues which must determine the choice of assignment.

INTERDEPENDENCE AND CONFLICT

If both countries in a two-country world conform to the extreme version of the Cambridge theory, the schematic world oscillates between zero and infinity because there is no net leakage to bring about convergence to a stable point.[7] Stability may be imparted by allowing for a savings leakage in the foreign country while there is no such leakage in the home country. This asymmetrical situation was implicit when the extreme Cambridge version was examined earlier in the context of a single country without regard to repercussions abroad. But the symmetrical case in which there are savings leakages in the private sectors of both countries, only rather low ones, so that each country's XX curve remains steeply sloped, is also in the spirit of the Cambridge theory.

The static properties of such a system are the same under both the Cambridge and the conventional assignments (assuming that equilibrium can be reached under either assignment). If the balance of payments targets of the two countries are consistent so that they boil down to one target, we have three instruments – fiscal policy at home, fiscal policy abroad and the exchange rate – pursuing three targets-domestic balance at home, domestic balance abroad and a common external balance – and all three targets are in principle attainable. But the dynamics of the system may be very different under each assignment. Particular attention should be drawn to the prospect of conflict at various points of the dynamic path if both countries adopt the Cambridge assignment; the conflict arises because in such a case they attempt to use the same instrument (the exchange rate) in response to deviations from two independent targets (their respective domestic balance targets). Consider, for example, a point on the dynamic path at which the foreign country is on its domestic balance locus but the home country suffers from unemployment. The home country allows its currency to depreciate but this exports unemployment to the foreign country; which, in turn, in keeping with the Cambridge assignment, causes the movement of the exchange rate to be reversed. A succession of competitive depreciations may ensue.

Joan Robinson labelled the use of currency depreciation for employment creation a 'beggar-my-neighbour remedy for unemployment'.[8] In the present context an attempt to refute this charge may be made along two lines. The first is that though the exchange rate is assigned to the domestic balance target, when used, as it is here, in conjunction with fiscal policy, there is some combination of the instruments which reconciles the domestic and external targets of both countries. This is true (provided that their external targets are consistent; if they are not, nothing can bring about a reconciliation) but there can be conflict on the way and the conflict may prevent the system from converging to the mutually acceptable point.

The second line is that when the savings leakage is very small, a depreciation of the currency does not have a significant adverse effect on employment abroad because the expansion of the home economy is so great that it ends up by increasing its imports by nearly as much as the depreciation has raised its exports, thereby imposing only a negligible deflation on the rest of the world. This is true in the limiting case where the savings leakage is zero in the home country; in such a case no unabsorbed output can be generated in the home country to sustain a surplus in its trade balance and imports will expand by as much as exports. But it need not be even approximately true for positive but low savings leakages in both countries because the deflationary impact of depreciation on the rest of the world is greatly magnified as a result of the small savings leakage abroad.[9]

Thus, under the Cambridge assignment, there is a presumption that conflict will be greater than under the conventional assignment. The presumption may be slight, however, because it is hardly possible, no matter the arrangement, to avoid dynamic conflict when the instruments employed to attain domestic balance in one country impinge upon the domestic balance abroad.

MONEY AND MONETARY POLICY

Where does money come in? The extreme version of the Cambridge theory implies incremental asset self-sufficiency of the private sector. Growth in the demand for net assets is satisfied by the generation of new assets inside the private sector through new investment. What about switching of the stock of assets which at any point of time the private sector has inherited from the past? Can switching of the inherited portfolio between private sector securities, government debt, central bank debt and foreign assets coexist with incremental asset self-sufficiency? The strict answer is no, since inherited assets and new assets are traded in the same markets and do not bear identifying tags. Less strictly one could conceive incremental asset self-sufficiency side-by-side with switches among government debt, central bank debt and foreign assets but not between private sector securities and other assets. Such coexistence implies that the net private sector demand for private sector securities is identically equal to the inherited stock of private sector securities plus current private sector savings, while the demand for other assets responds to a variety of influences.

In the strict interpretation there is no way whereby the private sector's stock of central bank money can change; the income and wealth velocity of circulation of central bank money would be infinitely variable and monetary policy would have no role to play *vis-à-vis* the private sector.

A budget deficit would have to be financed by money creation or borrowing from abroad. If it is financed by borrowing from abroad, the current account deficit in the balance of payments (which in the extreme Cambridge version must equal the budget deficit) will be exactly offset by a capital account surplus. It will look as if the country was on its external balance locus but, like all schemes for offsetting a balance of payments deficit by inducing an inflow of capital, the economy encounters the barrier that the interest rate climbs toward infinity as a given annual inflow becomes more difficult to induce, the higher the accumulated foreign debt.

If the budget deficit initially is financed by money creation, it will effectively be financed by running down of foreign exchange reserves through the operations of the exchange stabilisation fund. In this case a central bank which is independent of the government can prevent a long run deviation from the zero deficit balance of payments locus by refusing to purchase new government debt. However, either the government acts the way it is in ignorance that the economy will move away from its chosen external balance locus, in which case explanation, not countervailing action, is called for by the central bank, or the government's external balance locus differs from the zero deficit locus in which case, if it is a democratically elected government, it is not clear why its policy should be frustrated by the central bank.

When the home country's budget deficit is financed (proximately) by money creation and (ultimately) by reduction of exchange reserves, the foreign country has a balance of payments surplus and has the choice of sterilising (provided it has the appropriate money market mechanisms, which is by no means universally the case in the real world) or not sterilising the associated money inflow. The only interesting observation that can be added to this much discussed topic is that in the Cambridge framework sterilisation does not obstruct an equilibrating mechanism as in the gold standard-inspired models. This is because the balance of payments does not depend on the things through which non-sterilisation would exercise its equilibrating function: it does not depend on relative prices or the level of economic activity; not even on relative interest rates, when we adhere to the strict interpretation under which there is no switching whatsoever of the private sector portfolio. In an important sense, therefore, monetary interdependence is smaller in this model than in more conventional ones.

CONCLUSION

If reality is captured in the hypothesis, central to the new Cambridge view, that the private sector spends all its income on goods and services, then the case for reversing the conventional assignment rule is made: fiscal policy should be assigned to the balance of payments target and the exchange rate to the employment target. Under such an assignment, however, the risk of international conflict is increased. Monetary interdependence, on the other hand, is decreased.

NOTES

1. See R. Neild, letter to *The Times*, 26 Feb 1974. The view that this implication is central to the new theory is also taken by two critics – R. Kahn and M. Posner, 'Cambridge Economics and the Balance of Payments', *The Times*, 17 and 18 Apr 1974. It is, however, denied by one of the initiators of the new theory in an unpublished and provisional paper: W. Godley and M. Fetherston, 'Demand Management in the U.K.', p. 1.

2. In addition to the references in the previous footnote, see W. Godley and F. Cripps, *The Times*, 22 and 23 Jan 1974; M. H. Miller, 'A Note on the Macroeconomics of Godley and Cripps and the Cambridge "New School"' (unpublished). N. Kaldor has been closely associated with the development of the new ideas. For an earlier statement of the principles see W. M. Corden, 'The Geometric Representation of Policies to Attain Internal and External Balance', *Review of Economic Studies*, vol. XXVIII (1960–1) pp.1–22, especially pp. 16–18.

3. Implicit in the slopes of both curves is the assumption that the sum of the price elasticities of demand for exports and imports is numerically larger than one and that some money illusion is present to make a change of the exchange rate a workable instrument. It is not intended to imply that either assumption may be taken empirically for granted.

4. Cf. R. A. Mundell, 'The Monetary Dynamics of International Adjustment under Fixed and Flexible Exchange Rates', *Quarterly Journal of Economics*, vol. LXXIV (1960) pp. 227–57, reprinted with some modifications as ch. 11 in R. A. Mundell, *International Economics*, (New York: Macmillan Co., 1968). Cf. also W. M. Corden, op. cit., p. 17, and J. H. Levin, 'Monetary Policy and the Crawling Peg', *Economic Journal*, vol. 85, Mar. (1975) pp. 20–32.

5. It is sufficient for the Cambridge argument that this should be so at the margin. But it is difficult to see what mechanism or behaviour hypothesis could ensure a marginal propensity to spend of exactly unity side-by-side with an average propensity of less than unity. For the time being the hypothesis that the private sector spends what it earns has no theoretical underpinning and this is acknowledged as a weakness in the concluding paragraph of Godley and Fetherston (op. cit.); it rests only on limited empirical evidence in Great Britain.

6. A predetermined government revenue is awkward when income is variable. An important part of the criticism directed at the new Cambridge theory by Kahn and Posner (op. cit.) revolves around this point. There is however no difficulty in relabelling the horizontal axis 'budget surplus/deficit' since with a marginal propensity to spend of unity the balanced budget multiplier is zero. This does not remove all the difficulties since the budget surplus/deficit also depends on income. But as Godley and Fetherston (op. cit.) point out, budgetary plans and hence the planned surplus/deficit try to incorporate the income implications of budgetary action.

7. For the limited part of reality which is captured by the model we cannot rule out such

a violently oscillatory property merely by the observation that the real world (which contains many other parts) is not observed so to oscillate. But the search for principles of macroeconomic management in the framework of such a model would then be pointless.

8. 'Beggar-My-Neighbour Remedies for Unemployment' in Joan Robinson, *Essays in the Theory of Employment* (Oxford: Blackwell, 1937).

9. This can be easily shown in terms of the simplest Keynesian open economy model:

$$Y_h = E_h(Y_h) + B \tag{1}$$

$$Y_f = E_f(Y_f) - \frac{1}{r}B \tag{2}$$

$$B = M_f\left(\frac{1}{r}, Y_f\right) - r M_h(r, Y_h) \tag{3}$$

Equation (1) shows the equilibrium value of output in the home country as equal to planned expenditure by the residents of that country (which is itself a function of output) plus the trade balance. Equation (2) shows the same for the foreign country. Equation (3) expresses the trade balance in terms of the home currency (r units of which buy one unit of the foreign currency) and sets it equal to the difference between planned imports of the foreign and home countries respectively, the imports being dependent on the exchange rate and the level of output in each country. $dr > 0$ implies a depreciation of the home country's currency. Differentiating the three equations with respect to r and solving for $\dfrac{dY_f}{dr}$ (whilst assuming $B = 0$ and

$r = 1$ initially):

$$\frac{dY_f}{dr} = \frac{s_h(e_h + e_f + 1)}{s_h s_f + s_h m_f + s_f m_h} M_h \tag{4}$$

where s is the marginal propensity to save (net of any income-induced investment), m is the marginal propensity to import and e the price elasticity of demand for imports.

Clearly if $s_h = 0$, $\dfrac{dY_f}{dr} = 0$ and a depreciation by the home country does not beggar the foreign country. But if $s_h > 0$ and small and $s_f > 0$ and small also, then the expression in (4) will be negative (when the sum of the elasticities numerically exceeds unity) and could be large, thus suggesting the possible beggaring of the foreign country in a big way.

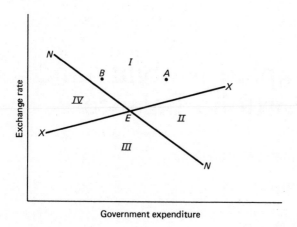

Figure 1

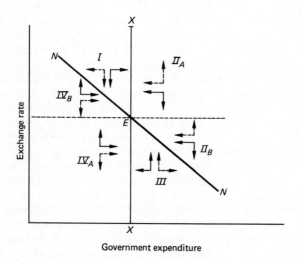

Figure 2

8 Capital Mobility and Portfolio Balance *

Rudiger Dornbusch

INTRODUCTION

In his work on monetary and fiscal policy in the open economy under fixed exchange rates Mundell has demonstrated the role of capital mobility.[1] Perfect capital mobility was shown to imply endogeneity of the world distribution of money and the ineffectiveness of monetary policy in a small country. The implications of capital mobility for macroeconomic questions were sufficiently forceful at a highly aggregative level for a detailed formulation of the implied portfolio balance relations to seem redundant. Attempts at monetary policy in individual countries reflect, too, the recognition of a high degree of capital mobility, and it is for this reason that policies have primarily taken the form of regulation of the financial industry, taxation of ownership or attempts at changing the relative yields of relatively non-tradeable securities over which domestic authorities may exert more leverage than over their tradeable counterparts.

The present paper develops a formal framework in which such asset market policies can be analysed. The framework is a partial equilibrium model of the asset markets that takes the real side of the economy as given. Conceptually it is therefore similar to studies of the money supply process or portfolio balance models.[2] The conclusions that emerge from such a formulation are not so much new insights about the operation of an open economy but rather pertain to the exact detail of the effects of policies and a description of the relevant parameters that determine the magnitude and direction of these effects. The model differs in two respects

* In preparing this paper, I have drawn on helpful discussions with Karl Brunner and Dale Henderson. I have benefited, too, from reading an unpublished paper by Girton and Henderson (1973).

from the standard macroeconomic treatment of these issues. First, there is an explicit development of the banking sector, and second, a non-traded asset is introduced in order to highlight the implications of capital mobility.[3]

In Section I the portfolio balance model under perfect capital mobility is restated and it is shown that the individual central bank, in order to be effective, has to change the world interest rate and that it will do so at a reserve loss inversely proportional to its effective size. In Section II a banking system is added and it is concluded that the analysis remains essentially unchanged except that now the authorities command more instruments.

In Sections III and IV non-traded assets are introduced. Section III analyses the small country case and develops the determination of the 'domestic' interest rate and the equilibrium stock of reserves. In Section IV that analysis is extended to the two country model and comparisons between open-market operations in traded and non-traded debt are made. It is concluded that interventions in non-traded debt yield a lower reserve loss and are more effective in changing the domestic rate of interest.

In Section V a model of the simultaneous determination of the yield on 'domestic' securities and the premium on forward exchange is developed. The model emphasises that these rates are determined by the conditions of portfolio equilibrium and permits the demonstration of the equivalence of open-market operations and interventions in the forward market.

I   CAPITAL MOBILITY AND PORTFOLIO BALANCE

The purpose of this section is to review the concept of capital mobility as it has been developed by Mundell. Perfect capital mobility is understood as an integrated *world* market for the existing stocks of assets and accordingly equalisation of yields on identical assets independent of location. The counterpart of the integration of markets or the 'law of one price' is the endogeneity of both the quantity of money and the distribution of central bank reserves.

This concept of capital mobility may readily be formulated by adopting a partial equilibrium approach and restricting the analysis to asset markets.[4] We assume there is one kind of debt instrument in the world and two monies. The demand for money in each country is a function of the opportunity cost of holding money, r, income Y, and wealth, W

$$L = L(r;Y_0,W_0) \tag{1}$$

$$L^* = L^*(r;Y_0^*,W_0^*)$$

where an asterisk denotes the foreign country and where we treat income and wealth as parametrically given.

In the absence of a banking system the money supply is equal to the central bank's holdings of reserves, R, and domestic credit, D:

$$M = R + D \tag{2}$$

$$M^* = R^* + D^*. \tag{3}$$

Finally we assume that the world stock of reserves, $\overline{R}$, is given so that

$$\overline{R}_0 = R + R^*. \tag{4}$$

Given income, wealth, and world reserves the variables that are to be determined are the equilibrium interest rate, the distribution of reserves and the national money supplies and debt holdings. To determine these variables we study the equilibrium conditions in the money markets:

$$R + D_0 = L(r, Y_0, W_0). \tag{5}$$

$$\overline{R}_0 - R + D_0^* = L^*(r, Y_0^*, W_0^*). \tag{6}$$

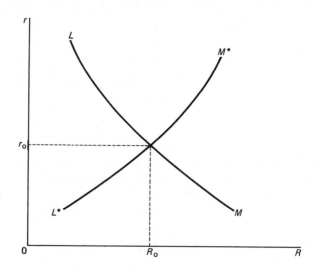

Figure 1

In Figure 1 we show as the LM schedule equation (5) and as L^*M^* schedule equation (6). The home country's money market equilibrium schedule is negatively sloped since an increase in reserves raises the money supply and thus requires a reduction in the interest rate to encourage the public to hold the increased quantity of money. The foreign money market equilibrium schedule is positively sloped since by (4) and (3) an increase in domestic reserves implies a reduction in the foreign money supply, therefore requiring an increase in the interest rate to maintain foreign monetary equilibrium. The equilibrium interest rate and distribution of reserves, r_o and R_o, obtains when both money markets clear. That equilibrium is contingent on the income, wealth and domestic credit parameters.

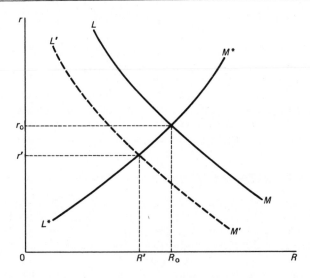

Figure 2

An increase in domestic credit in the home country, as shown in Figure 2, shifts the home country's money market equilibrium schedule to the left by the increase in domestic credit thereby creating an excess supply of money and an excess demand for debt. The equilibrium interest rate will decline to r' and the domestic stock of reserves will decrease to R'. The decline in reserves, however, is smaller than the increase in domestic credit and depends on the relative *effective size* of the two countries. Effective size is here defined as the product of the interest elasticity of the demand for money and a country's share in the world money supply and will be denoted by β and β^*, respectively. Using these definitions and differentiating equations (5) and (6) we obtain the effect of credit expansion on reserves:

$$dR = -\frac{\beta^*}{\beta + \beta^*} dD + \frac{\beta}{\beta + \beta^*} dD^*. \tag{7}$$

It is important to note that this framework does not suggest that a small country cannot modify the world interest rate or its quantity of money. What it does say is that the cost of doing so in terms of reserve losses (or gains) is inversely proportional to its effective size. Thus as a limiting case in (7) domestic credit expansion is met by an equal loss of reserves – the 'small country' case to which Mundell has drawn attention.

The change in the domestic quantity of money due to credit creation is independent of the origin of that credit creation:

$$dM = dR + dD = \frac{\beta}{\beta + \beta^*}(dD + dD^*).\tag{8}$$

According to (8) the increase in the domestic quantity of money is a fraction of the *world* credit creation where the fraction in turn is determined by relative effective size.

The analysis so far has been conducted in terms of the money markets. It is revealing, however, to use the budget constraint and translate the analysis into the world market for debt. In each country the excess supply of money is equal to the excess demand for debt so that, using (1) to (4) the world excess demand for debt, $\overline{B}$, is equal to:

$$\overline{B} = \overline{R} + D + D^* - L - L^*.\tag{9}$$

The world excess demand for debt is independent of the distribution of reserves and domestic credit and given the parameters D, D^*, Y, Y^*, W, W^* will only be a function of the rate of interest. Accordingly, the world debt market equilibrium schedule will be a horizontal line in Figures 1 and 2 and will pass through the intersection of the money market equilibrium schedules. It follows that we may use equation (9) to determine the equilibrium interest rate and either (5) or (6) to determine the equilibrium distribution of reserves. With this formulation the equilibrium may be described as follows: the interest rate is such that the world stock of debt is willingly held and the distribution of reserves is such that the supply of money equals the demand for money in each country.

II   FINANCIAL INTERMEDIATION

In this section we introduce financial intermediation in the form of a commercial banking system. This modifies the foregoing analysis in two respects. The money supply will now be determined by the monetary base and commercial bank reserve preferences. At the same time commercial banks appear as suppliers of loans or demanders of debt.

With these modifications we can write the money market equilibrium conditions of the previous section as follows:

$$m(r, v)(R + D) = L(r, \dots)\tag{5'}$$

$$m^*(r, v^*)(\overline{R} - R + D^*) = L^*(r, \dots)\tag{6'}$$

where m and m^* are the money multipliers.[5] They are functions of the yield on debt and central bank controls summarised in the parameters v and v^*.

The characteristics of the model developed in the previous section are not essentially altered by the introduction of a banking system except in two respects: a source of disturbance arises now from portfolio shifts on the part of the banking system between bank reserves and securities. The central bank, on the other hand, gains a further instrument in its ability to influence or regulate the banking systems' reserve ratio and balance sheet.

Consider now the effect of increased reserve requirements in the home country. At the initial equilibrium interest rate commercial banks will relinquish earning assets for high-powered money in the world market thereby creating an excess supply of debt. The equilibrium interest rate will increase and so will the domestic stock of reserves while the money supply declines in both countries. The private sector's holdings of debt rise in both countries. In both countries the size of the banking system contracts; in the home country earning assets decline relative to deposits while they increase abroad.

The effects of restrictive monetary policy remain essentially unaltered by the existence of financial intermediation; the instruments of monetary policy become larger in number but it continues to be true that a central bank, in order to be effective, has to change the world interest rates. To change this feature of the model we introduce in the next section 'domestic assets'.

III   DOMESTIC ASSETS AND THE SMALL COUNTRY MODEL

The preceding analysis is modified in this section to allow for the existence of 'domestic' or 'non-traded' debt. We will specifically assume that it is held by the commercial banking system and the central bank and is supplied by the domestic private sector. Both commercial banks and the central bank hold along with domestic debt internationally tradeable debt; the commercial banks may, however, hold negative amounts of internationally tradeable debt to the extent that they borrow in the world market in order to finance local loans. The private sector holds money and internationally tradeable debt and is a net supplier of non-tradeable debt. The analysis will proceed first to determine the equilibrium in a 'small' economy that faces a given rate of interest in the world market, $\bar{r}$.

Given the rate of interest in the world market, $\bar{r}$, we require to determine for the small country the equilibrium interest rate on non-tradeable debt, i, and the equilibrium stock of foreign exchange reserves. Given these variables and given the central bank's policy variables we will have determined the money supply and commercial bank credit and holdings of securities.

The interest rate on domestic assets and the stock of foreign exchange reserves are jointly determined by the equilibrium in the markets for domestic money and debt. The domestic money supply is proportional to high-powered money

$$M = m(r, i, v)(R + D + N) \tag{10}$$

where the multiplier reflects now the yields on both types of assets commercial banks will hold and where N is the central bank's holdings of domestic debt. The demand for money, similarly, reflects the alternative costs of holding money:

$$L = L(r, i, Y, W). \tag{11}$$

The supply of domestic loans by the commercial banking system, K, is proportional to the base and is an increasing function of the yield on domestic loans and a decreasing function of the yield on internationally tradeable debt:

$$K = \phi(r, i, v)(R + D + N). \tag{12}$$

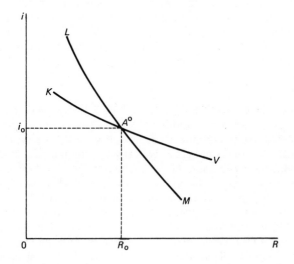

Figure 3

The private sector's excess demand for loans, V, will be a function of the same arguments as the demand for money and is increasing in the world interest and decreasing in the cost of domestic loans:

$$V = V(r, i, Y, W). \tag{13}$$

The equilibrium yield on domestic loans and the equilibrium stock of reserves are determined by the equilibrium conditions in (14) and (15) given the parameters $v°, Y°, W°, N°, D°$:

$$m(r,i,v)(R+D+N)=L(r,i,Y,W) \tag{14}$$

$$\phi(r,i,v)(R+D+N)=V(r,i,Y,W)-N. \tag{15}$$

The determination of the equilibrium is graphically shown in Figure 3, where the *KV* schedule corresponds to the equilibrium in the domestic credit market shown in (15) while the *LM* schedule reflects monetary equilibrium as shown by (14). Both schedules are negatively sloped since an increase in the interest rate yields an excess supply and thus has to be accompanied by a reduction in the base in order to maintain market equilibrium. The relative slopes assume that the credit market is more responsive to the yield on debt than the money market.[6]

Point $A°$ shows the equilibrium yield on domestic debt and the equilibrium stock of reserves such that the money and domestic loan markets simultaneously clear. That equilibrium is contingent on the values of the parameters so that we can now turn to the comparative static effects of altering those parameters.

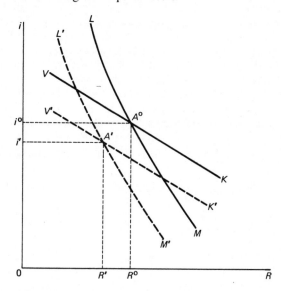

Figure 4

To study the working of the model consider the effect of an open-market purchase of domestic debt by the central bank, or in terms of the notation of (14) and (15) an increase in N. At point $A°$, in Figure 4, there is now an excess supply of both money and domestic credit so that both market equilibrium schedules shift to the left, the VK schedule shifting relatively more than the LM schedule.[7] The new equilibrium at point A' is one of a lower interest rate and a decrease in the stock of reserves. The change in reserves will depend on the elasticities of excess demand with respect to the interest rate and the domestic loan multiplier. Calculating from (14) and (15) the effect on reserves of an increase in N we have:

$$\frac{dR}{dN} = -\left[1 - \frac{\varepsilon}{\phi(\lambda - \varepsilon)}\right] \equiv -\gamma; \quad -0 \le \gamma \le 1 \qquad (16)$$

Several features of (16) are worth noting. First, if domestic and foreign assets are highly substitutable we revert to the one-asset model where an open-market operation is matched by an equal reserve loss. In general, the reserve loss will be a fraction of the open-market operation so that we have less than a full offset. With imperfect substitutability between domestic and international assets, the yield on domestic assets will decline and in response to that decline the public will wish to hold larger stocks of both money and foreign assets. The increased money holding is financed directly by the open-market operation. The reserve loss is the counterpart of increased holdings of foreign assets since, in the aggregate, the only way the country can acquire external assets is by relinquishing reserves. Of a given open-market purchase of domestic assets, therefore, a fraction γ is substituted into foreign assets and a fraction $1 - \gamma$ is held in the form of additional money balances. The relative size of the additional holdings of money and foreign assets will depend on the excess supply elasticities of domestic assets and money which between themselves imply an elasticity of demand for foreign assets. Given the excess supply elasticity of money a larger excess supply elasticity of domestic assets implies a larger reserve loss or, equivalently a relatively large addition to foreign assets and a relatively small addition to money holdings.

Table 1

	v	D	N	$\bar{r}$	Y
K	−	o	+	−	+
R	+	−	−	−	+
M	−	o	+	−	+
i	+	o	−	+	+

Table 1 summarises the effects of alternative changes in parameters on the endogenous variables. In particular we consider an increase in reserve requirements or reserve preferences, v, open-market purchases of D and N as well as increases in the world interest rate, $\bar{r}$, and domestic income.

The relevant endogenous variables are domestic loans of the commercial banking system, reserves, the money supply and the domestic interest rate.[8]

The basic features of the model can be further emphasised by considering policies that are specific to the banking system or to the distinction between tradeable and non-tradeable assets. While that distinction is already emphasised by a comparison of the effects of open-market operations in tradeable and non-tradeable debt it is further enhanced by considering tax, subsidy and regulatory devices. As a particular example consider a policy of taxing resident holdings of international debt or subsidising bank holdings of tradeable debt. These policies, at a given world interest rate, will change the desired portfolio composition of both the private sector and banks and thereby affect the equilibrium yield on domestic debt, the quantity of money and the stock of reserves.

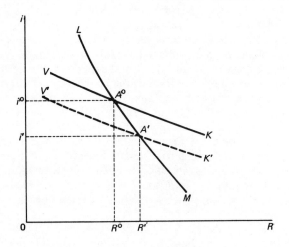

Figure 5

Consider next the regulation of the commercial banking system's earning assets and assume that the authorities reduce the banking system's holdings of tradeable debt in favour of non-tradeable debt. Such a policy will affect the domestic credit market as shown in Figure 5. At the initial interest rate there will be an excess supply of domestic loans so that the VK curve shifts to $V'K'$ and the equilibrium interest rate declines to i'.[9] Along with the decline in the yield on domestic loans we have an increase in the demand for money and the stock of reserves. Such a policy is of obvious interest to a country that wishes to lower domestic interest rates without impairing its reserve position.

The reserve changes that are induced by the policies we have considered require financing and it is important to recognise that for the consolidated home country we only have a change in the composition of assets between reserves and tradeable debt. For the policy described in Figure 5, the financing of reserve acquisitions is primarily via the commercial banks' liquidation of their holdings of tradeable debt. For other changes in parameters such as an increase in income, the reserve acquisition may be financed predominantly by private liquidation of international debt and commercial bank borrowing in the world market.

The possibility of commercial bank borrowing in the world market for the purpose of financing domestic loans proves to be a serious impediment to the effectiveness of monetary policies. In terms of Figure 3, it amounts to a high substitutability between domestic loans and tradeable assets and thus generates a rather flat VK schedule. The leverage that the central bank can gain by operating in the market for domestic loans may thus be offset by a high substitutability between domestic and international assets in intermediaries' portfolios. To regain that leverage, one policy that has been used is the imposition of ceilings on domestic loans by the commercial banking system. Such a policy should prove successful, the ingenuity of the market notwithstanding, if commercial banks play a substantial role in the retail credit market.

We conclude this section by a summary of its main message. In a small country the leverage of monetary policy is likely to come from the existence of non-tradeable assets. To the extent that these assets are, however, close substitutes for tradeable assets in the portfolios of financial intermediaries and particularly commercial banks that leverage may be easily lost and more specific policies and in particular regulation or taxation are required to implement policies and the banking system offers a suitable body on which to perpetrate these interventions.

IV DOMESTIC ASSETS AND THE WORLD MODEL

The analysis of the preceding section assumed that the world rate of interest was parametrically given and independent of the home country's actions. We alter that assumption now by considering a two-country model similar to that in Section II but with the addition that we allow for one tradeable asset and one non-traded asset in each country.

The equilibrium conditions in this model will be that the money market clears in each country and that the market for non-tradeable debt clears in each country. The budget constraint implies that when these conditions are satisfied the world market for tradeable debt will clear identically. These equilibrium conditions are given in (17) to (20):

$$m(r,i,v)(R+D+N)=L(r,i,Y,W) \tag{17}$$

$$m^*(r,i^*,v^*)(\overline{R}-R+D^*+N^*)=L^*(r,i^*,Y^*,W^*) \tag{18}$$

$$\phi(r,i,v)(R+D+N)=V(r,i,Y,W)-N \tag{19}$$

$$\phi^*(r,i^*,v^*)(\overline{R}-R+D^*+N^*)=V^*(r,i^*,Y^*,W^*)-N^*. \tag{20}$$

To develop the analogy with Sections I and II we draw on the results in the previous section to express the equilibrium interest rate on domestic debt as a function of the parameters v, N, Y, r:

$$i=i(v,N,Y,r) \tag{21}$$
$$i^*=i^*(v^*,N^*,Y^*,r). \tag{22}$$

Substituting these reduced form expressions for the domestic interest rates in (17) and (18) allows us to discard the domestic loan market equations (19) and (20), the equilibrium of which is implicit in the expressions for the domestic interest rates. Performing this substitution leaves us then with a system formally identical to equations (5) and (6) but with the particular interpretation that in the background the markets for non-tradeable debt clear.

We can proceed to ask in what manner the introduction of non-tradeable assets alters the conclusions of Sections I and II and in what manner the world model differs from the small country case. For that purpose it is instructive to compare the reserve loss arising from open-market purchases of domestic and tradeable debt respectively:[10]

$$\frac{dR}{dN}=-\gamma\frac{\delta^*m}{\delta^*m+\delta m^*};\ 1>\gamma>0;\quad \frac{dR}{dD}=-\frac{\delta^*m}{\delta^*m+\delta m^*}. \tag{23}$$

We note from (23) that open-market interventions in domestic debt will produce a smaller reserve drain than those in tradeable debt and that for both cases the reserve loss, barring the small country case, is less than proportionate to the open-market operation. Relative to the small country case we note that the reserve losses will be smaller in the present model as can be seen by a comparison between (16) and (23). This is so since an open-market operation in either form of debt will lower the world interest rate and thus further increase the demand for money and hence the derived demand for high-powered money.

The counterpart of the observation that interventions in domestic debt minimise the reserve loss associated with open-market operations is the fact that they are more effective, too, in lowering the domestic interest rate. It can be shown that per dollar open-market operation an intervention in domestic debt lowers the domestic interest rate by more than a purchase of tradeable debt. Conversely international debt is the more effective asset with respect to the yield on tradeable debt.

Some further comparative static results of this model are summarised in Table 2 and are derived in detail in Appendix I (p. 120).

We summarise the main conclusions of this section in noting that non-traded assets and a banking system can readily be added to the more conventional models of perfect capital mobility and that such an addition is useful because it emphasises the differential impact central banks will achieve depending on whom they regulate or what asset they intervene in. While the differential impact is emphasised it is true at the same time that the basic message of Mundell regarding capital mobility and the endogeneity of the quantity of money continues to hold.

Table 2

	v	D	N	Y
R	$+$	$-$	$-$	$+$
r	$+$	$-$	$-$	$+$
i	$+$	$-$	$-$	$+$
M	$-$	$+$	$+$	$+$
i^*	$+$	$-$	$-$	$+$

V   THE FORWARD MARKET AND ASSET MARKET EQUILIBRIUM

The models of the previous section can readily be extended to incorporate a forward market for foreign exchange and the effects of uncertainty about future spot rates on the allocation between alternative assets. To develop this extension we simplify the preceding models by omitting the banking system and introduce a 'domestic' security that is denominated in terms of domestic currency and that is an imperfect substitute for foreign assets. This domestic security is held by domestic and possibly foreign residents as well as by the domestic central bank. We further assume a fixed current spot rate and an interest rate on foreign assets that is, for the small country under consideration, exogenously given.

The excess demand for domestic securities by domestic and foreign residents will depend on the yield on domestic securities, i, the given yield on foreign assets, r, as well as on the premium on forward exchange, the expected future spot rate and in addition the parametrically given income and wealth variables. In equilibrium the domestic and foreign excess supply of domestic securities will equal the central bank's holdings of that asset:

$$\overline{B} = B(i, r, p, \overline{p}, \ldots) + B^*(i, r, p, \overline{p}, \ldots) \tag{24}$$

where B and B^* denote the domestic and foreign excess supply of domestic securities and where $\overline{B}$ denotes the central bank's holdings. The premium on forward foreign exchange is denoted by p and the expected future spot rate expressed as a fraction of the current spot rate is $\bar{p}$.[11]

We will assume that an increase in the yield on domestic assets creates an excess demand for these securities while an increase in the premium on forward foreign exchange will create an excess supply since it lowers the covered return on domestic securities and raises the covered return on foreign securities. An increase in the expected future spot rate shifts people out of domestic securities in anticipation of the capital loss on securities denominated in domestic currency.

The excess demand for forward foreign exchange on the part of the domestic and foreign private sector will be an increasing function of the yield on domestic securities and a decreasing function of the premium on forward exchange. An increase in the expected future rate in turn will raise the excess demand for forward cover. In equilibrium the private excess demand for forward cover will equal the central bank's stock supply of forward contracts:

$$\bar{F} = F(i, r, p, \bar{p}, \ldots) \tag{25}$$

where F denotes the private excess demand for forward exchange and $\bar{F}$ the stock supply of forward foreign exchange contracts issued by the central bank.

The determination of the equilibrium yield on domestic securities and the forward premium is shown in Figure 6 for a given expected future rate, $\bar{p}^\circ$, and given stocks of central bank holdings of domestic debts, $\bar{B}^\circ$, and forward contracts, $\bar{F}^\circ$. Along the schedule FF the forward market is in equilibrium while along BB the domestic security market clears.

This framework of analysis is an extension of the Fleming–Mundell (1964) model in that it shows the simultaneous determination of interest rates and forward rates. It shares, however, with that model the emphasis on the determination of forward rates in the asset markets or the markets for *stocks* of debt and forward contracts. The model is useful for the analysis of the asset market effects of changes in asset supplies and it represents, too, a framework in which to investigate the effects of speculation.

Consider first the effects of open-market and forward-market operations on the part of the central bank. An increase in the central bank's holdings of domestic securities will create an excess demand for these assets and therefore, lower the equilibrium yield at each level of the premium. In terms of Figure 6 this corresponds to a shift in the BB schedule down and to the right and accordingly to a decline in the equilibrium yield and the premium. A sale of forward exchange will similarly cause the domestic interest rate and the premium to decline since it shifts the FF schedule up and to the left. We note therefore that forward and open-market operations are equivalent in their effects on interest rates and forward rates. This conclusion is well in the tradition of the Keynes – Jasay – Spraos advocacy of active 'managed forward markets'.

Consider next the implications for reserves of interventions in the domestic debt or forward markets. Here the effects are asymmetrical in that an open-market purchase of debt causes in general a reserve loss while a forward market operation causes a reserve gain. The reason for this asymmetry is that both policies by lowering the premium and the domestic interest rate will raise the demand for money, but whereas a forward intervention leaves the domestic base unaffected, the purchase of debt will directly increase the money supply. These points can be seen from the equation for the equilibrium stock of reserves that in this model is determined by the demand for money and the domestic source component of the base:

$$R = L(i, p, \bar{p}, r, \ldots) - \bar{B}. \tag{26}$$

Differentiating (26) we obtain the effect on reserves of interventions by the central bank:

$$dR/d\bar{B} = dL/d\bar{B} - 1 \tag{27}$$

and

$$dR/d\bar{F} = dL/d\bar{F} > 0 \tag{28}$$

where the terms $dL/d\bar{B}$ and $dL/d\bar{F}$ will depend on the parameters of the demand for money and the comparative statics of (24) and (25). We will assume that an increase in either the yield on domestic securities or the premium will reduce the demand for money. With these restrictions we know from (28) that a forward market sale will raise reserves. To obtain the result that an open-market purchase of securities will lower reserves in (27) we require more restrictions on the system so as to make $dL/d\bar{B}$ smaller than unity.

Consider next the effects of a 'speculative attack' represented here by an increase in the expected future spot rate, $\bar{p}$. The anticipation of depreciation will shift the public out of domestic securities and will increase the excess demand for forward exchange. It will therefore shift in Figure 6 the FF schedule down and to the right and the BB schedule up and to the left so that the equilibrium interest rate and forward premium both increase. The effect of expected depreciation on interest rates and forward rates is akin to the 'Fisher effect' of expected inflation on nominal interest and arises for exactly the same reason, namely the anticipated depreciation of assets fixed in terms of domestic currency.

The expected depreciation will cause a shift out of money too, and to that extent will, by (26), cause a loss in reserves. That decline in the demand for money is due both to the direct effect of a change in $\bar{p}$ on the demand for money as well as to the induced changes in the demand for money that arise from the increase in interest rates and the premium. It is important to note that the loss in reserves is not due to a shift out of domestic into foreign securities directly, since the domestic stock of securities will have to be held, but rather operates through a change in the demand for money which, however, is not independent of the change in the equilibrium asset yields. This point is important since it shows that

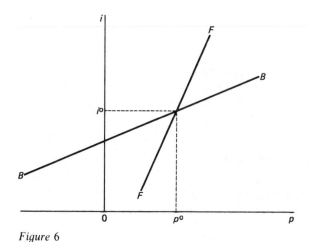

Figure 6

a policy that aims at maintaining reserves in the face of a loss of confidence in the domestic parity will have to aim at the demand and will have to operate via a reduction in domestic interest rates and/or the premium. The ideal policy then will be sales of forward exchange on a scale sufficient to *lower* the premium enough to compensate for the effect of expected depreciation on the demand for money. Provided $dL/d\bar{B}$ is smaller than unity such a policy can be supplemented by open-market sales of securities. This is obviously the standard policy package, at least in Britain, when the currency comes under attack.

CONCLUSION
This paper has developed a formal framework for the study of asset markets that are linked through an integrated world capital market and financial intermediation. The conclusions that emerge from this formulation uphold the Mundellian principle that 'the open economy leaks'. The disaggregation in asset markets that is proposed here shows further, however, that a distinction between domestic assets and

tradeable securities is of interest since it permits the formulation of the differential effect of open-market operations depending on the type of security the central bank intervenes in or the manner in which it regulates the banking system.

In linking the discussion to the forward market we show the simultaneous determination of domestic interest rates and the forward premium, and we show, too, the equivalence between open-market operations and forward-market interventions.

APPENDIX I

This appendix derives the comparative static results discussed in Section III of the paper. To derive these results we use the equilibrium conditions for the domestic money and loan markets, repeated here for convenience:

$$m(r,i,v)(R+D+N)=L(r,i,Y,W). \tag{A-1}$$

$$\alpha(r,i)(m(r,i,v)-1)(R+D+N)=V(r,i,Y,W)-N. \tag{A-2}$$

We further use the following notation, definitions and restrictions:

$$\phi=\alpha(m-1);\quad H\equiv R+D+N;\quad K\equiv\phi H$$
$$\lambda\equiv(\phi_i H-V)i/K>0$$
$$\varepsilon\equiv(m_i H-L_i)i/M>0$$
$$\eta\equiv(m_r H-L_r)r/M>0$$
$$\rho\equiv-(\phi_r H-V_r)r/K>0$$
$$m_v<0;\quad L_Y=V_Y>0;\quad \phi-m<0,\quad \lambda-\varepsilon>0.$$

Differentiating the equilibrium conditions in $(A-1)$ and $(A-2)$, and solving for the change in the equilibrium interest rate on domestic debt yields:

$$\frac{di/i}{dN}=-\frac{1}{\phi H(\lambda-\varepsilon)}<0;\quad \frac{di/i}{dY}=\frac{m-\phi}{m\phi H(\lambda-\varepsilon)}\quad L_Y>0 \tag{A-3}$$

$$\frac{di/i}{dv}=-\frac{m_v}{m\phi(\lambda-\varepsilon)}>0;\quad \frac{di/i}{dr/r}=\frac{\eta+\rho}{\lambda-\varepsilon}>0.$$

The change in the equilibrium stock of reserves is equal to:

$$\frac{dR}{dN}=-\gamma\quad<0;\quad \frac{dR}{dv}=\frac{m_v H(\alpha\varepsilon-\lambda)}{\phi(\lambda-\varepsilon)}>0 \tag{A-4}$$

$$\frac{dR}{dY}=\frac{L_Y(\phi\lambda-m\varepsilon)}{m\phi(\lambda-\varepsilon)}>0;\quad \frac{dR}{dr/r}=-\frac{H(\varepsilon\rho+\lambda\eta)}{\lambda-\varepsilon}<0$$

where we assume that:

$$\gamma \equiv 1 - \frac{\varepsilon}{\phi(\lambda - \varepsilon)} > 0; \quad \phi\lambda - m\varepsilon > 0.$$

For the discussion of Section IV it is convenient to define some reduced form expressions. We are interested in the change in the excess supply of money allowing the market for non-tradeable debt to clear. The effect of a change in the rate of interest on tradeable debt on the excess supply of money is:

$$\left[r(m_r H - L_r) + i(m_i H - L_i) \cdot \frac{di/i}{dr/r} \right] dr/r \tag{A–5}$$

and reduces after substitution from (A–3) to

$$\left[M \frac{\eta\lambda + \varepsilon\rho}{\lambda - \varepsilon} \right] dr/r \equiv \delta \, dr/r.$$

Proceeding in a similar manner we derive the following expressions for the remaining parametric changes:

$$\left[i(m_i H - L_i) \frac{di/i}{dN} + m \right] dN = m\gamma dN \tag{A–6}$$

$$\left[i(m_i H - L_i) \frac{di/i}{dv} + m_v H \right] dv = m_v \gamma H dv \tag{A–7}$$

$$\left[i(m_i H - L_i) \frac{di/i}{dY} - L_Y \right] dY = \frac{\varepsilon m - \phi\lambda}{\phi(\lambda - \varepsilon)} L_Y dY \equiv \Phi dY. \tag{A–8}$$

We can now proceed to determine the effects of policy and parameter changes in the two country model in a manner similar to Section I. The equilibrium conditions we shall use are those for the two money markets:

$$m(r, i, v)(R + D + N) = L(r, i, Y, W) \tag{A–9}$$

$$m^*(r, i^*, v^*)(\bar{R} - R + D^* + N^*) = L^*(r, i^*, Y^*, W^*) \tag{A–10}$$

To ensure that the comparative static results derived from (A–9) and (A–10) satisfy the equilibrium conditions in the respective markets for non-tradeable debt we will use (A–5) to (A–8). Differentiating the above equilibrium conditions and substituting from (A–5) to (A–8) we obtain the following results:

$$\frac{dr/r}{dN} = -mm^*\gamma/\Delta < 0; \quad \frac{dr/r}{dv} = -m^* m_v \gamma H/\Delta > 0 \tag{A–11}$$

$$\frac{dr/r}{dD} = -mm^*/\Delta < 0; \quad \frac{dr/r}{dY} = -m^*\Phi/\Delta > 0$$

$$\frac{dR}{dN} = -\delta^* m\gamma/\Delta < 0; \quad \frac{dR}{dv} = -\delta^* m_v \gamma H/\Delta > 0$$

$$\frac{dR}{dD} = -\delta^*m/\Delta < 0; \quad \frac{dR}{dY} = -\delta^*\Phi/\Delta > 0$$

where $\Delta \equiv \delta^*m + \delta m^* > 0$.

NOTES

1. See Mundell (1968). For a recent review and extensive references to the literature, see Myrhman (1975).

2. For studies of the money supply process see Burger (1971) and Brunner (1973). A model of portfolio balance is developed in Tobin (1969).

3. The concept of non-traded assets is used, too, in Branson (1972, 1977), Boyer (1975) and Dornbusch (1975). I am indebted to Walter Salant for pointing out that 'nontransferable assets' play a key role in Scitovsky (1969).

4. The following formalisation is a one-bond variant of the model developed in Girton and Henderson (1976), who consider a world with perfect capital mobility and two imperfectly substitutable bonds. It is, too, the asset market description of the model developed in Mundell (1968) and tested in Kouri and Porter (1974).

5. For a convenient discussion of money and credit multipliers, see Burger (1971).

6. In addition to the restrictions on the signs of the partial derivative of the behavioural equations in (10) to (14), we impose the restriction implicit in the relative slopes of the LM and VK curves in Figure 3:
$-\phi/(\phi_i H - V_i) > -m/(m_i H - L_i); \quad H \equiv R + D + N$. Defining the elasticity of excess supply of money and credit, respectively, as:

$$\varepsilon \equiv (m_i H - L_i)(i/M) \text{ and } \lambda \equiv (\phi_i H - V_i)i/K).$$

We can write this restriction as: $\lambda > \varepsilon$ so that we are assuming that the elasticity of excess supply of credit exceeds that of money.

7. The LM schedule shifts by $dR = -dN$ and the VK schedule by $dR = -(1 + 1/\phi)dN$.

8. In deriving these results we have imposed additional structure on the supply of domestic loans in assuming that $\phi(r, i, v) = \alpha(r, i)(m-1)$ so that the allocation of earning assets between domestic and international loans is independent of v. We further assume that $L_Y = V_Y$. The reader will recognise that these restrictions have a ready interpretation in terms of the relative shifts of the LM and VK schedules. See, too, Appendix I (p. 120).

9. The analysis assumes that the money multiplier m is unaffected by the regulation. See note 8.

10. For a derivation of (23) and the definition of symbols, see Appendix I (p. 122).

11. The expected future spot rate is treated as an exogenous variable along with other parameters of the distribution that are implicitly suppressed into the functional form of (24).

REFERENCES

Boyer, R., 'Commodity Markets and Bond Markets in a Small Fixed Exchange Rate Economy', *Canadian Journal of Economics* (Feb. 1975).

Branson, W., 'Macroeconomic Equilibrium with Portfolio Balance in Open Economies', Institute for International Economic Studies, Stockholm (1972).
— 'International Transmission of Inflation: A Keynesian Approach', forthcoming in L. Krause (ed.) *World Inflation: Theory and Recent Experience* (Brookings, 1977).
Brunner, K., 'Money Supply Processes and Monetary Policy in an Open Economy', in M. Connolly and A. Swoboda (eds) *International Trade and Money* (Allen & Unwin, 1973).
Burger, A., *The Money Supply Process* (Wadsworth, 1971).
Dornbusch, R., 'A Portfolio Balance Model of the Open Economy', *Journal of Monetary Economics* (Jan 1975).
Fleming, M. and Mundell, R. A., 'Official Intervention on the Forward Foreign Exchange Market', *I.M.F. Staff Papers* (Mar 1964).
Girton, L. and Henderson D., 'Financial Capital Movements and Central Bank Behaviour in a Class of Two Country, Short Run Portfolio Balance Models', *Journal of Monetary Economics* (Jan., 1976).
Kouri, P. and Porter, M., International Capital Flows and Portfolio Equilibrium', *Journal of Political Economy* (May/June 1974).
Mundell, R. A., *International Economics* (Macmillan, 1968).
Myrhman, J., 'Monetary Policy in Open Economies'. Unpublished manuscript, Institute for International Economic Studies, Stockholm, 1975.
Scitovsky, T., *Money and the Balance of Payments* (Allen & Unwin, 1969).
Tobin, J., 'A General Equilibrium Approach to Monetary Theory', *Journal of Money, Credit and Banking* (Feb 1969).

9 Interrelations Between Domestic and International Theories of Inflation

Robert J. Gordon

National governments are held responsible by their electorates for the attainment of full employment, price stability, and real economic growth. Conflicting guidance for policy-makers is provided by two quite different approaches to inflation theory, the first school of thought which is based on the domestic Phillips curve as the fundamental driving force of inflation with little or no reference to external influences, and the second approach of the 'monetary theory of the balance of payments', in which the only determinants of domestic inflation are the rate of change of the exchange rate and of world prices.

The simplest static version of the domestic approach warns policy-makers that full employment and price stability cannot be simul-taneously achieved because the rates of inflation and unemployment are not independent targets; the choice of one predetermines the other. A more sophisticated dynamic version holds that the choice of more rapid inflation will yield reduced unemployment only temporarily, since the adjustment of expectations will cause the short-run tradeoff curve to shift upwards until unemployment has returned to the 'natural rate'. Unem-ployment and inflation targets are not determined jointly as in the static version but rather represent two independent policy problems, one to be handled by a group of labour economists who study the possibility of altering the natural rate of unemployment by reducing search costs and the mismatch of workers and jobs by location and skill, and the second by a group of monetary economists who compute the optimum rate of inflation as depending on the interest rate paid on money and the administrative and allocative costs of levying taxes other than the 'inflation tax'. The determination by the second group that actual inflation is proceeding faster than the optimum rate calls for domestic policy sufficiently deflationary to reduce inflation to the optimum, although in a society with a positive rate of time preference the near-term costs of lost output in a recession may sufficiently counterbalance the long-term benefits of optimum inflation as to recommend a policy in which inflation is reduced only part of the way toward the optimum. A third independent branch of the policy-making agency can maintain external balance by the suitable choice of an exchange rate.

The monetary approach to balance of payments theory, henceforth labelled 'the international approach', presents policy-makers with radically different conclusions. The only point of agreement is that alterations in the unemployment rate in the long run depend on improving the efficiency of the labour market and cannot be achieved by monetary policy. Otherewise, the roles of domestic monetary policy and exchange rate policy are reversed. Since the price of goods in terms of domestic currency is equal to the price of those goods in terms of foreign currency times the exchange rate (the domestic currency price of foreign exchange), the rate of domestic inflation can be reduced below the rate of world inflation only by means of a continuous currency appreciation. With a fixed exchange rate the application of restrictive domestic monetary policy, the cure for excessive inflation proposed by the domestic theory, actually has no effect on the inflation rate but rather attracts an inflow of foreign capital which causes a balance-of-payment surplus. If, on the other hand, the exchange rate is floating, the capital inflow appreciates the exchange rate and, by reducing the price level of traded goods, give the domestic monetary authorities a direct lever on the domestic inflation rate.

An attempt to reconcile the domestic and international approaches has particular relevance in the aftermath of the oil inflation of 1973–5, which has caused most oil-consuming nations to suffer both from accelerated rates of inflation and payments deficits. The domestic approach would propose to reduce the inflation rate by monetary restriction while allowing a devaluation (or downward sinking of a floating rate) to maintain external balance. The international approach would agree on the necessity of a deceleration in the growth of domestic credit, assigning it to the maintenance of external balance, but would recommend a currency *re*valuation (or upward float) to reduce the domestic rate of inflation.

The purpose of this paper is an examination of the theoretical underpinnings of both theories, of the assumptions necessary for their validity, and of the consequences of loosening the most restrictive assumptions. Such a comparison might appear to be unnecessary on the grounds that the domestic approach was intended for application to closed economies and could never have been taken seriously as a explanation of inflation in economies open to foreign trade. But this overlooks the awkward historical fact that the domestic approach based on the Phillips curve was popularised by Phillips and Lipsey in an application to wage data for the open UK economy, and even in the last few years has remained the dominant framework for empirical analysis of the inflation process in every major open economy.[1] Another possible objection to the comparison is that the two theories are intended to apply to different time horizons, with the Phillips curve approach relevant to a short-run disequilibrium in which unemployment and real output can vary from their full-employment levels, and the international monetary theory intended explicitly for the comparison of long-run equilibrium positions. But policy-makers care about the short run before the next election and need a theory which simultaneously takes account of an economy's openness to commodity and capital movements but which at the same time loosens the restrictive assumption that output is always fixed.

The last third of the paper attempts a reconciliation of the two theories which combines the characteristics of the money market and traded-goods market of the international monetary theory with those of the non-traded (home) goods market described by domestic Phillips curve theory. The result is a hybrid which corresponds more closely to the real world than either extreme view from which it is derived. The domestic inflation rate can only temporarily diverge from the rate in the world traded-goods market, but unemployment can nevertheless develop as the economy adjusts to changes in world prices or as a consequence of restrictive domestic monetary policy.

OUTLINE OF THE DOMESTIC PHILLIPS CURVE APPROACH

Early theoretical and empirical work in the Phillips curve tradition was almost exclusively concerned with the relationship between the unemployment rate and the change in nominal wage rates, implicitly holding constant the expected rate of inflation. The early approach was static, in contrast to the 'natural rate' hypothesis, introduced by Friedman (1968) and Phelps (1967), which emphasises the dynamic consequences for the unemployment – wage change tradeoff of a change in the expected rate of inflation, and which provides an explanation of points which had appeared to be 'off' the static tradeoff curve. The following brief outline describes the theory implicit in my own empirical attempts (1971), (1972) to reconcile the natural rate hypothesis with the US data.[2] In contrast to previous expositions of the domestic approach, it places much more emphasis on the importance of both direct and indirect taxes as determinants of prices and wage rates.

In domestic inflation theory the rate of inflation is typically determined in separate wage and price equations, with the wage equation providing the 'driving force' of the inflation process, and the price equation a less important appendage in which the distribution of income depends on the response of the price level to changes in unit labour cost. The wage equation can be interpreted as tracing the disequilibrium adjustment path of the wage rate when the demand and supply of labour are out of balance. An interesting question, which we discuss below, is the source of the asymmetry which selects the labour market disequilibrium, rather than the concurrent commodity market disequilibrium, as the dominant feature of the adjustment mechanism.

We begin with standard neoclassical demand and supply functions for labour in the domestic nonfarm sector of the economy, in which output (X_h) is assumed to be produced by labour, another fixed factor, and 'technology' $(\hat{Q})$, which is assumed to be Hicks-neutral and advance at an exponential rate of (q).

$$X_h = \hat{Q}\psi(N), \tag{1}$$

where N is the quantity of labour input in the domestic non-farm sector. Non-farm labour receives a nominal wage (W) equal to the expected value of its marginal product during its period of service:

$$W = (1 - \tau_E^e)P_h^e\hat{Q}\psi'(N), \tag{2}$$

where P_h is the gross-of-tax price of non-farm output, the superscript (e) denotes an expected variable, and τ_E^e is the expected excise tax rate. (2) can be inverted and written as a demand for labour function:

$$N^d = N^d[WT_E^e/(P_h^e\hat{Q})], \quad N_1^d < 0, \tag{3}$$

where $T_E^e = 1/(1 - \tau_E^e)$.

Workers in the domestic non-farm sector consume goods produced outside the sector, both farm products and imports, and base their labour supply decisions on the expected real wage defined in terms of a consumer price index which includes an appropriately weighted average of the prices of farm and non-farm products, as well as imports, relative to the productivity trend $(\hat{Q})$. If the real expected wage rises at the same pace as $\hat{Q}$, labour supply is assumed unchanged, but a faster increase in the real expected wage induces an increase in labour supply. In addition to the excise tax, the government which levies a direct payroll tax on labour at rate τ_P which is paid by workers.[3]

The expected real wage relevant for labour supply decisions is calculated after taxes:

$$N^s = N^s[W/(T_P^e P_c^e\hat{Q})], \quad N_1^s > 0, \tag{4}$$

where $T_P^e = 1/(1 - \tau_P^e)$, and P_c^e is the expected level of the consumer price index. The excess demand for labour (Z) can be written as a ratio:

$$Z = N^d[WT^e_E/(P^e_h\hat{Q})]/N^s[W/(T^e_p P^e_c \hat{Q})]. \tag{5}$$

(5) can be converted into a relationship between the proportional rates of growth of the demand for and supply of labour:

$$Z = -(a+\beta)(w-\hat{q}) + \alpha p^e_h + \beta p^e_c - \alpha t^e_E + \beta t^e_p, \tag{6}$$

where lower-case letters indicate rates of change $(w = dW/W)$, and α and β are, respectively, the real-wage elasticities of labour demand and supply. A standard disequilibrium adjustment hypothesis is that the speed at which a disequilibrium disappears depends on its size.

$$Z = -\gamma(Z), \quad \gamma(1) = 0. \tag{7}$$

When (6) and (7) are combined and solved for the change in the nominal wage, we obtain after some rearrangement:

$$w - \hat{q} = p^e_c + \frac{1}{\alpha + \beta}\left[\alpha(p^e_h - p^e_c - t^e_E) + \beta t^e_P + \gamma(Z)\right]. \tag{8}$$

The wage equation (8) has been estimated for US data in an earlier paper (Gordon, 1971) and has been simulated in a more recent paper (Gordon, 1972) to estimate the effect of the US wage – price control experiment of 1971–3.[4] The real wage defined in terms of consumer prices can rise relative to the productivity trend $(\hat{q})$ if there is a net excess demand for labour. If the labour supply curve is vertical $(\beta = 0)$, the nominal wage depends only on the domestic non-farm price level, and the burden of an increase in farm or import prices relative to domestic non-farm prices is entirely borne by employees, as is the burden of an increase in either tax rate. If the labour demand curve is vertical, on the other hand, the burden of higher external prices or tax rates is entirely shifted to employers.

In non-competitive labour-market settings an increase in external prices and in tax rates might be partially shifted forward even if labour were supplied inelastically. In unionised industries, for instance, unions might use their strike weapon to pass through some or all of a tax or external price increase in higher wages. Unions are not necessary, however, since competitive firms might offer risk-averse employees a wage contract partially indexed to the after-tax consumer price index, trading this 'real wage insurance' for a reduction in the average real wage.[5]

The price equation is based on the hypothesis that the price level net of excise taxes is marked up over 'standard' unit cost, the latter consisting of (1) 'standard' unit labour cost, i.e. the wage rate (W) divided by productivity (Q^s) defined for some 'standard' level of capacity utilisation, (2) the expected nominal user cost of the capital services required to provide that level of capacity, i.e. the expected domestic non-farm price level multiplied by the expected real user cost (P^e_k), and (3) the expected unit cost of materials purchased from outside the sector in question (P_f^e). External materials would include, for instance, all non-manufactured materials in a price equation for the manufacturing sector, and farm products and imports in a price equation for the domestic non-farm sector. The mark-up fraction is assumed to depend on an index of the excess demand for commodities (V).[6] According to this approach the price equation for the domestic non-farm sector is:

$$q^s = bq + (1-b)\hat{q}, \tag{10}$$

The production process is assumed to be characterised by constant returns to scale, i.e. that there is a unitary elasticity of price to an equi-proportionate increase in the prices of all three inputs. Note that pricing at a mark-up over average cost is equivalent to marginal cost pricing if the production function is Cobb–Douglas.

The price equation (9) can be expressed in terms of observable variables if we assume, first, that firms estimate the rate of growth of standard productivity to be a weighted average of rates of growth of actual (q) and trend $(\hat{q})$ productivity,

$$P_h = T_E^e V^\phi (W/Q^s)^\eta (P_h^e P_k^e)^\mu P_f^{(1-\eta-\mu)}. \tag{9}$$

and that the real price of capital services (P_k) equals the real interest rate plus the depreciation rate adjusted for taxation of capital.[7] When (9) is converted into a relationship between proportional rates of growth, into which (10) is substituted, we obtain an expression for the domestic non-farm rate of inflation:

$$p_h = \eta(w-\hat{q}) - \eta b(q-\hat{q}) + (1-\eta-\mu)p_f^e + \phi v + t_E^e + \mu(p_h^e + p_k^e). \tag{11}$$

I have estimated for the domestic US non-farm economy an equation which includes the first, second and fourth terms on the right-hand side of (11).[8] The rate of change of excess commodity demand (v) is proxied by the rate of change in the ratio of unfilled orders to capacity and implies significant procyclical variation in the mark-up fraction, sufficient to cause a reduction of about 2 per cent in the price level relative to the wage rate during a typical post-war US recession. The contribution of actual productivity in the estimation of standard productivity apears to be about 20 per cent; i.e. about 80 per cent of the above-trend growth of productivity during an economic expansion flows through to profits. My empirical work was performed for a sample period during which multicollinearity and insufficient variation prevented reliable estimates of the effects of external prices and the user cost of capital services.

The interpretation of the domestic approach is straightforward when (8) and (11) are combined into a single reduced-form equation for the rate of domestic non-farm inflation:[9]

$$p_h = [\eta\varepsilon(\alpha+\beta a)+\mu]p_h^e + \{\eta[\varepsilon\beta(1-a)-1]+1-\mu\}p_f^e$$
$$+ \phi v + \eta\varepsilon\gamma(Z) - \eta b(q-\hat{q}) + (1-\eta\varepsilon\alpha)t_E^e + \eta\varepsilon\beta t_p^e + \mu p_k^e. \quad (12)$$

(12) can be viewed as a short-run Phillips curve relating the rate of domestic non-farm inflation (p_h) to the excess demand for labour (Z) for a given rate of expected inflation (p_h^e). The short-run tradeoff can be shifted not only by a change in external inflation (p_f), but also by a change in the excess demand for commodities or in the rate of productivity growth relative to trend, as well as by changes in tax rates and the real user cost of capital. In contrast to the conventional wisdom that the existence of the inflation – unemployment tradeoff prevents the authorities from dampening inflation without increasing unemployment, a reduction in either tax rates or the real user cost of capital (e.g. through lower interest rates or taxes on capital) can *temporarily* shift the tradeoff. Depending on the size of the multiplier effect of the tax or interest rate reduction on income, which raises inflation by increasing the net excess demand for labour and commodities, the total effect of these policy changes may be either to raise or reduce the rate of inflation.[10] The authorities can take advantage of the differing total inflationary impacts of the alternative fiscal and monetary measures, achieving a downward shift in the short-run Phillips curve by, for example, reducing excise tax rates while at the same time raising income tax rates or by reducing the growth rate of the money supply.

In the long run, the actual and expected rates of domestic inflation are equal, and the inflation – unemployment tradeoff is:

$$p_h = p_f^e + \frac{\phi v + \eta\varepsilon\gamma(Z) - \eta b(q-\hat{q}) + (1-\eta\varepsilon\alpha)t_E^e + \eta\varepsilon\beta t_p^e + \mu p_k^e}{1-\mu-\eta\varepsilon(\alpha+\beta a)}. \quad (13)$$

INTERPRETATION OF THE 'DOMESTIC APPROACH'

The foregoing immediately raises a basic question when viewed from the perspective of the monetary approach to balance of payments theory, can domestic and world prices permanently diverge? Central to the first question is the existence of a long-run tradeoff between inflation and unemployment. In an entirely closed economy no external prices enter into the determination of standard variable cost in (9), and there is no discrepancy between the non-farm and consumer price indices in (8). When all tax and interest rates are constant, the long-run tradeoff disappears, and (12) can be rewritten:

$$p_h - p_h^e = \phi v + \eta\varepsilon\gamma(Z). \quad (14)$$

Long-run equilibrium occurs only if $v=0$, i.e. if the excess demand for commodities is constant and the excess demand for labour is at the level consistent with equilibrium in the labour market, i.e. Friedman's (1968) 'natural rate' of unemployment. Any attempt by policy-makers to maintain the unemployment rate at a level permanently below the natural rate causes $p_h > p_h^e$ in (14), which can occur permanently in the presence of an adaptive mechanism for the formation of p_h^e only if the actual rate of inflation permanently accelerates, and similarly a permanent *excess* of unemployment requires a permanently accelerating deflation.

Now consider the long-run tradeoff in an open economy, i.e. the solution of (13) when tax rates and interest rates are constant:

$$p_h = p_f^e + \frac{\phi v + \eta \varepsilon \gamma(Z)}{1 - \mu - \eta \varepsilon (\alpha + \beta a)} \tag{15}$$

(15) yields one result which is consistent with the monetary approach to balance of payments theory, i.e. a unitary response of domestic inflation to an increase in the rate of inflation of external prices ($\partial p_h / \partial p_f = 1$). Ignoring farm prices, the external price equals the world price level in foreign currency (P_w) times the exchange rate (G, the domestic currency price of foreign currency), and (16) can be rewritten:

$$p_h = p_w + g + \frac{\phi v + \eta \varepsilon \gamma(Z)}{1 - \mu - \eta \varepsilon (\alpha + \beta a)} \tag{16}$$

If domestic policy-makers are unwilling to accept a domestic inflation rate equal to the imported rate, and insist on maintenance of a fixed exchange rate, they have the option of raising the unemployment rate. A permanent reduction in the domestic inflation rate below the imported rate requires a *permanent* recession.

Can the divergence of domestic and world prices continue for ever? The long-run relationship of prices and wages in the traded and non-traded goods sectors, more fully explored below, implies that a continual divergence of domestic inflation at a rate below the imported inflation rate causes a continual shift of resources from the non-traded to traded goods sectors and a growing surplus in the balance of trade. Leaving aside the question of capital movements for subsequent discussion, in a fixed-rate regime the resulting inflow of foreign exchange must be fully sterilised, or otherwise the domestic money supply will expand, the unemployment rate will fall, and the domestic inflation rate will converge to the world rate. Since sterilisation cannot be maintained for ever, the true long-run equilibrium in an open economy occurs at the natural unemployment rate, as in the closed economy described in (14).[11] In a floating rate regime, on the other hand, currency appreciation will further reduce the domestic inflation rate relative to the world rate.

Thus the logical consequences of the domestic theory appear to be incompatible with the international monetary approach only as the consequence of a partial equilibrium approach which ignores the effects of higher imported inflation on the domestic commodity and money markets. When the full interaction with the other markets is taken into account, there can be no permanent divergence between domestic and world inflation in a fixed rate regime; a one-shot devaluation causes an acceleration in the domestic rate of inflation until the domestic price level converges with the higher prices of traded goods expressed in domestic currency; and only a continuous currency appreciation allows a permanent reduction of domestic inflation below the world rate.

How has this set of conclusions escaped the attention of the numerous analysts working with econometric models based on wage and price equations identical in specification to (8) and (11)? The conditions required for a unitary elasticity of domestic to imported inflation (holding constant the unemployment rate) are implicit in (12) above: first, the coefficients on unit domestic and external costs in the price equation must sum to unity and, second, the coefficient on expected inflation in the wage equation must be unity.

Econometricians have rarely bothered to impose the first condition in the estimation of their price equations, probably due to their pre-occupation with short-run forecasting and relative disinterest in long-run simulation.[12] The consistent finding in econometric work, at least until recently, that the coefficient on expected inflation in the wage equation is less than unity, may be partly due to errors in the estimation of expected inflation, but is due more basically to the standard econometric practice of constraining coefficients to be constant. Because of costs of contract renegotiation, individuals do not bother to incorporate their perceptions of expected inflation into their labour supply decisions unless that expected rate exceeds a 'threshold' level which depends on the adjustment costs. Since the aggregate expected inflation rate relevant for supply decisions is a weighted average of the individual expected rates of those whose perceptions are above and below the threshold, the elasticity of wage rates to expected inflation is a variable, equal to zero when the inflation rate is low enough to leave all individuals below their threshold and equal to unity when inflation is sufficiently rapid to raise all individuals above their threshold.[13] Econometricians who erroneously estimate (8) with a fixed parameter on p_c^e will obtain an estimate equal to the mean proportion of individuals above their threshold during the sample period. I have estimated (1971, pp. 404–6) a wage equation with a variable coefficient on expected inflation, the estimated size of which implies that the elasticity reaches unity in the US when the inflation rate reaches roughly 7 per cent. This variable coefficient approach has the advantage that it reconciles (*a*) the partial adjustment observed in most post-war econometric studies of wage behaviour in the US and other countries, (*b*) the steady increase in the size of the partial adjustment coefficient as the sample period is extended into the late 1960s, and (*c*) the long-run 'natural rate of unemployment' hypothesis summarised in (14) above.

The failure of most existing econometric wage – price models for open economies to satisfy either of these two conditions guarantees in advance that any attempt to tie together national models to simulate the international transmission of inflation, as in the case of Project LINK (Ball, 1973), will reach erroneous conclusions. For example, recent models for the UK lament the apparent 'breaking down' of the Phillips curve relationship without any systematic attempt to analyse the channels by which world inflation influences the domestic economy. An extreme example is the London Business School model (Ball 1971) in which the full feed-through of world prices to domestic prices is prevented by the remarkable assumption that wage changes are exogenous! Another is the observation by Dicks-Mireaux that 'perhaps the least obvious' channel by which inflation may be imported is the influence of export-sector wages on national wages.

THE MONETARY APPROACH TO BALANCE OF PAYMENTS THEORY

There is no connection between the domestic and international varieties of monetarism. Domestic monetarism attributes changes in nominal income to changes in the supply of money engineered by the domestic monetary authority, and determines the division of those changes in nominal income by a Phillips curve-type inflation equation like (12). International monetarism removes both the domestic money supply and inflation rate from the control of domestic authorities, claiming that an expansion in the domestic assets of the central bank will be offset by an outflow of international reserves, and that changes in the domestic inflation rate simply mirror those in world prices (adjusted for any changes in exchange rates). The domestic and international theories converge only in the trivial sense that the rate of inflation of the world, which is a closed system and can be analysed without mental strain by domestic monetarists, depends on the rate of world monetary expansion, world output growth and the world's income elasticity of the demand for money.

The international analysis begins with a demand function for real balances which depends on real output (X) and the nominal interest rate ($R + p^e$). The nominal money supply consists of two components, one backed by international reserves (S) and the other by the domestic assets of the central bank (D), and is equal in equilibrium to the domestic price level (P) times the demand for real balances:[14]

$$S + D = PL(X, R + p^e).\qquad(17)$$

In its simplest version for a static economy the theory assumes that only a single composite traded good is produced, the price of which (P) is rigidly pegged to the world price level ($P = GP_w$). Capital is also freely mobile between countries, thus pegging the domestic interest rate to the world level. The third basic assumption is that real output (X) is fixed. If the exchange rate is fixed, then (21) contains only two slack variables, S and D. Any attempt by the authorities to increase domestic credit must lead to an outflow of reserves. In a dynamic growing economy the same assumptions imply that any attempt to create domestic credit at a faster percentage growth than the growth rate of the nominal demand for money will cause a reduction in the share (θ) of the money supply consisting of international reserves:

$$s = \frac{m - (1 - \theta)d}{\theta} = \frac{g + p_w + \rho_X x - (1 - \theta)d}{\theta} \tag{18}$$

where ρ_X is the real-output elasticity of the demand for money and the nominal interest rate is assumed fixed. The absolute level of reserves will decline, i.e. the nation will suffer a payments deficit, only if $d > m/(1 - \theta)$.

Several major conclusions follow from this analysis, including:

(1) Nations have only themselves to blame for payments deficits in a fixed-rate regime, since deficits can be caused only by excessive domestic credit expansion. Devaluation cannot improve the balance of payments of a country like the UK by making its traded goods more 'competitive', since national authorities have no control of the foreign-currency prices of traded goods.

(2) Any attempt to reduce the domestic rate of inflation below the world rate by pursuing restrictive domestic credit policy is doomed to failure, since domestic inflation depends only on world inflation and the rate of change of the exchange rate. The subject nation is assumed to be sufficiently small so that the effect of its own restrictive domestic credit policy on the rate of growth of the world money supply, and hence on the world rate of inflation, can be neglected.

(3) Domestic turmoil, e.g. the three-day week in the UK during the 1974 coal miners' strike, causes a payments deficit only if the rate of growth of domestic credit continues unchanged, since the decline in real output reduces the demand for money and hence causes an outflow of reserves. Reduction in domestic credit expansion along with the reduction in money demand would prevent any emergence of a payments deficit.

(4) The achievement of an 'optimum quantity of money', i.e. of a domestic rate of inflation which balances the marginal 'shoe leather' cost of the inflation tax against the marginal administrative and allocative costs of other taxes, depends on the choice of an appropriate rate of currency appreciation or depreciation, not on domestic monetary policy.

When its conclusions are applied to the disequilibrium induced by the recent increase in the world price of oil, the international monetary theory suggests that restriction of the growth of domestic credit is the appropriate policy response for oil-consuming nations, but that the large payments deficits recently experienced by the UK, France, Italy, and others stand as evidence that domestic credit restriction has not been carried far enough. This interpretation raises at least two important questions: can domestic credit restriction achieve balance of payments equilibrium in an individual small country without inducing a recession, and can simultaneous domestic credit restriction by many oil-consuming nations together reduce the world rate of inflation without causing a worldwide recession or depression?

The basic version of the international monetary theory refers to long-run equilibrium positions and is unsuitable as it stands for the analysis of some short-run disequilibrium problems. The domestic Phillips curve theory, on the other hand, provides estimates of adjustment speeds but is inconsistent with the international monetary theory in its long-run implications. A useful function would be served by the development of a hybrid approach which combines the best features of each theory. The analysis of the international monetary theory with two classes of goods, both traded and non-traded, serves as a useful point of departure for this exercise, since it clarifies the channels by which a devaluation or an exogenous increase in the world rate of inflation influences domestic wages and the prices of non-traded goods. After an exposition of the conventional full-employment flexible-price version of the two-sector model, we shall explore a version in which prices are slow to adjust and unemployment can arise. (The following is adapted from Salter (1959) and Dornbusch (1973) and (1974).)

A TWO-SECTOR MODEL WITH FLEXIBLE PRICES

All production and expenditure is divided into two classes of goods, traded and non-traded, the former with prices determined on world markets, and the latter with prices determined entirely by internal supply and demand. The terms of trade are assumed unaffected by the domestic economy, allowing both exportables and importables to be amalgamated into a single traded good.[15] Both classes of goods are treated as composite commodities, implying that the relative prices of goods within each class are fixed. Although the capital stock in each of the two sectors is fixed and immobile, the homogeneous labour force is perfectly mobile between sectors, maintaining a single nominal wage rate (W) and thus serving as the basic economic link between the sectors. There are separate production functions in each sector, competitive factor pricing, and a fixed supply of labour (N_0), implying the following labour-market equilibrium condition:

$$N^s = N_0 = N_h^d(W/P_h) + N_f^d(W/P_f), \tag{19}$$

where the subscripts f and h now refer to the traded and non-traded ('home') goods sectors, and the superscripts s and d refer to supply and demand. Defining the relative price of non-traded goods as

P^* $(P^* = P_h/P_f)$, and the real wage in terms of traded goods as ω^* $(\omega^* = W/P_f)$, (19) can be rewritten as:

$$N^s = N_0 = N_h^d(\omega^*/P^*) + N_f^d(\omega^*).\tag{20}$$

The labour-market is illustrated in the north-east quadrant of Figure 1, with a market-clearing real wage ω_0^* corresponding to the assumed initial relative price P_0^*. (20) can be solved for P^* in terms of ω^* and N:

$$P^* = P^*(\omega^*, N); \quad P_1^* > 0; \quad P_2^* < 0.\tag{21}$$

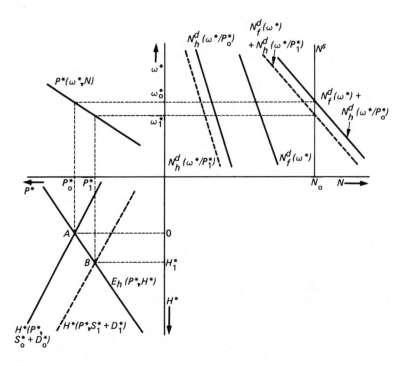

Figure 1

This labour-market equilibrium condition is illustrated in the north-east quadrant of Figure 1. For any fixed labour force (N_0) an increase in the real wage (ω^*) reduces the demand for labour in both sectors, and the reattainment of equilibrium requires a disproportionate increase in the relative price (P^*), so that ω^*/P^* is reduced by enough to raise employment in the non-traded goods sector by the amount needed to regain full employment. Growth in the labour force causes the $P^*(\omega^*, N)$ schedule to pivot counter-clockwise, since a reduction in the real wage is necessary to prevent the emergence of an excess supply of labour. The area north-east of the $P^*(\omega^*, N)$ schedule represents unemployment, and the area south-west an excess demand for labour.

Up to this point the model determines a relationship between the real wage and the relative price, but not a unique value for each. The additional element needed to close the model is the relationship between the relative price and domestic hoarding, i.e. the flow excess demand for money. Let us assume a fixed interest rate and a unitary income elasticity of the demand for money, making the demand for money a fixed fraction (k) of nominal income. The nominal flow excess demand for money is:

$$H = \ell\left[k(P_f X_f + P_h X_h) - S - D\right], \tag{22}$$

where X_f and X_h are respectively the real quantities of traded and non-traded goods. Real output and the real money supply in the terms of traded goods can be written:

$$X^* = X_f + P^* X_h = X^*(P^*); \quad S^* + D^* = (S + D)/P_f. \tag{23}$$

Now the expression for desired nominal hoarding in (23) can be rewritten in real terms:

$$H^* = \left[kX^*(P^*), S^* + D^*\right] = H^*(P^*, S^* + D^*); \quad H_1^* > 0; \quad H_2^* < 0. \tag{24}$$

When the real money supply (i.e. the nominal money supply relative to the nominal price of traded goods) is held constant, an increase in the relative price of non-traded goods raises the demand for money and induces positive hoarding, as illustrated by the schedule labelled H^* in the southwest quadrant of Figure 1. This hoarding relationship indicates the connection between desired hoarding and the relative price but does not represent equilibrium in the money market, which occurs only when $H^* = 0$.

A second schedule relating real hoarding to the relative price of non-traded goods is obtained from the market-clearing conditions in the commodity market. An increase in real hoarding represents a decrease in real expenditure ($X^* - H^*$) relative to real income (X^*), thus causing an excess supply of non-traded goods if the marginal propensity to spend on non-traded goods is positive. Since the excess supply of non-traded goods in turn is a function of their relative price, the commodity-market equilibrium condition is:

$$0 = E_h(P^*, H^*) = X_h^s(P^*) - X_h^d(P^*, X^* - H^*); \quad E_{h_1} > 0; \quad E_{h_2} > 0. \tag{25}$$

The excess supply created by an increase in real hoarding can be eliminated by a decline in the relative price, which reduces the supply of the non-traded good and raises its demand.

What are the consequences of an increase in the domestic currency price of traded goods, induced either by a devaluation or some exogenous increase in foreign demand? Starting from an initial equilibrium in Figure 1 at P_0^*, w_0^*, and $H^* = 0$, denoted at point A in the southwest quadrant, an increase in the domestic currency price of traded goods reduces the supply of real balances and shifts the hoarding schedule to the right, raising hoarding from zero to H_1^*, the counterpart of which is a balance of payments surplus. The relative price declines from P_0^* to P_1^* to maintain equilibrium in the domestic non-traded goods market, i.e. equilibrium in the south-west quadrant occurs at point B. Labour market equilibrium requires that workers shift to the traded goods sector, reducing the real wage in terms of traded goods from ω_0^* to ω_1^*. As indicated by the slope of the $P^*(\omega^*, N)$ schedule in the north-west quadrant of Figure 1, the relative price of non-traded goods falls by more than the real wage, thus raising the real wage in terms of non-traded goods, reducing the demand for labour in that sector, and averting an aggregate excess demand for labour.

The new situation is not one of sustainable long-run equilibrium, however, since the trade surplus associated with positive hoarding leads to an inflow of reserves. If the real quantity of domestic credit remains fixed, the real supply of money will increase relative to the demand, and the economy will return to its original position at point A, as hoarding is eliminated. The domestic monetary authority can reduce domestic credit as reserves flow in, but sterilisation must eventually come to an end (see note 11 below). Thus an increase in the domestic currency price of traded goods, whether brought about by devaluation or an exogenous external increase in demand, has no long-run real effect. The nominal rate of inflation in the two sectors is identical, of course, when the relative price is constant (i.e. either at P_0^* or P_1^*), and so any divergence of the rates of inflation of the two sectors is strictly a transitory phenomenon requiring a continuous change in real hoarding.

DISEQUILIBRIUM ADJUSTMENT IN THE TWO-SECTOR MODEL

In the previous section the wage rate and the price of non-traded goods were assumed to be perfectly flexible, allowing the continuous maintenance of equilibrium in the labour and commodity markets in the wake of an exogenous increase in the price of traded goods. In the real world, however, labour and commodity market disequilibria are not instantaneously eliminated. A more realistic model is obtained if we abandon the assumption of perfectly flexible wages and prices, and instead adopt a Phillips curve-type mechanism for the non-traded goods sector, with the adjustment of the wage rate assumed to eliminate only a portion of a labour-market disequilibrium in any given time period (the same adjustment assumption written in equation (7) above). In contrast to the previous section, in which the *price* of non-traded goods is a residual which adjusts to clear the market for non-traded goods, here the non-traded goods price is assumed (as in (9) above) to be 'marked up' over the wage rate, so that a disequilibrium can persist not only in the labour market but also in the market for non-traded goods. Since the wage rate and the non-traded goods price level are now determined by behavioural adjustment hypotheses, it is the level of non-traded goods *output* which becomes the residual. While firms in the traded-goods sector still behave as competitors, expanding employment to the point at which the wage rate equals the value of labour's marginal product, their unlucky colleagues in the non-traded goods sector will face a sales constraint if the residual output level (X_h) happens to be less than the amount they would like to produce at the going real wage, and the amount of labour they will hire will be given along their 'effective' labour demand curve $\tilde{N}_h^d(X_h)$.[16]

The excess demand for labour when a sales constraint is operative is the demand for labour in the two sectors minus the fixed supply of labour:

$$Z = N_f^d(W/P_f^e) + \tilde{N}_h^d(X_h) - N_o, \qquad (26)$$

where the level of demand for non-traded goods is assumed to be sufficiently low to prevent firms from operating on their 'notional' demand curve, i.e. from hiring all the labour they would like at the given real wage. The wage rate is assumed to adjust to eliminate a portion (γ) of the excess demand for labour:

$$-\psi\alpha(w - p_f^e) + (1 - \psi)\pi^{-1}x_h = z = -\gamma(Z), \qquad (27)$$

where α is the real-wage elasticity of the demand for labour, π is the elasticity of output to a change in labour input (the production function is assumed to be the same in both sectors), and ψ is the share in total labour demand of the traded goods sector.

Upon rearrangement (31) becomes a wage equation:

$$w = p_f^e + v^{-1}x_h + \hat{\gamma}(Z), \qquad (28)$$

where $v^{-1} = (1 - \psi)/\psi\alpha\pi$ and $\hat{\gamma}(Z) = \gamma(Z)/\psi\alpha$, for notational convenience. The rate of change of the wage rate can diverge from the rate of change of traded-goods prices in a regime of excess labour supply $(Z < 0)$ unless $x_h = -v\hat{\gamma}(Z)$. Must the nominal wage rate rise following an increase in the traded goods price? While eventually it must increase by the same proportion, in the short run it might decrease if the positive direct effect of a higher traded goods price in (32) is offset by sufficiently large negative values of the rate of change of non-traded goods output (x_h) and of the excess demand for labour (Z).

In Figure 2 the north-east quadrant depicts the labour market, where the vertical schedule at N_0 represents the fixed total supply of labour, and the supply of labour available for non-traded goods production is determined by the subtraction of the demand for labour in the traded goods sector, which for any given nominal wage depends on the exogenous traded goods price. The $(N_0 - N_f^d)$ 'available supply' curve shifts upward by the exact proportion of the higher traded-goods price P_{f_1}, and at the same time the effective non-traded labour demand curve shifts leftward by an amount to be determined below. At the initial wage W_0 the result may be either an excess supply of or demand for labour in the two sectors taken together, with the first possibility illustrated by the distance CD in Figure 2.

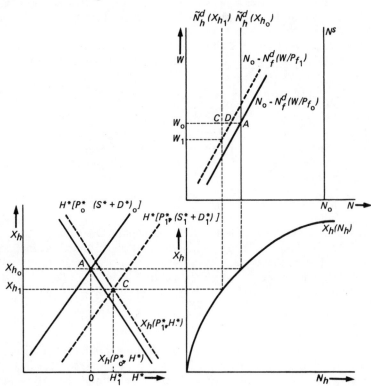

Figure 2

The 'first-round' decline in non-traded goods output following from imported inflation depends on the relative strength of the decline in the real money supply, which brings about a decline in non-traded goods output, as opposed to the stimulating effect on the demand for non-traded goods of their lower relative price.

The real rate of hoarding in the money market depends only on the relative price of non-traded goods (P^*), the level of non-traded goods output, and the real supply of money in terms of non-traded goods. (28) above can be rewritten to allow for a variable level of X_h:

$$H^* = \ell \left\{ k[X_f(P^*) + P^* X_h] - (S^* + D^*) \right\}$$
$$= H^*(P^*, X_h, S^* + D^*), \qquad (29)$$
$$H_1^* > 0; \quad H_2^* > 0; \quad H_3^* < 0.$$

The solid H^* schedule in the south-west quadrant of Figure 2 is positively sloped, representing the increase in hoarding associated with an increase in X_h when prices are held constant. An increase in the price of traded goods for any given level of X_h raises the real rate of hoarding:

$$h^* = \left\{ \lambda_{X*} \left[(1-a)v + a\left(\frac{x_h}{p_f} - 1 \right) \right] + 1 \right\} p_f, \qquad (30)$$

where:

h^* = dH^*/M^* = the change in M real hoarding relative to the initial real money supply.

λ_{X*} = the elasticity of the real demand for money to a change in real income.

a = the share of spending on non-traded goods in total income.

The first term in (30) represents the positive effect on the demand for money of the increase in real traded-goods output induced by a higher traded-goods price; the second represents the negative impact on money demand of the lower output and relative price of non-traded goods; the third (+ 1) represents the positive effect on excess money demand of the decline in the real money supply ($S^* + D^*$) measured in terms of traded-goods prices. In Figure 2 the net downward vertical movement of the H^* schedule (i.e. when $dH^* = 0$) in the case of a unitary real-income elasticity of real money demand reduces to:

$$\frac{x_h}{p_f} = \frac{-(1-a)(1+v)}{a}. \qquad (31)$$

The greater the elasticity of traded-goods output to their price (v), the greater the demand for money in that sector, and the more non-traded goods output must fall to clear the money market.

A second relationship between non-traded goods output and hoarding is obtained from market-clearing conditions in the commodity market. In contrast to the previous section, in which the relative price adjusted to equate the demand for non-traded goods output with the amount firms desired to sell at that relative price, now (25) is rewritten to set the supply equal to the demand at the given relative price:

$$X_h = X_h^d(P^*, X^* - H^*) = X_h(P^*, H^*); \quad X_{h_1} < 0, \quad X_{h_2} < 0. \quad (32)$$

The X_h schedule has a negative slope in Figure 2, reflecting the reduction in the demand for home-goods output when hoarding increases, with a steeper slope when the marginal propensity to spend is relatively high. An increase in the price of traded-goods could raise or lower the X_h schedule:

$$\frac{x_h}{p_f} = \frac{\sigma_P - \sigma_X[1 - (1-a)v/a]}{1 - \sigma_X}, \quad (33)$$

where σ_P = the elasticity of the demand for home goods to a change in their relative price (sign reversed)

   σ_X = the elasticity of the demand for home goods to changes in income.

A higher price in the traded-goods sector raises real home demand through the direct substitution effect (first term) and by raising real income generated in the production of traded-goods (third term), but reduces demand by reducing the real value of a given income denominated in home prices.

The direction of the change in non-traded goods output depends on the relative strength of the terms in equations (31) and (33), with a decline in output occurring if:

$$\sigma_P < \sigma_X + [(1-a)/a][1 + v(1 - \sigma_X)]. \quad (34)$$

The smaller the substitution effect, i.e. the stimulus to the demand for non-traded commodities provided by their reduced relative price, the more likely is their output to decline in the wake of an increase in the price of traded-goods. In Figure 2 the new level of non-traded goods output is denoted by point C, which is less likely to be above A, the weaker is the substitution effect.

The change in the excess demand for labour resulting from an increase in the traded-goods price depends on the relative strength of the increase in the demand for labour in the traded-goods sector and the reduction in the demand for labour in the home-goods sector:

$$\frac{z}{p_f} = (1-a)\alpha + \frac{ax_h}{\pi p_f}, \quad (35)$$

where, combining the money-market condition in (30) with the commodity market condition in (32), we have:[17]

$$\frac{x_h}{p_f} = \frac{\sigma_P + \sigma_X\left\{\frac{(1-a)}{a}[\alpha(1-k)] - 1\right\}}{1 - \sigma_X(1-k)}. \quad (36)$$

When there are minimal possibilities for substitution between labour and capital, and between traded and non-traded goods ($\alpha = \sigma_P = 0$), the excess demand for labour decreases unambiguously. It is more likely to increase, the larger are the elasticities of substitution between labour and capital and between the two types of goods. The formal condition necessary for an initial increase in excess labour demand is:

$$\alpha > \frac{a\{\sigma_X - a\sigma_P + (1-a)[1 - \sigma_X(1-k)]\}}{(1-a)[a + (1-a)\sigma_X(1-k)]}, \tag{37}$$

which is more likely to be satisfied with large values of α and σ_P.

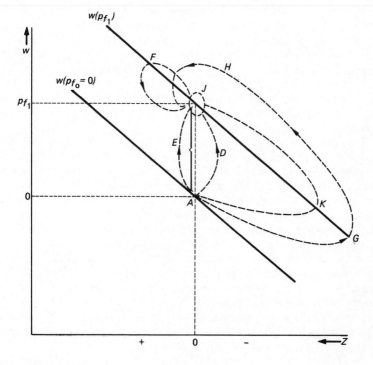

Figure 3

Three alternative paths of adjustment of the nominal wage are illustrated in Figure 3, where two Phillips curves from (28) above are drawn for a constant initial traded-goods price level ($p_{f_0} = 0$) and an increasing level ($p_{f_1} > 0$). Starting from an initial point A with zero excess labour demand and a fixed traded-goods price, the response of the wage rate to a higher traded-goods price could follow:

(1) The path AEJ if condition (37) is satisfied. The net demand for

labour increases even if (34) is satisfied and the level of non-farm output falls.[18]

(2) The path ADJ if condition (37) is not satisfied. Although the level of non-traded goods output and the net demand for labour both decline, they are too weak along path ADJ to offset the direct upward pull on the wage rate of the higher traded-goods price.

(3) The path AKJ if condition (37) is not satisfied and if the negative influence of excess labour supply and lower non-traded goods output are sufficiently strong to reduce the nominal wage. At point K the net demand for labour reaches its minimum point and begins to increase, both because of the stimulus to home-goods demand of lower home-goods prices ($p_h = w$) and because of the stimulus to labour demand in the traded-goods sector of the lower real wage (W/P_f). If the real-wage elasticity of labour demand in the traded-goods sector is sufficiently high, the economy may arrive at a position of balance in the labour market while the *level* of the real wage rate ($\omega^* = W/P_f$) is still below its initial value, a result equivalent to point B in Figure 1 above; the real wage (ω^*) and relative price (P^*) have both fallen by enough to clear the labour market.

Point K, however, does not represent the end of the story, for the increased rate of production in the traded-goods sector causes a balance of payments surplus which, if it is not sterilised, raises the level of real balances. In Figure 2 the H^* schedule begins to shift leftward toward its original position, raising home-goods demand, creating an excess demand for labour, and raising the wage rate relative to the exogenous traded-goods price. This process continues until production of traded-goods returns to the initial level, requiring a sufficient increase in the nominal wage rate to return the real wage rate (ω^*) to its initial level. A stationary position requires a zero excess demand for labour, which requires in turn that the level of home-goods demand return to its initial level, which occurs when the level of nominal money and the home-goods price rise by the same percentage as the traded-goods price. In Figure 3 this increase in the nominal wage relative to the traded-goods price is represented by the loop labelled JFJ.

(4) If the real-wage elasticity of the demand for labour is very low, the economy may follow a path like $AGHJ$ in Figure 3. In this case the falling real wage (ω^*) does not stimulate any appreciable reduction in the excess supply of labour. If, in addition, there is little substitution in demand between traded and home goods (i.e. σ_P is low), the falling relative price of home goods (P^*) does not add any appreciable strength to the demand for home goods. Thus the economy could 'get stuck' at a point like G in Figure 3 until the trade surplus creates sufficient reserves to raise the real money supply and hence the demand for home-goods output.

This analysis assumes throughout that capital is immobile between the two sectors. The fundamental cause of the emergence of an excess supply of labour when (41) is not satisfied is the inability of firms in the traded-goods sector profitably to employ all of the workers made redundant in the home-goods sector, due to the presence of diminishing returns to labour when their capital stock is fixed. Any movement of capital between the two sectors raises their demand for labour and increases the number of workers who may be profitably hired. In (37) this is equivalent to an increase in α and raises the likelihood that a devaluation or exogenous increase in the traded-goods price will create an excess demand rather than an excess supply of labour.

COMPARISON OF THE DOMESTIC AND INTERNATIONAL DISEQUILIBRIUM APPROACHES

In the domestic approach (15) above is the long-run relationship between domestic and foreign inflation when tax rates and interest rates are constant, and it is rewritten here:

$$p_h = p_f^e + \frac{\phi v + \eta \varepsilon \gamma(Z)}{1 - \mu - \eta \varepsilon(\alpha + \beta a)}. \tag{15}$$

The tradeoff in the international approach is (28), which can be rewritten as a price equation if the home-goods price is always marked up by a constant fraction over the wage rate:

$$p_h = w = p_f^e + v^{-1} x_h + \hat{\gamma}(Z). \tag{38}$$

Except for the size of the coefficients, the only difference between the two equations is the appearance of the rate of change in excess commodity demand (v) in (15) and the rate of change of non-traded goods output (x_h) in (38). Assuming that v and x_h are closely related, there appears to be no difference at all between the two approaches. Nevertheless interesting questions of interpretation arise.

(1) In the domestic approach p_f refers to the prices of goods produced outside the domestic non-farm sector, i.e. farm products and imports. The direct influence of external prices on domestically produced exportables and import substitutes is ignored, in contrast to the international approach, which treats imports, import substitutes, and exportables as a composite good.

(2) The derivation of the domestic approach ignores the distinction between notional and effective labour demand curves. Since wages are not perfectly flexible, any decrease in domestic demand imposes on producers a sales constraint which pushes them off of their notional labour demand curve on to an effective labour demand curve. Since the position of the latter depends only on sales, not the real wage, any changes in variables which shift only the notional demand curve (expected product prices, sales tax rates) should have no effect on the adjustment of wage rates. Tax rates and expected prices affect wage rates

only if they shift the notional labour supply curve, and hence influence the size of the disequilibrium between effective demand and notional supply. For instance, a reduction in the personal income tax would tend to reduce wages by shifting the notional supply curve to the right (assuming that the latter is positively sloped), but it would also tend to raise wages to the extent that it increases domestic demand and hence the effective demand for labour.

(3) Equation (15) for the domestic approach is a long-run tradeoff schedule; in the short run the behaviour of wage rates depends also on the expected rate of change of domestic prices. What is the role of expected home-goods prices in the international approach? Labour supply was assumed fixed in the derivation of (38) to simplify the exposition of the previous section, but a more general treatment would allow the supply of labour to depend on the real expected wage. To the extent that expectations adapt slowly to actual events, the inclusion of expected home-goods inflation in (38) would slow down the adjustment of the economy to a devaluation or other external shock and would prolong any period of excess labour demand or supply. Nevertheless, condition (37) is still relevant to determine whether the nominal wage initially rises or falls in the wake of a higher traded-goods price.

(4) Both approaches share the common assumption that the wage equation is the main instrument determining the economy's adjustment to a disequilibrium, and that the price equation is a mere appendage primarily driven by changes in the wage rate. The statement of the mark-up hypothesis in (9) above allows the size of the commodity market disequilibrium to affect the price *level* (not its rate of change), and the international theory could be amended to allow a similar term. While the mark-up hypothesis is clearly unrealistic for many primary products, e.g. wheat and copper, the prices of which are sufficiently flexible to clear markets almost continuously, there is nevertheless a limit to the price flexibility of products with a major input of purchased labour and materials. For a given level of wage rates and materials prices a firm can reduce its price only in so far as it is able to sustain losses. There is no similar limit on the ability of labour, a primary input, to sustain a decline in the real wage. This distinction is the basis of the asymmetry in the development of both (15) and (38), in which prices set by a mark-up hypothesis and wages are allowed to adjust to eliminate the labour-market disequilibrium.

POLICY IMPLICATIONS OF THE DISEQUILIBRIUM INTERNATIONAL APPROACH

In the pure monetary theory of the balance of payments, a nation running a balance of payments deficit under fixed exchange rates has only itself to blame. Since output, prices and interest rates are exogenous, the growth in the demand for money is given, and extra reserves can be attracted simply by reducing the creation of domestic credit below the increase in the demand for money (see (18) above). There is no danger that restrictive domestic credit policy can cause unemployment because, first, the free flow of world capital prevents the domestic central bank from affecting its own nominal money supply, since one dollar of reserves flows in to replace each dollar by which the supply of domestic credit is reduced. Second, even if the supply of money can be affected, its reduction causes a temporary reduction in the home-goods price level and in the wage rate, as described by the flexible price story of Figure 1 above. Resources flow into the traded goods sector and a trade surplus attracts more reserves until the money supply and price level return to their original situation. In contrast our disequilibrium analysis illustrates another possibility, that a reduction in the real money supply can cause involuntary unemployment. Thus unemployment in the two-sector international model cannot occur unless the domestic authorities can control the money supply without a complete dollar-for-dollar offset of reserve flows for changes in domestic credit creation.

Empirical evidence in favour of the zero-unemployment version would demonstrate that a restrictive domestic credit policy automatically generates offsetting reserve flows, in which case the possibility of unemployment is irrelevant, since an excess demand for money never occurs. In one empirical test Zecher (1976) estimated (18) above and found that d and s were negatively correlated in Australia. But since this amounts to fitting a rearranged money demand function, it demonstrates nothing more than the long-accepted fact that the money demand function is stable. Other evidence provides examples in which capital flows only partially offset domestic actions. Brunner (1974) presents evidence that between the second quarter of 1964 and the fourth quarter of 1966 only half of the net reduction in the 'domestic source component' of the German monetary base was offset by a change in the 'international source component' of the base. Similarly, Argy and Kouri (1974) find that 'capital flows have partly offset the effects of monetary policy on the monetary base'. Argy and Hodjera (1972) provide evidence that interest rates, while highly correlated across countries, have nevertheless diverged in several cyclical episodes. One of the most careful studies, that of Kouri and Porter (1974), concludes that 'our results indicate that while monetary policy has a strong effect on the capital account in all the four countries there is still some room for independent monetary policy, if only in the short run, if the Central Bank is willing to tolerate the large reserve movements which that policy entails'.

Since most medium-sized countries can exert at least partial control over their money supplies, the disequilibrium approach predicts that the consequence of restrictive credit creation policy would not be an effortless cure for balance of payments deficits, but may involve a temporary recession with involuntary unemployment. Similarly, unemployment may occur in the wake of an exogenous change in the traded-goods price level, or of a devaluation or revaluation, with the direction of the effect depending on the elasticities of substitution between labour and capital, on the one hand, and between traded and non-traded goods, on the other hand.

Whether or not a single nation can control its own money supply and create a domestic recession, it cannot be disputed that simultaneous monetary restriction by the major industrial nations of the world can create a world recession. The partial derivative of the world money supply to the rate of domestic credit expansion is a nation's share of total world money times the share of domestic credit in the domestic money supply (see Johnson, 1972). If a number of important nations simultaneously decelerate the growth of domestic credit, the size of the former fraction will be substantial enough to cause a marked slowdown in the growth rate of the world money supply. The domestic Phillips curve approach then comes into its own, since the world is a closed economy. Unless the adjustment of expectations is instantaneous, a worldwide monetary deceleration reduces output growth in the short run, violating the basic assumption in the flexible-price international monetary approach that output is fixed.

The rapid conversion of many international economists to the flexible-price monetary theory of the balance of payments, as popularised by Johnson (1972), suggests how much easier it is to publicise and 'sell' simple ideas than more complex notions. It has become common, for example, to chide the British in retrospect for their repeated balance of payments crises under the fixed-rate regime, since the Johnson version of the monetary theory suggests that all their problems would have been cured by the simple expedient of a restrictive domestic credit policy. But there are two awkward flaws in this prescription: (1) credit contraction in a nation the size of Britain is not completely offset by reserve inflows, and (2) a lower supply of money may lead to involuntary unemployment which may be short-lived or of indefinite duration, depending on the size of the monetary shock and the parameters of the wage-adjustment mechanism. Politicians who object to the tight money remedy cannot be waved aside by platoons of international monetary theorists carrying banners labelled 'flexible prices' and 'perfect capital mobility', but rather the theorists should be locked up in their ivory towers to reconsider the relevance of their prescriptions for a world in which capital is less than perfectly mobile and home-goods prices are less than perfectly flexible.

NOTES

1. Every national model in the LINK project contains one or more wage equations with independent variables including the unemployment rate or some other proxy for excess labour demand, as summarised by Ball (1973). Empirical work in the UK is dominated by the Phillips curve approach with only passing reference to the influence of external inflation, as in most of the papers in the Johnson – Nobay conference volume (1971).

2. Other empirical work for the US by DeMenil – Enzler, Andersen – Carlson, and others is contained in Eckstein (1972). Other closely related empirical papers are those by Eckstein – Brinner (1972) and Perry (1970), the conclusions of which are compared to mine in detailed sensitivity tests in my (1972).

3. The income tax, any payroll taxes paid by firms, and taxes on capital are ignored here to simplify the notation but should be taken into account in empirical work.

4. The original equation appears in my (1971, table 1, equation (11)). It was re-estimated, subjected to sensitivity tests, and compared with alternatives proposed by other authors in my (1972, tables 1–3). In the estimated equation expected price changes are estimated by a distributed lag on past actual price changes, using weights estimated alternatively in nominal interest rate equations and in the wage equation itself; several different unemployment variables are used as a proxy for excess labour demand; and separate coefficients are estimated for changes in the 'employee tax rate' (personal income tax and employees' social security contributions) and the 'employer tax rate' (employers' social security contributions). Lipsey (1960) first suggested this method for the derivation of a relationship between the nominal wage and excess labour demand; Hines (Johnson and Nobay, 1971) and others generalised Lipsey's formulation to take account of changes in the expected rate of inflation; and Parkin, Sumner and Ward (1976) produced an explicit derivation of an equation very similar to mine by adding tax rates and the distinction between producer and consumer prices to the simpler Lipsey – Hines formulation. The Parkin – Sumner – Ward paper and other papers by Parkin and associates also contain successful empirical tests of the equation for the United Kingdom.

5. The idea of wage insurance as a justification for rigid wage was independently suggested in the context of a single-sector closed economy by three papers written simultaneously (Azariardis, 1975; Baily, 1974; Donald F. Gordon, 1975).

6. The assumption that businessmen practice mark-up or 'full cost' pricing is supported by numerous empirical studies. The following are representative conclusions: 'It is impossible not to be struck by the devastating completeness of entrepreneurs' uncertainty about matters usually assumed to be known in the textbooks. In this fog of uncertainty the full cost principle may provide a guiding beacon – indeed it often does so' (Harrod, 1939, pp. 5–6). 'We concluded that the twelve firms studied did normally fix the price of their products with the guidance of the full cost principle' (Cook *et al.*, 1956, p. 142). 'There can be no doubt that it is an almost universal custom to use as a basis for price fixing a figure . . . which would be described by an economist as a long-period average cost' (Pearce, 1956, p. 114).

7. The exact definition of P_k depends on the details of the tax system, and takes account of the effect of investment allowances and tax credits, and of the value of depreciation deductions. See Hall and Jorgenson (1967).

8. See my (1971, p. 129).

9. For notational convenience $\varepsilon = 1/(\alpha + \beta)$, and a is the share of domestic prices in the consumer price index: $p_c = ap_h + (1-a)p_f$.

10. For an exact statement of the ambiguity for the case of an income tax in a simple comparative static model, see Blinder (1973).

11. Sterilisation by the sale of the central bank's domestic assets ends when the assets run out; by an increase in reserve requirements ends when reserve requirements reach 100 per cent; and by a reduction in bank borrowing ends when borrowing reaches zero.

12. In my long-run simulations (1971, p. 413), the estimated coefficient on standard unit labour cost (0.964) is raised to 1.0 to maintain a constant distribution of income between labour and capital.

13. This argument is stated more formally in my (1972).

14. A symbol is saved by the assumption that commercial bank reserve requirements are fixed at 100 per cent.

15. Dornbusch (1975) has more recently explored a model in which the terms of trade can vary.

16. Barro and Grossman (1975) explore in detail such a model for a one-sector closed economy.

17. In deriving (40) the expression was simplified by the assumptions that (1) $\lambda_X = 1$; (2) the production function is Cobb–Douglas, which implies $\pi = (\alpha - 1)/\alpha$; and (3) that $M^*/X_h = k/a$, an identity when the change occurs from an initial situation where $P_h = P_f = 1.0$.

18. The path AEC assumes that in (32) the positive effect of the p_f and Z terms dominates any negative effect of the x_h term in the case of a decline in real output.

REFERENCES

Argy, Victor, and Hodjera, Zoran, 'Financial Integration and Interest Rate Linkages', *International Monetary Fund Staff Papers*, vol. 20 (1972) pp. 1–77.

— and Kouri, Pentti J. K., 'Sterilisation Policies and the Volatility in International Reserves', in R. Z. Aliber (ed.) *National Monetary Policies and the International Financial System* (Chicago: University of Chicago Press, 1974) pp. 209–30.

Azariadis, Costas, 'Implicit Contracts and Underemployment Equilibria', *Journal of Political Economy*, vol. 83 (Dec 1975) pp. 1183–1202.

Baily, Martin N., 'Wages and Employment Under Uncertain Demand', *Review of Economic Studies*, vol. 41 (Jan 1974) pp. 37–50.

Ball, R. J., 'The Economic Models of Project LINK', in R. J. Ball (ed.) *The International Linkage of National Economic Models* (Amsterdam: North-Holland, 1973) pp. 65–108.

— 'Inflation and the London Business School Model', in Johnson and Nobay (1971) pp. 43–51.

Barro, Robert J., and Grossman, Herschel, *Money, Employment, and Inflation* (Cambridge: Cambridge University Press, 1976).

Blinder, Alan, 'Can Income Tax Increases Be Inflationary?' *National Tax Journal*, vol. 26 (June 1973) pp. 295–301.

Brunner, Karl, 'Monetary Management, Domestic Inflation, and Imported Inflation', in R. Z. Aliber (ed.) op. cit., pp. 179–208.

Cook, A. C., Dufty, N. F., and Jones, E. H., 'Full Cost Pricing in the Multiproduct Firm', *Economic Record*, vol. 32 (May 1956) pp. 142–7.

Dornbusch, Rudiger, 'Devaluation, Money, and Non-traded Goods', *American Economic Review*, vol. 63 (Dec 1973) pp. 871–80.

— 'Real and Monetary Aspects of the Effects of Exchange Rate Changes', in R. Z. Aliber (ed.) op. cit., pp. 64–81.

— 'Exchange Rates and Fiscal Policy in a Popular Model of International Trade', *American Economic Review*, vol. 65 (1975).

Eckstein, Otto, *The Econometrics of Price Determination Conference* (Washington: Federal Reserve Board, 1972).

— and Brinner, Roger, *The Inflation Process in the United States*. A Study Prepared for the Use of the Joint Economic Committee, 92 Congress, 2 session, 1972.

Friedman, Milton, 'The Role of Monetary Policy', *American Economic Review*, vol. 58 (Mar 1968) pp. 1–15.

Gordon, Donald F., 'A Neo-Classical Theory of Keynesian Unemployment', in Karl Brunner and Alan Meltzer (eds) *The Phillips Curve and Public Policy* (Amsterdam: North-Holland, 1975)

Gordon, Robert J., 'Inflation in Recession and Recovery', *Brookings Papers on Economic Activity*, vol. 2 (1971, no. 1) pp. 105–66.

— 'Wage-Price Controls and the Shifting Phillips Curve', *Brookings Papers on Economic Activity*, vol. 3 (1972, no. 2) pp. 385–421.

— 'Can Econometric Policy Evaluations be Salvaged?', in Karl Brunner and Alan Meltzer (eds) *The Phillips Curve and Public Policy* (Amsterdam: North-Holland, 1976) pp. 47–61.

Hall, Robert E., and Jorgenson, Dale W., 'Tax Policy and Investment Behaviour', *American Economic Review*, vol. 57 (June 1967) pp. 391–414.

Harrod, R. F., 'Price and Cost in Entrepreneurs' Policy', *Oxford Economic Papers*, vol. 2 (May 1939) pp. 1–11.

Hines, A. G., 'The Determinants of the Rate of Change of Money Wage Rates and the Effectiveness of Incomes Policy', in Johnson and Nobay (1971) pp. 143–75.

Johnson, Harry G., 'The Monetary Approach to Balance-of-Payments Theory', *Further Essays in Monetary Economics* (London: Allen & Unwin, 1972) pp. 229–49.

— and Nobay, A. R. (eds) *The Current Inflation* (London: Macmillan, 1971).

Kouri, Pentti J. K., and Porter, Michael G., 'International Capital Flows and Portfolio Equilibrium', *Journal of Political Economy*, vol. 82 (May/June 1974) pp. 443–68.

Lipsey, R. G., 'The Relation Between Unemployment and the Rate of Change of Money Wage Rates in the United Kingdom, 1862–1957', *Economica*, n.s., vol. 27 (Feb 1960) pp. 1–31.

Parkin, M., Sumner, M., and Ward, R., 'The Effects of Excess Demand, Generalised Expecations, and Wage-Price Controls on Wage Inflation in the UK', in K. Brunner and A. Meltzer (eds) *The Economics of Price and Wage Controls* (Amsterdam: North-Holland, 1976) pp. 193–222.

Pearce, I. F., 'A Study in Price Policy', *Economica*, vol. 23 (May 1956) pp. 114–27.

Perry, George, 'Changing Labour Markets and Inflation', *Brookings Papers on Economic Activity*, vol. 1 (1970, no. 3) pp. 411–41.

Phelps, Edmund S., 'Phillips Curves, Expectations of Inflation, and Optimal Unemployment Over Time', *Economica*, n.s., vol. 34 (Aug 1967) pp. 254–81.

Salter, W. E. G., 'Internal and External Balance: The Role of Price and Expenditure Effects', *The Economic Record*, vol. 35 (Aug 1959) pp. 226–38.

Zecher, J. R., 'Australian Reserve Flow Experience: A Test of the Monetary Approach to the Balance of Payments', in J. Fienkel and H. G. Johnson (eds), *The Monetary Approach to the Balance of Payments* (London: Allen & Unwin, 1976) pp. 287–97.

Part III

THE EMPIRICAL SIDE OF MONETARY INTERDEPENDENCE

10 The Interdependence of Monetary, Debt and Fiscal Policies in an International Setting

John Helliwell and Robert McRae

There are a number of theoretical and empirical frameworks available for assessing the economic interdependence of nations. The theoretical models are noted for the variety of their assumptions and a corresponding dispersion of results. Most of the empirical frameworks are based entirely on international transmission through trade flows.[1] There have been studies of international capital movements, but usually not in a framework wherein the interaction of trade and capital flows can be assessed. To our knowledge, the linked RDX2 – MPS system is the only mechanism currently available for tracing international repercussions in the full context of trade, capital flows and migration.[2] The two component models, and the nature of their linkage, have been described elsewhere, and are summarised briefly in the Appendix (p. 167), so that it is only necessary to note here that the two models are reasonably comparable in terms of aggregation, and that both have well-developed financial sectors, and a variety of channels whereby the financial and real sectors influence one another.

One of the main advantages of a system with detailed and comprehensive links between economies is that it can be used to test whether there are important mechanisms suppressed in the simpler models more commonly employed. In the present paper, we study especially the linkages among monetary, debt and fiscal policies, and see what effects these interactions have domestically and abroad.

In the first section we provide, by way of background, a summary of earlier experiments with linked systems, and explain why we came to perform the particular experiments reported now.

In the second section we consider two different ways of accommodating monetary to fiscal policy. In both cases we assume that one country or the other undertakes a fiscal policy; in one case we hold nominal interest rates constant and in the other we hold constant the supply of money. By measuring how much the income, price and employment effects depend on the nature of the accommodating monetary policy, we get some idea how important it is to take monetary consequences into account when assessing the effects of fiscal policies. In the simulations reported in the second section we assume that the same type of monetary policy is applied in Canada as in the United States.

In the third section, by contrast, we see what would happen if the monetary strategy applied in Canada were the reverse of that applied in the United States. Then we assess these consequences for fiscal policies originating in each country, with either the money stock or the rate of interest held constant in the country initiating the policy. These experiments give some idea whether the type of monetary rule adopted by the passive country makes much difference to the size of the shock transmitted, and whether these results depend on which monetary strategy is used by the country initiating fiscal policy.

In Section 4 we turn to the often ignored issue of debt management, and ask whether the term structure of government interest-bearing debt issued to finance expenditure has a material impact on the domestic and international consequences of that expenditure. These experiments are conducted only for fiscal plus money and debt policies initiated in Canada, because only in RDX2 do the relative supplies of bonds and other assets materially affect the structure of interest rates and asset yields.

I   BACKGROUND

The first quantitative results for the linked RDX2 – MPS system were presented at Wingspread 1 in 1972 and have subsequently been published (Helliwell and Maxwell (1974*b*)). The main aim of the early experiments was to assess the operation of rigidly fixed, gliding peg, adjustable peg and flexible exchange rate systems. Two of these foreign exchange models were directly estimated from Canadian data: the flexible exchange system being estimated using data from the 1950s and since 1970, and a Bretton Woods pegged exchange rate system based on Canadian experience between 1962 and 1970. The results of these simulations exposed problems in the operation of a gliding peg system, and showed that exchange rate movements within the margins of the Bretton Woods system have been large enough to make that system materially different from a rigidly fixed exchange rate regime. The flexible exchange rate system differed in action less than sometimes thought from the pegged exchange rate, because of the short-term capital flows implied by the apparently substantial lags in clearing trade and long-term capital flows through the foreign exchange market. Stabilising exchange rate expectations and institutional factors combine to allow private short-term capital flows to play an exchange rate smoothing role under flexible and pegged exchange rates alike, reducing the relative importance of official foreign exchange support as a determinant of short-term movements in the foreign exchange rate.

The experiments reported in 1972 were based on the transmission of monetary policies originating in one country or the other. There was a problem posed by the fact that monetary policies were modelled somewhat differently in RDX2 and MPS. Subsequent experiments using bond-financed fiscal policies to test alternative exchange rate systems broadly supported the earlier results. In both of these early studies, however, there was some uncertainty about our understanding of the dynamics of both models. And we were also anxious to improve the comparability of the two models, to understand better how each model worked on its own, and to disentangle the various components of the linkage process. Furthermore, we wished to establish better comparability of monetary policies in the models.

The next stage in our experiments involved assessing the separate importance of trade flows, long-term capital flows, short-term capital flows, and migration flows as channels through which policy shocks originating in Canada or the United States are transmitted to the other economy and subsequently reflected back. Most empirical models of linkage are based entirely on trade flows, and most theoretical models concentrate entirely on trade and long-term capital flows. The striking feature of our results disentangling the quadruple linkage was the very large effect that migration flows and short-term capital flows have on the size and timing of the transmission of economic policies from one country to the other. We also discovered in the course of these experiments that the nature of the monetary assumption radically affects the consequences of fiscal policy in both the originating and passively recipient countries.

In the first version of Helliwell (1974), the fiscal policy in MPS was accompanied by a rigidly fixed money supply (M1) while the fiscal policy in RDX2 was accompanied by a money supply rule that came close to achieving the same result. The RDX2 rule involved successive revisions to interest rates in order to approach a money growth target, without forcing money growth to be always on target. Although this rule is more applicable in practice, it turns out that relatively small differences in money supply have rather marked effects on the impact of fiscal policy at home and abroad. We were impressed enough by these differences to make them the main focus of the present paper. Perhaps others have been as prone as we had been to make fairly casual assumptions about the nature of accommodating monetary policies, and to consider fiscal and monetary policies in rather separate terms. So much for background. We proceed now to present the results, starting first with our assessment of how much money matters.

II   HOW MUCH DOES MONEY MATTER?

Putting the matter in its simplest terms, how steep is the *LM* curve? Does the answer depend on how long the policies have been in operation? Does the change in the nature of an accommodating monetary policy have different effects at home and abroad?

The experiments used are reported in Tables 1–A and 1–B (pp. 174, 175); in Table 1–A we report the results of a reduction of US Federal Government expenditure, 1963 to 1970, where the sustained cut is equal to 1 per cent of 1963 US GNE. For all of the simulations reported in this paper, the two models are linked by a flexible exchange rate system based on parameters estimated using Canadian data from the 1950s and since 1970. The US fiscal policy has effects both at home and abroad. The left-hand side of Table 1–A shows the effects in the United States and the right-hand side shows the effects in Canada. On either side of the table there are two columns. The left-hand column, entitled 'Fixed M1' shows the effects when the accommodating monetary policy in both countries is assumed to be a supply of money (currency plus demand deposits) equal to that in the control solution of the linked models. In the right-hand column in each side of the table we show the results of a simulation in which the nominal interest rate is set equal to control values in both countries. The details of the assumed policies, and the definitions of the main variables reported in Tables 1–A and 1–B are described in the second section of the Appendix (p. 170).

If we wish to interpret the results in the context of a simple *IS–LM* diagram, the 'Fixed M1' results show the decreases in real income and nominal interest rates that accompany the intersection of the shifted *IS* and the pre-existing *LM* curve. In the 'Fixed R' case, we are shifting the *IS* curve with a horizontal *LM* curve. Ignoring the dynamics of the system, if we were to find real multipliers twice as large with a pegged interest rate as with a fixed money supply, we could conclude that the *LM* and *IS* curves had about the same steepness in the relevant region. And that is about as far as we can carry the analogy with the *LM – IS* analysis as that framework ignores the distinctions between nominal and real interest rates, suppresses the dynamics of portfolio adjustment, savings and growth, and bypasses the important disequilibrium dynamics of investment, employment, trade and capital flows.

Although the flow dynamics of the quarterly models are rather suppressed by our decision to report only average values for the second, fourth, sixth and eighth years of the simulation, even the figures reported indicate rather complex dynamic patterns which differ materially according to the nature of the monetary policy used. Looking first at Table 1–A, we see that the multiplier values in the second year are not sharply different with fixed money supply and fixed treasury bill rates but quickly differ thereafter as the monetary ease causes the real multipliers to peak sooner and to turn around more dramatically. The difference in the induced price effects is rather smaller while the induced effects on the US trade balance are generally about two-thirds as large with a fixed money supply as with a fixed interest rate.

The peak effects of US fiscal policy on US real business output (-4.4 per cent) are in the seventh year of the simulation with pegged nominal interest rates, while the response in the fixed M1 simulation follows a faster cyclical pattern with a smaller amplitude, reaching peaks of about -2.1 per cent in the second and sixth years, and turning positive part way through the eighth year. The effects on the unemployment rate follow the same pattern. Turning to prices and nominal GNE there is once again a marked difference between the two monetary regimes, a difference that becomes larger as the simulations proceed. In the fourth year, the expected US rate of inflation (PDOT in MPS) is reduced by 0.78 per cent with fixed R and by 0.63 per cent with fixed M1. After eight years, PDOT is down by 1.71 per cent with a fixed R and by 0.94 per cent with fixed M1. With fixed interest rates, nominal aggregate income is 1.95 per cent below control in the eighth year, compared to 4.7 per cent with a fixed M1. More than half of this gap represents real output rather than price level differences.

The effects on the US balance of trade are very marked in both simulations, and reflect a mixture of price and activity effects. Real exports are up, in the eighth year of the fixed interest rates simulation, by about 900 million 1958 $US per year, 700 million going to countries other than Canada. These changes are almost entirely due to the decline in US prices, offset to some extent by the induced declines in Canadian prices and capacity utilisation. In the eighth year of the simulation with fixed M1, US real exports are once again higher by 900 million 1958 $US, but this time 400 million of the increase is to Canada. Exports to third countries are up less because US prices have fallen less, while exports to Canada are higher because the Canadian economy is more buoyant than in the fixed interest rate simulation. The greater buoyancy of the Canadian economy in the fixed M1 case is partly due to the smaller real US multipliers in that case, and partly to the fact that the fixed M1 policy in Canada provides greater insulation for a given export shock. These factors must remain entangled until the Table 1–A results are used in the next section to separate the effects of shock size from those of monetary policy response.

In the various demand-determined theoretical models of internal and external balance, it is a matter of uncertainty whether a country that cuts government expenditure but leaves money supply unchanged will incur an appreciation or depreciation of its currency (gain or lose reserves under fixed exchange rates) as a consequence. With sufficiently interest responsive capital flows, the cut in government spending with fixed M1 could lead to a depreciation of the domestic currency. With domestic prices free to move downward to restore balance between aggregate supply and demand, depreciation would not take place without a greater degree of capital mobility. Full results for the United States are not available from our linked system, for MPS does not yet contain equations for capital flows between the United States and countries other than Canada. However, to the extent that the bilateral linkages with Canada are symptomatic of the links between the United States and the rest of the world, we can make use of the Table 1–A results for the movements of PFX, the price of US dollars in terms of Canadian dollars. Throughout the simulation of US government expenditure cut with fixed M1, we see that the value of the US dollar is lower, while it is higher in the case where both countries peg their nominal interest rate. Thus the US represents a case of sufficient capital mobility, at least in its bilateral links with Canada, that fiscal cuts with unchanged money supply lead to depreciation of the US dollar. By the end of eight years, the price of the US dollar in terms of Canadian dollars has depreciated by 1.9 per cent in the fixed M1 case compared to an appreciation of 1.1 per cent in the fixed R case. This 3 per cent difference in exchange rates between the two cases is greater than a 2 per cent difference in aggregate prices under the two monetary rules, but rather closer to the difference in the prices of tradeable goods.

The results in Table 1–B show the effects of a cut in Canadian government expenditure, once again assuming that both countries adopt the same monetary policy, which is either to fix the money supply (as shown in the left-hand column of each pair) or the nominal interest rate. The results indicate that money matters even more in RDX2 than in MPS, in the sense that the real GNE multipliers in the first six years of the simulation are almost three times larger with a fixed R than with a fixed M1. For MPS this ratio is more cyclical than for RDX2, but averages about 2.0 over the first six years of the simulation. With no monetary contraction, the value of the real multiplier in RDX2 reaches a peak in the second year and never exceeds 1.0. In the fixed R simulation, the peak multiplier (2.7) is reached in the fourth year. By the end of the eight years, both multipliers are below 1.0, and the money supply in the fixed rate case has returned to its control solution value. One interesting difference between the results in Tables 1–A and 1–B is that non-monetary forces come more into play in eventually limiting the multiplier process in the RDX2 fixed R simulation so that the final extent of monetary contraction is much less than in the MPS fixed R simulations. As always, it is difficult to know whether to attribute this contrast to characteristics of models or to characteristics of economies. In part it may be due to the greater use of explicit endogenous aggregate supply measures in RDX2, so that demand for investment recovers when the capital stock drops sufficiently. The main capacity measure in MPS (XBC) is a very slowly moving distributed lag function of business output. Thus under the fiscal cut, potential output in RDX2 (UGPPD), which drops because of reduced investment, reduced labour force participation, and reduced immigration, moves as much as 3 per cent below the control solution in the fifth year, and has fallen below aggregate demand (UGPPA) by that time. By contrast, in the simulation of US fiscal cut with fixed R, XBC is only 1 per cent below control in the fifth year, and never falls as far as XB during the eight years.

Consistent with the greater degree of endogenous supply response in RDX2, the Canadian fiscal cut has greater employment effects in Canada than has the corresponding cut in the US, under either type of monetary policy; but these effects are reversed sooner as migration alters and reduces the Canadian population. At the same time similar adjustments are taking place in the other elements of aggregate supply. This reversal of employment effects is sharper in the case of pegged interest rates because the initial effects are larger. It appears to be a general feature of the RDX2 domestic results of alternative monetary rules that pegging interest rates produces a larger but more sharply reversed set of consequences to fiscal shock.

The international effects are consistent with this pattern, so that the effects of Canadian policy on the US are larger and more cyclical if both countries peg interest rates than if both countries peg the money supply. This can be seen from the movement in the bilateral balance of trade in Table 1–B.

Canada appears to be like the United States with respect to the exchange rate consequences of a fiscal cut with unchanged money supply, at least for the first six or so years of the simulation. By the end of the simulation experiments reported in Table 1–B, the exchange rates based on the two monetary rules differ less from one another than in the case of US fiscal policy results reported in Table 1–A. This is consistent with the price level differences reported earlier.

The overall conclusion from Tables 1–A and 1–B must be that the nature of the monetary concomitants of fiscal policy dramatically affects both the size and timing of the domestic and international effects of policy changes initiated in either country. This is so even though fiscal policy without monetary expansion has substantial real and price level effects spanning several years.

III INTERDEPENDENCE OF NATIONAL MONETARY STRATEGIES

In this section we consider the effects of differing rather than parallel monetary strategies being used in Canada and the United States. Table 2–A (p. 176) shows the effects of the US fiscal policy. In the case where the United States adopts a fixed M1 policy, Canada pegs the short-term interest rate, and vice versa. Table 2–A in conjunction with Table 1–A allows us to see the effect that the Canadian monetary strategy has on both the US and the Canadian effects of US fiscal policies. Tables 2–B and 1–B allow the same sort of analysis for the effects of a fiscal policy originating in Canada.

First comparing Tables 1–A and 2–A, we can note the following results.

(1) The US effects of US fiscal policy are unaltered by the nature of the Canadian monetary response, reflecting the relative unimportance of the trade sector in the United States and the high proportion of US trade carried on with countries other than Canada.

(2) Canadian real income, employment and prices are more insulated from the effects of US fiscal policies if Canada keeps a fixed money supply. This is true whether the United States keeps a fixed money supply or a fixed nominal interest rate. The basic reason for this is that Canadian multipliers are smaller when Canada uses a money supply rule.

(3) The bilateral exchange rate effects of US fiscal policy are larger if Canada follows a monetary policy opposite to that used by the United States. This is true whichever monetary strategy is used by the United States.

Turning to a comparison of Tables 1–B and 2–B, showing the effects of a Canadian fiscal policy, we find the following results.

(1) The Canadian real income and employment effects of Canadian fiscal policy are smaller for the first four years and thereafter larger if the United States keeps a constant money supply rather than a constant interest rate. This result follows whether Canada fixes M1 or R.

(2) US real income, employment, and prices are more insulated from the effects of Canadian fiscal policies if the United States keeps a fixed money supply.

(3) The exchange rate effects of Canadian fiscal policy are generally larger if the United States follows a monetary strategy opposite to that used by Canada.

Putting the results from Tables 2–A, 2–B, 1–A and 1–B together, the conclusions of general applicability appear to be:

(1) A money supply rule provides better insulation from foreign shocks than does the pegging of nominal interest rates, even if the shock originates in a country with pegged nominal interest rates.

(2) The use of parallel monetary strategies in both countries reduces the exchange rate impacts of foreign fiscal policies.

If the monetary authorities focus on the exchange rate, or the level of reserves, as their primary target, they will tend to keep their interest rates in line with those in other countries. However one of the consequences of such a policy is that the real domestic economy will be more strongly affected by economic shocks originating abroad. Although such a conclusion can be reached from a variety of simplified theoretical models, our simulations indicate that it appears also to be applicable to Canada and the United States as modelled in RDX2 and MPS.

IV   HOW MUCH DOES DEBT MANAGEMENT MATTER?

The macroeconomic theory of portfolio balance, owing much of its development to Tobin (e.g. Tobin (1969)), makes considerable use of the fact that real and financial assets, and different types and maturities of financial assets, are not perfect substitutes for one another. Diversification and other considerations combine to produce desired portfolio proportions of assets and liabilities consistent with total wealth and each set of expectations about asset yields and income. In such a model, asset yields are determined endogenously and are influenced in an essential way by the relative supplies of the various asset stocks. It is therefore somewhat surprising that empirical macroeconomic models usually provide little or no role for asset supplies. Even in MPS, which possesses the most ambitious financial structure of all existing econometric models of the United States, relative supplies of financial assets play no direct role in determining the long rate of interest and the capitalisation rate for expected dividend streams, the two key rates linking the financial and real sectors of the model.

Given the structure of MPS, there is no way of testing the propositions of Tobin (1963) and others about the effect of debt management on the yield curve and hence on the pattern of investment, savings and international capital flows.

The structure of RDX2 is somewhat better suited for the analysis of debt management, as there are three main endogenous mechanisms by which changes in the size of the government debt influence the economy.

(1) The relative sizes of government debt and business capital stock, as measured by the earnings streams to which each gives rise, is an important determinant of the relation between a long-term government bond rate and the supply price of capital to business. An increase in the size of the government's interest-bearing debt relative to the size of the business capital stock increases long rates of interest relative to the supply price of capital.

(2) The amount of long-term government debt outstanding, relative to the total resident-held portfolio of liquid assets, affects the long-term interest rate (RL) relative to the expected value of future short rates. Our efforts to estimate such an effect in the first version of RDX2 were not successful, but subsequent research by L. Christofides (1973) convinced us that the influence of the term structure of the debt was there to be found, and was too important to be ignored. Our present equation is not fully satisfactory and work is under way to improve it so as to better

extend, with Christofides, his study of the 1958 Conversion Loan, a massive but not widely studied extension of the average term of the Federal Government debt. In the present RDX2 equation for RL an increase of 500 million dollars in the size of non-bank holdings of federal debt with a maturity over ten years, given the total supply of liquid assets, leads to an increase of approximately 5 basis points (0.05 per cent) in 1963 and about half as much in 1970 given the doubling of the relevant nominal asset supplies over that period. This effect, while statistically very significant, is somewhat smaller than Christofides's estimate (1973, ch. 3) that the Conversion Loan of 1958 increased the long rate in Canada by more than 50 basis points, from an increase of about 3 billion or more in private holdings of debt in the longest-term category.

(3) Finally any change in long-term interest rates leads to capital gains or losses on the outstanding debt, which in RDX2 is broken down into four maturity classes each of which has a valuation ratio suitably derived from the relevant interest rates and terms to maturity. These market valuation ratios serve to define the market value of federal debt which in turn enters into the definition of permanent non-wage disposable income used in explaining consumption. However, our efforts to find a direct role for capital gains and losses in the consumption equations have so far been unsuccessful.

Debt management narrowly defined includes alterations of the term and nature of the government's interest-bearing debt; thus only the second and third of the channels listed above are brought into play during a debt management operation, except to the extent that the debt management changes the required total of interest payments.

The simulations in Table 3 differ from those in Table 1–B in their assumptions about the maturity distribution of the net debt change implied by alterations in government expenditure, taxes and money supply. In the version of RDX 2 used for Tables 1 and 2, treasury bills are the residual asset in the government balance sheet; for the purposes of Table 3, we use treasury bills as a source of interim finance for the current quarter, and then translate the entire shock-control change in government current cash requirements into a change in the amount outstanding of the government's longest-term debt category. We continue to treat the amount of Canada Savings Bonds outstanding as demand determined from the private sector's liquid asset portfolio allocation model in sector 15. This demand is conditional upon the exogenous interest rate on Canada Savings Bonds. In keeping with our plans to make the C.S.B. rate an endogenous policy variable, we assume for the Table 3 (p. 178) simulations that any increase or decrease in private demand for Canada Savings Bonds is offset by a change in the stock of treasury bills outstanding.

By the end of the eight-year simulation with fixed short-term interest rates, the long-term rate RL is about 13 basis points below control, consistent with the reduction of almost 3 billion dollars in the stock of the longest-term category of federal debt. This is a fairly extreme change in the term structure of the debt, by most standards, as it is larger than the 1970 publicly held stock of federal direct debt in that maturity class. In relation to the size of the relevant portfolios, however, it is less than half as large as the Conversion Loan of 1958. Nevertheless, the effects of the debt management on the domestic economy, and on the main international trade and capital flows, are not very large in the simulated circumstances, where the term structure of the debt changes slowly over the years, cumulating to large amounts only towards the end of the eight-year simulation. The general direction of the differences are clear, for the reduction of federal long debt reduces interest rates and the supply price of capital below what they would have been with treasury bill financing. These reductions are not nearly as great as those caused by changing from a fixed money supply rule to a fixed interest rate. They are also much smaller than the effects of the 1958 Conversion Loan, which altered RL at the outset by amounts sufficiently large to lead to substantial macroeconomic repercussions.

Our tentative conclusion in this section is that the debt management aspects of a fiscal policy are apparently not crucial to the size and timing of the domestic and foreign effects of a monetary and fiscal policy package.

V   CONCLUSION

The simulations reported in Tables 1, 2 and 3 represent only a first step in the analysis of the international interdependence of economic policy choices. We have progressed from assessing the domestic and international effects of one country's policies to a consideration of the influences that the policy strategy of the second country have on the dynamic pattern of outcomes for both countries. As suggested by the work of Hamada (1974) and others, the next logical step might be to assess more complicated policy responses for the passive country, leading to a chain of explicit policy choices by both countries. Some progress in this direction is undoubtedly worth while, but eventual limits will be set by the complexity of the process and by the resulting difficulty of disentangling model structure from particular steps in the assumed pattern of interdependent policy choices. It is important to first understand more fully the main empirical characteristics of the linked economies. The present paper is offered as a gesture in that direction.

APPENDIX

This appendix has two sections. In the first, we describe the versions of RDX2 and MPS used in our simulations, and indicate the changes that have been made to the most recently published versions. In the second section, we describe the mechanics of the linkage simulations, including the methods that we have used to implement policies, and the definitions of the variables reported in the tables.

1   RDX2 AND MPS

The model is basically that described in Helliwell *et al.*, (1971), as revised and estimated to 4Q70 and presented in Helliwell and Maxwell (1974*a*). The main change we have made for our linked simulations is to build in a new equation for Canadian exports to the United States, excluding motor vehicles and energy products. Energy exports to the United States increased rapidly after 1970, and we wish to be able to simulate easily within the linked system the consequences of alternative policies relating to energy trade between the two countries. By treating energy exports as a separate exogenous series, we are able to facilitate these simulations and to obtain a more satisfactory equation for the main southbound flow of goods, including data to 4Q72. The price elasticity of the new equation is -1.09 with respect to a 16-quarter moving average of the ratio of the Canadian export price to the Canadian dollar equivalent of the price of US non-farm business product. Interestingly enough, this same long lag on relative prices also worked best in explaining exports of goods from the United States to countries other than Canada.

We are using version 'S' of the MPS model, with a mimeographed equation list dated January 1973. The equation for the dividend/price ratio dates from mid-1973. Our earlier experiments used a version for which the equation list was dated January 1971. There is no published version of the current model, but Albert Ando (1975) has recently written a useful paper on the theoretical structure of the model, and Ando and Modigliani (1974, 1975) have recently published an extended paper on the financial structure of the model, and have a book in progress. The MPS model has four equations for imports, split between goods and services and between Canada and other countries. For our current simulations, the model was run either with M1$ exogenous and the residuals added back to the RTB equation, or with the treasury bill rate itself as the exogenous policy variable, as described later in this appendix. Structural alterations made especially for our simulations include:

(1) The equations for imports from Canada are replaced by the RDX2 equations for the same flows, with an exogenous series used to adjust for data discrepancies.

(2) All US exports of goods and services are now endogenous to the linked system. The constant-dollar total of Canadian imports from the United States, as determined from the nine RDX2 equations for these items, is adjusted by fixed proportionate seasonal adjustment factors and divided by 258.05 to convert the flow into US exports to Canada, measured as a quarterly flow at annual rates. This series is subtracted from EEX, the series for total US exports, to obtain X23, a new series for exports to countries other than Canada. This series is explained by a log-

linear equation showing an elasticity with respects to total world imports (excluding North America) of 0.77, and a price elasticity of − 0.90 with respect to a 16-quarter moving average of PEEX/PWXG. This lag length gave better fit and higher price elasticity than did longer or shorter lags, whether based on moving averages or Almon variables. The dock strike variable JDOCK also contributes significantly to the equation, which has an RB2 of 0.969 in its log form.

(3) The MPS export price index is made endogenous by an estimated equation that explains PEEX in terms of the main US price PXBNF and the UN index for the price of world exports of goods. That index (PWXG in RDX2) is defined in terms of US dollars, so that no exchange rates are used in the equation for PEEX. The MPS export price index is not used in explaining trade flows to Canada, because RDX2 makes use of more disaggregated import prices, but is needed in the equation for US exports to the rest of the world, and to obtain an appropriate distinction between changes in the value and volume of trade in the US national income and expenditure accounts.

(4) The MPS import price is left exogenous for imports from countries other than Canada. To deflate imports from Canada for national accounts purposes, PEIM is replaced by EPEIM*PXNMV12/PFX, where EPEIM is a new exogenous series defined so as to make the substitution exact in terms of historical data.

(5) The 90-day London Eurodollar rate (REUR in RDX2) is made endogenous for our linked simulations by means of an identity: REUR = 0.72*RTB2 + EREUR, where EREUR is a new exogenous series defined to make the equation fit exactly over the historical period. The coefficient on the US treasury bill rate is based on recent work by Herring and Marston. We selected a coefficient that excludes periods of extreme credit tightness in the United States and abstracts from the effects of US interest rates on European central bank discount rates.

We are in the course of further research intended to make the structure of MPS more compatible with that of RDX2, and to complete the linkage between MPS and the non-Canadian world. Some notable prospects for change include:

(1) The wage/price dynamics and theory differ too much between the models. The main MPS price equation is constrained to have an elasticity of 1.0 with respect to normal unit labour costs, while the wage rate has an elasticity much less than 1.0 with respect to consumer prices, even after all lags are worked out. In RDX2, by contrast, the long-term elasticity of the wage rate with respect to consumer prices is constrained to be 1.0, while the average elasticity of the aggregate output price with respect to normal unit labour costs is about equal to labour's share in value-added. John Lester has been experimenting with a number of alternatives for MPS that are more consistent with RDX2.

(2) Possible explanation of migration, or at least an attempt to

allocate some of Canadian migration to US sources or destinations.

(3) Modelling US capital flows, and integrating them with a more fully specified portfolio model of US wealth allocation among domestic and foreign assets.

(4) Development of measures of capacity output more closely relate to aggregate factor supplies. The present variable (XBC) is a weighted average of past levels of actual output.

(5) Perhaps an application of the RDX2 factor demand and dis-equilibrium adjustment framework to MPS.

2   MECHANICS OF LINKAGE AND POLICY SIMULATIONS

In each quarter, MPS is solved first; then subroutines are called to define the US variables used in RDX2 in terms of the solution values from MPS. RDX2 is then solved, and subroutines called to translate the RDX2 output to the form required for MPS. MPS is then solved again, and the process continues until the linked system converges. The procedure is repeated for each quarter.

Canadian monetary policy was modelled in the control solutions by replacing the estimated reaction function for RS by the following equation based on a target rate of growth for the sum of currency held by the non-bank public and demand deposits at the chartered banks.

$$RS = J1L(RS) - 0.001*(1.065*J4L(ANFCUR + DDB) - (0.963*Q1 + 1.048*Q2 + 1.009*Q3 + 1.046*Q4)*J1L(ANFCUR + DDB))$$

In the first version of Helliwell (1974), the above monetary policy rule was also used for the shock simulations, as a reasonably operational counterpart of the MPS monetary assumption that M1$ is held constant when fiscal policy is changed. In the final version of the paper, the Canadian money supply M1$C is forced to be identical in shock and control solutions. Although this type of accommodating monetary policy may be harder to put into practice, given the lags between monetary changes and the final adjustments to M1, it makes the RDX2 results more closely comparable to the MPS results.

The US fiscal shock was accomplished by subtracting 5.51 from the exogenous series for constant-dollar federal government expenditure.

The Canadian fiscal policy was modelled by subtracting 111.*J1L*PGCNWF from the equation for GCNWF. For both models, the changes had the effect of subtracting, on a continuing basis, a constant-dollar amount equal to 1 per cent of the country's 1963 constant-dollar GNE. The object of using a shock defined in constant dollars is to facilitate the calculation of real multiplier effects with unambiguous definitions.

MPS is solved with the treasury bill rate exogenous by recoding the demand for money equation with MD$ instead of RTB as the left-hand variable, renormalising three monetary identities, and solving for excess reserves (ZMS) as an endogenous variable.

Tables 1 to 3 show income and price figures in terms of percentage differences between shock and control. To compare the sizes of the effects in the two countries, it is necessary to know that the control solution value for 1963 GNE is 590 billion $US in MPS, 46.8 bill. $C in RDX2, while the 1963 value for the flexible exchange rate is 1.047 $C./$US.

The multipliers are calculated by dividing the shock-control results for real GNE (XOBE in MPS and UGNE = YGNE/PGNE in RDX2) by the size of the constant-dollar cut in government expenditure.

The variables reported in the Tables are as follows:

Real private business output is XB in MPS and UGPP in RDX2.

The price of GNE is PGNE in RDX2 and POBE in MPS.

Unemployment rate results are shown in simple shock minus control format based on ULU in MPS and RNU in RDX2.

The short-term interest rate reported is the treasury bill rate (RTB) in MPS and the 0–3 year rate (RS) in RDX2.

The US balance of trade (XBAL$2) is current dollar exports (PEEX*EEX) minus the sum of the current-dollar import series in MPS.

The bilateral balances are the RDX2 variables XBAL12 and UBAL12, the former a new identity defined for these simulations. XBAL12 is the bilateral balance of trade in goods and services, while UBAL12 is the basic bilateral balance of trade and long-term capital flows.

The Canadian real trade balance (XBAL) is X – M, reported in millions of 1961 dollars.

The exchange rate (PFX) is $C per $US, reported in percentage shock-control format.

NOTES

1. For example, the Project LINK system used to forecast developments in the world economy involves national econometric models of varying complexity linked by trade in goods and services (Johnson and Klein (1974), Hickman (1974), and chapter 13 of Ball (1973)). The models of Taplin (chapter 7 of Ball (1973)) and of Morishima and Murata (1972) also embody multilateral trade linkages, but short-circuit most of the economic structure in the component nations. There have also been models of smaller groups of nations linked by trade flows, as with the Common Market models by Barten and d'Alcantara (1973) and by Waelbroeck and Dramais (1974), and the linked simulation of Japanese and US models reported by Moriguchi and Tatemoto in chapter 11 of Ball (1973).

2. Many people have contributed to the project over several years. The main outline of the project, and of the nature of the linkages between the models, is reported in chapter 12 of Ball (1973). The Canada Council has provided substantial financial support for the work. We have benefited from extensive collaboration on a continuing basis with the Research Department of the Bank of Canada, and have enjoyed the co-operation of Albert Ando and his MPS group. J. L. Bolduc has been an important contributor to the simulations underlying this paper.

REFERENCES

Ando, A., 'Some Aspects of Stabilisation Policies, the Monetarist Controversy, and the MPS Model', *International Economic Review* (1975).

Ando, A., and F. Modigliani, 'Some Reflections on Describing Structure of Financial Models', in *The Brookings Model: Perspective and Recent Developments* (North-Holland, Amsterdam, 1974).

Ando, A., and F. Modigliani, 'The MPS Econometric Model: Its Theoretical Foundation and Empirical Findings' (1975).

Barten, A. P., and G. d'Alcantara, 'The Linkage of Models of the EEC Countries', mimeo (1973).(C.O.R.E., Louvain.)

Ball, R. (ed.) *InternationalLinkage of National Economic Models* (North-Holland, Amsterdam, 1973).

Christofides, L. N., 'The Canadian Conversion Loan of 1958: A Study of Debt Management', Ph.D. dissertation, University of British Columbia (1973).

Hamada, K., 'Alternative Exchange Rate System and the Interdependence of Monetary Policies', in Aliber, R. (ed.) *National Monetary Policies and the International Financial System* (University of Chicago, Chicago, 1974).

Helliwell, J., 'Trade, Capital Flows, and Migration as Channels for International Transmission of Stabilisation Policies', in Ando, A., Herring, R., and Marston, R., (eds) *International aspects of Stabilisation Policies* (Federal Reserve Bank of Boston, 1974, Conference Series no. 12).

Helliwell, J., H. Shapiro, G. Sparks, I. Stewart, F. Gorbet, and D. Stephenson, 'The Structure of RDX2' (Bank of Canada, Ottawa, 1971).

Helliwell, J., and T. Maxwell, 'The Equations of RDX2 revised and estimated to 4Q 1970' (1974*a*) (Bank of Canada, Ottawa).

Helliwell, J., and T. Maxwell, 'Monetary Interdependence of Canada and the United States under Alternative Exchange Rate Systems', in Aliber, R. (ed.) *National Monetary Policies and the International Financial System* (University of Chicago, Chicago, 1974*b*).

Hickman, B. G., 'International Transmission of Economic Fluctuations and Inflation', in Ando, A., R. Herring and R. Marston (eds) *International Aspects of Stabilization Policies* (Federal Reserve Bank of Boston, 1974, Conference Series no. 12).

Johnson, K., and L. R. Klein, 'Stability in the International Economy: the LINK Experience', in Ando, A., R. Herring and R. Marston (eds) *International Aspects of Stabilization Policies* (Federal Reserve Bank of Boston, 1974, Conference Series no. 12).

Morishima, M., and Y. Murata, 'An Estimation of the International Trade Multiplier, 1954–1965', in M. Morishima, Y. Murata, T. Nosse, and M. Saito, *The Working of Econometric Models* (Cambridge U.P., London and New York, 1972).

Mundell, R., *International Economics* (New York, Macmillan 1968).

Tobin, J., 'An essay on principles of debt management', in *Commission on Money and Credit, Fiscal and Debt Management Policies* (Englewood Cliffs; Prentice-Hall, 1963).

Tobin, J., 'A General Equilibrium Approach to Monetary Theory', *Journal of Money, Credit, and Banking*, 1 (1969) pp. 15–29.

Waelbroeck, J., and A. Dramais, 'Desmos: A Model of Policy Coordination for the EEC Countries', in Ando, A., R. Herring, and R. Marston, (eds) *International Aspects of Stabilisation Policies* (Federal Reserve Bank of Boston, 1974, Conference Series no. 12).

TABLE 1–A   *US fiscal policy with parallel monetary policies*

Reduction of US Federal Government Expenditure, 1963–70
Sustained cut equal to 1 % of 1963 US GNE
Both countries use the same monetary policy, setting either the money supply (M1) or a short-term interest rate (R) equal to control.

Change in variables	Effects in US		Effects in Canada	
	Fixed M1	Fixed R	Fixed M1	Fixed R
Real private business output (% of control)				
2nd year	−2.11%	−2.58%	−.21%	−.36%
4th year	−.84%	−2.23%	+.19%	−.19%
6th year	−1.99%	−3.70%	−.09%	−.66%
8th year	+.92%	−3.81%	+.80%	−.42%
Real GNE multiplier (US), or induced effects as % of 1963 GNE (Can.)				
2nd year	+1.97	+2.47	−.16%	−.27%
4th year	+.88	+2.43	+.22%	−.11%
6th year	+2.31	+4.37	+.06%	−.49%
8th year	−1.09	+4.49	+1.25%	−.11%
Price of GNE (% of control)				
2nd year	−.21%	−.21%	+.01%	−.00%
4th year	−1.08%	−1.28%	−.20%	−.19%
6th year	−2.88%	−3.73%	−.54%	−.51%
8th year	−5.55%	−7.31%	−1.41%	−1.27%
Unemployment rate (percentage points)				
2nd year	+.484	+.577	+.110	+.169
4th year	+.364	+.691	−.021	+.126
6th year	+.531	+.975	+.185	+.324
8th year	+.113	+1.020	+.020	+.498
Short-term interest rate (%age points) or money supply (% of control)				
2nd year	−.29	−1.62%	−.02	−.18%
4th year	−.32	−2.70%	−.03	−.31%
6th year	−.99	−5.34%	−.09	−.80%
8th year	−1.79	−8.87%	−.07	−1.19%

Balances of trade with all countries (in mill. current dollars per year)

	US trade balance		Canadian trade balance	
	Fixed M1	Fixed R	Fixed M1	Fixed R
2nd year	+907.	+959.	−1.	+5.
4th year	+1191.	+2107.	−178.	−125.
6th year	+4149.	+6166.	−191.	−132.
8th year	+5510.	+8863.	−480.	−444.

Bilateral balances of trade and long-term capital, in mill. Can. dollars

	Balance of trade		Basic balance	
	Fixed M1	Fixed R	Fixed M1	Fixed R
2nd year	−8.	−8.	−24.	−37.
4th year	−152.	−143.	−70.	−107.
6th year	−202.	−235.	−178.	−259.
8th year	−416.	−647.	−192.	−597.

Canadian real trade balance and exchange rate

	XBAL (1961 $)		PFX ($C/$US, % ch)	
	Fixed M1	Fixed R	Fixed M1	Fixed R
2nd year	−63.	−41.	−.37%	+.05%
4th year	−241.	−190.	−.35%	+.20%
6th year	−338.	−263.	−.79%	+.57%
8th year	−679.	−699.	−1.86%	+1.14%

TABLE 1–B *Canadian fiscal policy with parallel monetary policies*

Reduction of Canadian Federal Government non-wage expenditure, 1963–70
Sustained cut equal to 1 % of 1963 Canadian GNE
Both countries use the same monetary policy, setting either the money supply (M1) or a short-term interest rate (R) equal to control.

Change in variables	Effects in US		Effects in Canada	
	Fixed M1	Fixed R	Fixed M1	Fixed R
Real private business output (% of control)				
2nd year	−.06%	−.13%	−1.28%	−2.84%
4th year	−.09%	−.14%	−.89%	−3.42%
6th year	−.40%	−.03%	−.83%	−2.05%
8th year	+.12%	−.04%	−.94%	−.56%
Real GNE multiplier (Can), or induced effects as % of 1963 GNE (US)				
2nd year	−.06%	−.13%	+.83	+2.02
4th year	−.10%	−.16%	+.58	+2.69
6th year	−.48%	−.03%	+.64	+1.81
8th year	+.14%	−.04%	+.84	+.81
Price of GNE (% of control)				
2nd year	−.00%	−.00%	−.61%	−.99%
4th year	−.04%	−.07%	−1.06%	−2.00%
6th year	−.21%	−.24%	−.73%	−.77%
8th year	−.64%	−.40%	−.67%	+.83%
Unemployment rate (percentage points)				
2nd year	+.016	+.036	+.627	+1.32
4th year	+.029	+.055	+.115	+.983
6th year	+.077	+.026	−.185	−.686
8th year	+.011	+.002	+.194	−.773
Short-term interest rate (%age points) or money supply (% of control)				
2nd year	−.01	−.07%	−.55	−2.99%
4th year	−.02	−.16%	−.60	−4.47%
6th year	−.15	−.24%	−.33	−2.67%
8th year	−.23	−.36%	−.12	+.93%

Balances of trade with all countries (in mill. current dollars per year)

	US balance		Canadian balance	
	Fixed M1	Fixed R	Fixed M1	Fixed R
2nd year	−61.	−247.	+199.	+303.
4th year	−94.	−140.	+327.	+606.
6th year	+334.	+574.	+318.	+298.
8th year	+454.	+236.	+184.	−432.

Bilateral balances of trade and long-term capital, in mill. Can. dollars

	Balance of trade		Basic balance	
	Fixed M1	Fixed R	Fixed M1	Fixed R
2nd year	+109.	+184.	+76.	+168.
4th year	+201.	+381.	+70.	+140.
6th year	+219.	+220.	+166.	+124.
8th year	+135.	−221.	+187.	−16.

Canadian real trade balance and exchange rate

	XBAL (1961$)		PFX ($C/$US, % ch)	
	Fixed M1	Fixed R	Fixed M1	Fixed R
2nd year	+313.	+393.	+1.23%	−.31%
4th year	+468.	+711.	+1.27%	−.88%
6th year	+359.	+237.	+.32%	−1.38%
8th year	+130.	−604.	−1.00%	−1.38%

TABLE 2–A   *US fiscal policy with differing monetary policies*

Reduction of US Federal Government expenditure, 1963–70
Sustained cut equal to 1 % of 1963 US GNE
Countries use the opposite monetary policy. If one country sets the money supply (M 1) equal to control, the other pegs the short-term interest rate (R). Thus, e.g. cols 1 and 3 are from the same simulation.

Change in variables	US policy and effects		Can. policy and effects	
	Fixed *M*1	Fixed *R*	Fixed *R*	Fixed *M*1
Real private business output (% of control)				
2nd year	−2.11%	−2.58%	−.26%	−.31%
4th year	−.84%	−2.23%	+.12%	−.09%
6th year	−1.99%	−3.70%	−.22%	−.44%
8th year	+.91%	−3.81%	+.43%	−.07%
Real GNE multiplier (US), or induced effects as % of 1963 GNE (Can.)				
2nd year	+2.03	+2.47	−.20%	−.23%
4th year	+.93	+2.43	+.17%	−.02%
6th year	+2.36	+4.36	−.07%	−.29%
8th year	−1.14	+4.62	+.84%	+.27%
Price of GNE (% of control)				
2nd year	−.21%	−.21%	−	+.01%
4th year	−1.08%	−1.28%	−.23%	−.15%
6th year	−2.88%	−3.73%	−.56%	−.46%
8th year	−5.55%	−7.31%	−1.50%	−1.19%
Unemployment rate (percentage points)				
2nd year	+.49	+.58	+.13	+.15
4th year	+.37	+.69	−	+.09
6th year	+.53	+.97	+.21	+.27
8th year	+.12	+1.02	+.17	+.40
Short-term interest rate (%age points) or money supply (% of control)				
2nd year	−.29	−1.62%	−.17%	−.03
4th year	−.32	−2.70%	−.19%	−.05
6th year	−.99	−5.34%	−.59%	−.12
8th year	−1.80	−8.87%	−.71%	−.21

Balances of trade with all countries (in mill. current dollars per year)

	US trade balance		Canadian trade balance	
	Fixed M 1	Fixed R	Fixed R	Fixed M 1
2nd year	+903.	+962.	+3.	+2.
4th year	+1186.	+2116.	−171.	−136.
6th year	+4134.	+6189.	−184.	−146.
8th year	+5470.	+8902.	−456.	−507.

Bilateral balances of trade and long-term capital, in mill. Can. dollars

	Balance of trade		Basic balance	
	Fix US M1	Fix US R	Fix US M1	Fix US R
2nd year	−5.	−10.	−19.	−41.
4th year	−148.	−150.	−69.	−111.
6th year	−196.	−246.	−165.	−278.
8th year	−397.	−658.	−170.	−614.

Canadian real trade balance and exchange rate

	XBAL (1961 $)		PFX($C/$US, % ch)	
	Fix US M1	Fix US R	Fix US M1	Fix US R
2nd year	−60.	−42.	−.43%	+.11%
4th year	−236.	−197.	−.42%	+.32%
6th year	−343.	−264.	−1.01%	+.89%
8th year	−671.	−690.	−2.26%	+1.63%

TABLE 2–B *Canadian fiscal policy with differing monetary policies*

Reduction of Canadian Federal Government non-wage expenditure, 1963–70
Sustained cut equal to 1% of 1963 Canadian GNE
Countries use the opposite monetary policy. If one country sets the money supply (M1)
equal to control, the other pegs the short-term interest rate (R).

Change in variables	US policy and effects		Can. policy and effects	
	Fixed R	Fixed M1	Fixed M1	Fixed R
Real private business output (% of control)				
2nd year	−.11%	−.09%	−1.30%	−2.83%
4th year	−.07%	−.13%	−.96%	−3.32%
6th year	−.02%	−.36%	−.74%	−2.14%
8th year	−.14%	+.25%	−.76%	−.88%
Real GNE multiplier (Can), or induced effects as % of 1963 GNE (US)				
2nd year	−.11%	−.08%	+.84	+2.01
4th year	−.08%	−.15%	+.64	+2.61
6th year	−.03%	−.43%	+.58	+1.87
8th year	−.17%	+.30%	+.71	+1.09
Price of GNE (% of control)				
2nd year	−.00%	−.00%	−.62%	−.98%
4th year	−.06%	−.05%	−1.08%	−1.97%
6th year	−.19%	−.25%	−.68%	−.82%
8th year	−.31%	−.68%	−.41%	+.51%
Unemployment rate (percentage points)				
2nd year	+.03	+.02	+.64	+1.31
4th year	+.04	+.04	+.13	+.95
6th year	+.02	+.08	−.27	−.59
8th year	+.02	−.00%	+.10	−.60
Short-term interest rate (%age points) or money supply (% of control)				
2nd year	−.06%	−.01	−.55	−4.19%
4th year	−.11%	−.03	−.61	−4.41%
6th year	−.18%	−.15	−.32	−2.76%
8th year	−.34%	−.21	−.06	+.52%

Balances of trade with all countries (in mill. current dollars per year)

	US balance		Canadian balance	
	Fixed R	Fixed M1	Fixed M1	Fixed R
2nd year	−137.	−169.	+181.	+321.
4th year	+35.	−275.	+365.	+564.
6th year	+542.	+317.	+432.	+189.
8th year	−61.	+645.	+142.	−365.

Bilateral balances of trade and long-term capital, in mill. Can. dollars

	Balance of trade		Basic balance	
	Fix C. R	Fix C. M1	Fix C. M1	Fix C. R
2nd year	+97.	+197.	+66.	+177.
4th year	+225.	+354.	+85.	+122.
6th year	+301.	+143.	+228.	+68.
8th year	+114.	−181.	+136.	+41.

Canadian real trade balance and exchange rate

	XBAL (1961$)		PFX ($C/$US, % ch)	
	Fix C. R	Fix C. M1	Fix C. M1	Fix C. R
2nd year	+296.	+409.	+1.26%	−.34%
4th year	+507.	+667.	+1.33%	−.94%
6th year	+477.	+124.	+.43%	−1.51%
8th year	+89.	−536.	−.84%	−1.71%

TABLE 3   *Canadian fiscal policy with alternative debt policies*

Reduction of Canadian Federal Government non-wage expenditure, 1963–70
using long-term bonds rather than treasury bills as residual source of funds.
Both countries use the same monetary policy, setting either the money supply (M 1) or
the short-term interest rate (R) equal to control.

Change in variables	Effects in US		Effects in Canada	
	Fixed M1	Fixed R	Fixed M1	Fixed R
Real private business output (% of control)				
2nd year	−.06%	−.13%	−1.20%	−2.76%
4th year	−.09%	−.14%	−.72%	−3.30%
6th year	−.40%	−.00%	−.68%	−1.96%
8th year	+.09%	−.02%	−.86%	−.40%
Real GNE multiplier (Can), or induced effects as % of 1963 GNE (US)				
2nd year	−.06%	−.12%	+.77	+1.95
4th year	−.10%	−.15%	+.44	+2.59
6th year	−.48%	−.01%	+.49	+1.72
8th year	+.10%	−.03%	+.73	+.64
Price of GNE (% of control)				
2nd year	−.00%	+.01%	−.60%	−.98%
4th year	−.03%	−.05%	−1.03%	−1.97%
6th year	−.20%	−.18%	−.77%	−.80%
8th year	−.65%	−.29%	−.80%	+.79%
Unemployment rate (percentage points)				
2nd year	+.01	+.02	+.60	+1.29
4th year	+.02	+.03	+.05	+.93
6th year	+.08	+.02	−.18	−.66
8th year	+.02	+.02	+.23	−.81
Short-term interest rate (%age points) or money supply (% of control)				
2nd year	−.01	−.07%	−.53	−4.12%
4th year	−.02	−.14%	−.56	−4.37%
6th year	−.15	−.19%	−.31	−2.59%
8th year	−.25	−.26%	−.12	+1.00%

Can. Govt long bond rate and nominal supply price of business capital (percentage points)

	Bond rate (RL)		Supply price (RHO)	
	Fixed M1	Fixed R	Fixed M1	Fixed R
2nd year	−.34	−.05	−.46	−.54
4th year	−.59	−.04	−.57	−.64
6th year	−.58	−.05	−.40	+.03
8th year	−.47	−.13	−.03	+.86

Bilateral balances of trade and long-term capital, in mill. Can. dollars

	Balance of trade		Basic balance	
	Fixed M1	Fixed R	Fixed M1	Fixed R
2nd year	+102.	+177.	+66.	+157.
4th year	+184.	+372.	+54.	+136.
6th year	+210.	+225.	+138.	+116.
8th year	+154.	−214.	+181.	−34.

Canadian real trade balance and exchange rate

	XBAL (1961$)		PFX ($C/$US, % ch)	
	Fixed M1	Fixed R	Fixed M1	Fixed R
2nd year	+301.	+382.	+1.22%	−.29%
4th year	+439.	+696.	+1.27%	−.83%
6th year	+357.	+255.	+.38%	−1.29%
8th year	+186.	−579.	−.86%	−1.27%

11 Monetary Interdependence among Major European Countries

Paul De Grauwe*

I INTRODUCTION

Two problems of the international monetary system have received widespread attention in the literature during the last decade. They are first the potential instability of the Bretton Woods system, which revealed itself at the end of the sixties and, second, the low efficacy of national monetary policies in an interdependent world.

A broad consensus has emerged identifying the source of these two problems as being a lack of flexibility of the post-war international monetary system. The argument, which is well known, runs as follows. In a fixed exchange rate system with downward inflexibility of nominal wages and prices, general deflationary measures to correct a balance of payments deficit will produce (or increase) unemployment. Since the authorities are committed to full employment, they have no other choice than to prevent this to happen. Exchange rate depreciations then become inevitable when the monetary authorities run out of reserves. As a result the fixed exchange rate system is transformed into a system of erratically flexible exchange rates, characterised by considerable instability of reserve flows between consecutive exchange rate changes. The conclusion readily follows that provisions for more systematic or 'orderly' exchange rate changes have to be introduced into the system, either by

* This study is based on my doctoral dissertation submitted in October 1973 to the Johns Hopkins University. A revised version was published in 1976–see De Grauwe (1976). I would like to acknowledge the stimulating comments and criticisms of my thesis committee chairman Professor Jurg Niehans and of Professor Bela Balassa. This paper also benefited from many helpful comments of Professor Carl Christ, Professor Ronald McKinnon, Hans Gerhard, John Hewson, Eisuke Sakakibara and Herman Verwilst.

letting exchange rates be freely determined by market forces or by making it dependent on some objective criteria or 'presumptive rule'. In addition, such schemes would eliminate the dilemma cases between internal and external equilibrium and enable monetary authorities to pursue independent monetary policies.

Implicit in this argument is that, although the rigidity of the fixed exchange rate system is related to the downward inflexibility of nominal wages and prices, the ultimate responsibility for the rigidity of the system lies in the attempts by national authorities to prevent the operation of the automatic adjustment mechanism. In other words, the rigidity of the Bretton Woods system is not inevitable, it is the result of particular policies of national authorities. The purpose of this study is to analyse how a particular class of national policies directly affects the rigidity of the system and, therefore, its stability. For that purpose, the working of a system (constructed to represent some essential features of the Bretton Woods system) will be studied in situations where monetary authorities systematically prevent the automatic adjustment to operate. More specifically we will analyse the effects on the stability of the system of policies aimed at offsetting the monetary effects of the balance of payments. At the same time, the question will be asked how effective these policies can be in an interdependent system where many countries tend to do the same.

Section II contains a theoretical model linking the monetary base of n countries. The basic model has been developed elsewhere.[1] This basic model is extended here to incorporate the case in which the group of European countries float jointly *vis-a-vis* the rest of the world.

In Section III the models are estimated for a group of European countries. In Section IV the effect of the use of sterilisation policies on the stability of the system is analysed. The question is also examined as to the usefulness of these policies in attaining greater monetary independence.

II   THE GENERAL MODEL

(1)   The following assumptions and concepts are used: (*a*) It is assumed that the monetary authorities have a full control over the credit they extent to the domestic economy; that is, they control the domestic component of the monetary base. However, they do not have a full control over the monetary base. In an open economy the latter is made up of a domestic and a foreign component. Changes in the domestic component of the monetary base induced by the monetary authorities generally lead to an opposite change in the foreign component, everything else remaining constant.[2] As a result, the monetary base of country i is not under the control of the monetary authorities of country i.[3] The main focus of this study is on the interdependence of the national monetary bases in a multi-country model. One of the essential ingredients of this interdependence is that changes in the monetary base in

any one country are the result of monetary policy actions of all the countries of the system. (*b*) It is assumed that a system of fixed exchange rates exists between the *n* countries of the system. Since one of the purposes of the model is to shed light on past developments in monetary relations between European countries, this is a natural assumption to make. In addition, considering the fact that a group of European countries, still maintains fixed exchange rates among each others' currencies, this assumption remains relevant. (*c*) The existence of a $(n+1)$th country (the United States) is assumed. Two alternative exchange rate regimes will be considered. One in which the price of the dollar in terms of European currencies is fixed; a second in which it is flexible.

An asymmetrical relationship between the United States and the European countries is assumed, i.e. it is assumed that the US monetary base is unaffected by monetary conditions in the European countries. This assumption can be justified on two grounds. First, the difference in size between the United States and any European country leads to only marginal influences of monetary policies of European countries upon the US monetary base. Second, the role of the US dollar as a reserve currency implies that a deficit (surplus) of the US balance of payments will not necessarily be reflected in a decrease (increase) in the US monetary base. The degree in which the US monetary base is affected by a balance of payments deficit (surplus) depends on the form in which European countries hold their reserves. If these are held as deposits in US commercial banks, a US deficit (surplus) will not affect the US monetary base since only a shift from domestic to foreign holders will occur (vice versa in the case of surplus). Similarly, if the European monetary authorities hold their reserves in the form of US Treasury securities, the US monetary base will be unaffected.[4] Only if a US balance of payments deficit (surplus) leads to a gold outflow (inflow) or to an increase (decrease) of European central banks' deposits at the Federal Reserve will the US monetary base be affected.[5]

(2) THE MODEL WITH A FIXED DOLLAR EXCHANGE RATE (MODEL I)

In the multi-country context that is considered here changes in the stock of international reserves of country *i* are the outcome of monetary policy actions of all the countries of the system. Therefore, there exists a set of equations.

$$R_i = R_i(D_1, \ldots, D_n, D_{n+1}) \tag{1}$$

$$\text{for } i = 1, \ldots, n$$

where R_i = the stock of international reserves of country *i*

D_i = the domestic component of the monetary base of country *i*; this variable is assumed to be under the full control of the monetary authorities of country *i*.[6]

In accordance with well-known theoretical results,[7] the partial derivatives can be assumed to have the following signs:

$$\frac{\partial R_i}{\partial D_j} \leq 0 \qquad \text{if } i=j$$
$$\qquad\qquad \geq 0 \qquad \text{if } i \neq j \tag{2}$$

i.e. an expansionary (contractionary) monetary policy in country j will result in a reserve outflow from (inflow into) country j and corresponding inflows into (outflows from) the other countries of the system, *ceteris paribus*.[8]

Clearly in an interdependent system additivity constraints on these partial derivatives exist. These are

$$\sum_{i=1}^{n} \frac{\partial R_i}{\partial D_j} - E_j = 0 \qquad \text{for all } j=1, \ldots, n \tag{3}$$

where $E_j \leq 0$ is the outflow (inflow) of reserves to (from) the United States resulting from an expansionary (contractionary) policy of country j.[9] E_j can also be interpreted as the change in the level of European reserves induced by a change in the domestic component of the monetary base of country j.

Differentiating (1) one obtains

$$dR_i = \alpha_{i1} dD_1 + \ldots + \alpha_{in} dD_n + \alpha_{i,n+1} dD_{n+1} \tag{4}$$
$$\text{for } i=1, \ldots, n$$

where $\quad \alpha_{ij} = \dfrac{\partial R_i}{\partial D_j}.$

The partial derivative $\alpha_{i,n+1}$, i.e. the effect of US monetary policy actions on country i's reserve position, can be written as

$$e_i E_{n+1}$$

where $\quad E_{n+1} = \dfrac{\partial E}{\partial D_{n+1}} \geq 0$, i.e. an expansionary (contractionary) US monetary policy increases (decreases) the total level of European reserves, *ceteris paribus*;

and $\quad e_i = \dfrac{\alpha_{i,n+1}}{E_{n+1}}$ i.e. the proportion of the US induced change in European reserves distributed to country i. Clearly $\Sigma e_i = 1$.
Equations (4) now become

$$dR_i = \sum_{j=1}^{n} \alpha_{ij} dD_j + e_i dE_a \tag{5}$$
$$\text{for } i=1, \ldots, n$$

where $dE_a = E_{n+1} dD_{n+1}$; this variable has to be interpreted as the total change in European reserves resulting from a change in US monetary policy, *ceteris paribus*.

Adding the definitional equations

$$dB_i = dR_i + dD_i \tag{6}$$

where $dB_i =$ the change in the monetary base of country i, the model (5)–(6) determines the changes in the monetary base of n European countries as a function of exogenous changes in the domestic component of the monetary base of n European countries and the US.

Since adjustments to changes in monetary policies take time to be fully implemented a lagged adjustment pattern has to be introduced. A distributed lag adjustment pattern is assumed. Using matrix notation and expressing variables in difference form, one obtains

$$R_t = A[\Lambda_o D_t + \ldots \Lambda_{t_o} D_{t-t_o}] + e\Delta E_{at} \tag{7}$$

where

$$B_t = \begin{bmatrix} \Delta B_{1t} \\ \vdots \\ \Delta B_{nt} \end{bmatrix}; \; D_t = \begin{bmatrix} \Delta D_{1t} \\ \vdots \\ \Delta D_{nt} \end{bmatrix}; \; R_t = \begin{bmatrix} \Delta R_{1t} \\ \vdots \\ \Delta R_{nt} \end{bmatrix}$$

$$A = \begin{bmatrix} \alpha_{11} & \cdots \cdots & \alpha_{1n} \\ \vdots & & \vdots \\ \alpha_{n1} & \cdots \cdots & \alpha_{nn} \end{bmatrix}; \; e = \begin{bmatrix} e_1 \\ \vdots \\ e_n \end{bmatrix} \geq 0$$

$$A_k = \begin{bmatrix} \lambda_{1k} & \cdots \cdots & 0 \\ & & \\ 0 & \cdots \cdots & \lambda_{nk} \end{bmatrix}$$

$\Delta E_{\alpha t} = \sum\limits_{k=0}^{t_0} \lambda_{a,k} E_{a,t-k}$, the supply of reserves to Europe resulting from present and past changes in US monetary policies;

and where $\sum\limits_{k=0}^{t_0} \lambda_{j,k} = 1$ for $j = 1, \ldots, n, n+1$

Equation (7) can also be written as

$$R_t = A_0 D_t + A_1 D_{t-1} + \ldots + A_{t_0} D_{t-t_0} + e\Delta E_{at} \tag{8}$$

Equation (8) together with the identities

$$B_t = IR_t + ID_t \tag{9}$$

yield the model to be used for empirical estimation. From the previous discussion on the signs of the partial derivatives α_{ij}, it follows that the diagonal elements of $A_0, A_1 \ldots A_{t_0}$ are negative or zero. The off-diagonal elements of $A_0 \ldots A_{t_0}$ are all non-negative. In addition, from (3) it follows that the column sums of $A_0 \ldots A_{t_0}$ are non-positive and equal to the net leakage with the US.

(3) THE MODEL WITH A FLEXIBLE DOLLAR EXCHANGE RATE (MODEL II)
If the price of the dollar in terms of European currencies (the dollar exchange rate) is assumed to vary, country i's stock of international reserves also depends on the dollar exchange rate, K.[10] Instead of equation (1) one has

$$R_i = K R_{fi}(D_1, \ldots, D_n, D_{n+1}, K) \tag{10}$$

where R_{fi} = the stock of international reserves of country i expressed in dollars
        K = the dollar exchange rate.
The same signs on the partial derivatives of R_{fi} with respect to D_j can be postulated as in (2), i.e.

$$\frac{\partial R_{fi}}{\partial D_j} \begin{array}{ll} \leq 0 & \text{if } i = j \\ \geq 0 & \text{if } i \neq j. \end{array} \tag{11}$$

The sign of the partial derivative of R_{fi} with respect to K is uncertain

$$\frac{\partial R_{fi}}{\partial K} \gtrless 0 \tag{12}$$

summation of R_i in (10) yields the function

$$\Sigma R_i = E = K E_f(D_1, \ldots, D_n, D_{n+1}, K) \tag{13}$$

which describes the total level of international reserves in Europe as a function of the $n+1$ monetary policy variable and of the dollar exchange rate.[11]

Joint floating of European currencies implies that the balance of payments of Europe as a whole is always in equilibrium, i.e. that

$$dE = 0 \tag{14}$$

This means that K in (13) is uniquely determined by the exogenous variables $D_1, \ldots, D_{n+1}$.

Without loss of generality it can be assumed that $K = 1$, i.e. that initially one dollar = one European currency. After differentiation the system consisting of equations (10), (13), and (14) can be solved to obtain the endogenous variables dR_i and dK, The solution is

$$dR_i = \sum_j \bar{\alpha}_{ij} dD_j + \bar{e}_i dE_a \tag{15}$$

and

$$dK = -\frac{1}{(1+\gamma)E_f}(\sum_j \sum_i \alpha_{ij}dD_j + \sum_i \alpha_{i,n+1}dD_{n+1}) \qquad (16)$$

where

$$\alpha_{ij} = \frac{\partial R_{fi}}{\partial D_j}, \quad \text{as in Model I} \quad \alpha_{ij}$$

represents the change in country i's total reserve position resulting from a change in the domestic component of the monetary base, everything else (including the dollar exchange rate) remaining constant.

$$\bar{\alpha}_{ij} = (\alpha_{ij} - m_i \sum_k \alpha_{kj}) \qquad (17)$$

$$\gamma_i = \frac{\partial R_{fi}}{\partial K}\frac{K}{R_{fi}} \qquad \gamma = \frac{\partial E_f}{\partial K}\frac{K}{E_f} \qquad (18)$$

i.e. γ_i and γ are the elasticities of the international reserves of country i, respectively Europe, with respect to the dollar exchange rate.

$$\bar{e}_i = e_i - m_i \qquad (19)$$

$$m_i = \left(\frac{1+\gamma_i}{1+\gamma}\right)\frac{R_{fi}}{E_f}, \qquad (20)$$

it can be proven that $\Sigma m_i = 1$[12]

$$e_i = \frac{\alpha_{i,n+1}}{\Sigma \alpha_{i,n+1}} \quad \text{and} \quad dE_a = \sum_i \alpha_{i,n+1} \ dD_{n+1}.$$

The interpretation of e_i and dE_a has been given earlier.

In (15) we obtain a system of equations which is similar to the system of equations (5) obtained under the assumption of a fixed dollar rate. However, the existence of joint floating has changed the system in several aspects.

(a) The system (15) is a closed system *vis-à-vis* the United States, i.e. the joint floating eliminates leakages to and from the United States. This can be seen from

$$\sum_i \bar{\alpha}_{ij} = \sum_i (\alpha_{ij} - m_i \sum_k \alpha_{kj}) = 0$$

i.e. a reserve outflow (inflow) from (into) country i resulting from a change in monetary policy in that country goes to (comes from) the other European countries in its entirety.

(b) The joint floating of European currencies affects the intra-

European reserve flows, i.e. it changes the size of the leakages. From (17) it can be deduced that

$$\left|\bar{\alpha}_{ii}\right| < \left|\alpha_{ii}\right| \qquad \text{since} \sum_k \alpha_{kj} < 0$$

and

$$\bar{\alpha}_{ij} > \alpha_{ij} \qquad \text{for } i \neq j.$$

This means that the joint floating results in two opposing tendencies as far as the European interdependence is concerned. On the one hand it decreases the total leakage of the countries' monetary policies. On the other hand it increases the flows to (or from) the other European countries resulting from these leakages.

(c) Although US monetary policies have no influence on the total European reserves, and, therefore, on the total European monetary base ($\Sigma \bar{e}_i = \Sigma e_i - \Sigma m_i = 0$), it may still have an effect on the reserve holdings of individual countries and, therefore, on their monetary base. The latter will happen if $m_i \neq e_i$. This will occur if the elasticities γ_i are different and/or if the relative openness of European countries *vis-à-vis* the United States is different (as measured by differences in e_i and $\dfrac{R_{fi}}{E_f}$). The significance of this result will be analysed when the model is simulated.

The system of equations (15) and (16) now can be transformed to its discrete form assuming a distributed lag adjustment. One obtains, in matrix notation

$$R_t = \bar{A}_o D_t + \bar{A}_1 D_{t-1} + \ldots \bar{A}_{to} D_{t-to} + \bar{e} \Delta E_{at} \tag{21}$$

$$\Delta K_t = -\frac{1}{(1+\gamma)E_f}(iA_o D_t \ldots + iA_{to} D_{t-to} + \Delta E_{at}) \tag{22}$$

where $\quad \bar{A}_i = (I - L)A_i \tag{23}$

and

$$L = \begin{bmatrix} m_1 & \cdots & m_1 \\ \vdots & & \vdots \\ m_n & \cdots & m_n \end{bmatrix} \quad \text{and } \bar{e} = \begin{bmatrix} e_1 & - & m_1 \\ & \vdots & \\ e_n & - & m_n \end{bmatrix} \tag{24}$$

$$i = \begin{bmatrix} 1 & \cdots & 1 \end{bmatrix}$$

Together with the definitional equations (9), (21)–(23) determine the monetary base of *n* European countries and the dollar exchange rate as a function of past and present monetary policies of the $n+1$ countries of the system.

III EMPIRICAL ESTIMATION

The two models developed in the previous section are estimated from empirical data relating to a group of European countries. It should be stressed that the estimations are not performed for their own sake. Rather, the intention is to obtain plausible numerical values of the coefficients of the model so as to make simulations possible.[13]

Except for two devaluations (United Kingdom in 1967 and France in 1969) and three appreciations (Netherlands and Germany in 1961 and Germany in 1969) the system prevailing during the period 1960–70 can be characterised as a fixed exchange rate system. Therefore, model I is estimated using data relating to this period. Joint floating is a recent phenomenon, so that direct estimation of model II is precluded. However, given the relationship between the parameters of the two models, the numerical values of the parameters of model II can be derived from a knowledge of the parameters of model I plus extraneous information of the parameters m_i.

(1) ESTIMATION OF MODEL I

Due to the large degree of multi-collinearity among the independent variables direct estimation of the system (8) was impossible, i.e. it was impossible to obtain significant estimates of the individual influences of the different countries' monetary policy variables on the changes in reserves of a particular country. Therefore, it was decided to estimate only the diagonal elements of the matrices $A_0, A_1, \ldots$, through a least squares method.[14] The off-diagonal elements of $A_0, A_1, \ldots$, were estimated indirectly by assuming that the reserve changes of a particular country induced by a change in its monetary policies are distributed over the rest of the system according to the relative size of the different countries. As a measure of size gross national product was selected.

The decision to estimate only the diagonal elements of the matrices A_0, $A_1, \ldots$, means that the equations to be estimated are specified as follows:

$$\Delta R_{it} = k_i + a_{io}\Delta D_{it} + \ldots + a_{ito}\Delta D_{i,t-to} + u_t \tag{25}$$

$$\text{for } i = 1, \ldots, n$$

The data used for the estimation of (25) are quarterly series. Therefore, seasonal dummy variables, SE_j, were introduced. In addition, in the case of two countries a speculative dummy variable was introduced. This proved to increase substantially the statistical quality of the equations. The model was estimated with lags of up to four quarters. However, no significant estimates were obtained for parameters corresponding to lags of two quarters or more. The final specification was, therefore, chosen to be

$$\Delta R_{it} = k_i + a_{i0}\Delta D_{it} + a_{i1}\Delta D_{i,t-1} + g_i\Delta E_t \tag{26}$$

$$+ \sum_{j=2}^{4} \zeta_{ij}SE_{jt} + \theta_i SP_{it} + u_{it}$$

where k_i = the constant

ΔE_t = the change in total European reserves.[15]

SP_{it} = a speculative variable which was introduced in the case of Italy and the United Kingdom. It was obtained by selecting those periods for which the residual in the regression without a speculative variable was twice as large as the mean absolute error. If the residual in these periods was negative (positive), a value of -1 ($+1$) was given.

Due to the existence of an inverse relationship between ΔD_{it} and ΔR_{it} resulting from the use of sterilisation policies during the sample period the equations in (26) were estimated with a two-stage least-squares method. GNP variables were selected as instrumental variables.

The equations were estimated for seven European countries: Belgium, France, Germany, Italy, Netherlands, Switzerland and the United Kingdom during the period 1959–70. The results of the estimation of (26) are presented in Table 1.[16] It is seen that the estimated leakages a_0 and a_1 have the right sign in all cases but two, and in eight out of fourteen cases they are significantly different from zero at the 95 per cent confidence level.

As mentioned in the beginning of this section, the off-diagonal elements of A_0 and A_1 were estimated using extraneous information, i.e. using an indicator of the relative size of the different countries of the system. It will be remembered that the model (8) is an open model in the sense that a net flow of reserves between the European system and the US can occur. Therefore, the degree of integration between the US and the European countries is an important parameter in the model. Instead of trying to estimate such a parameter, several alternative values will be assumed.

The degree of integration between the US and a particular European country i will be represented by

$$\varepsilon_i = 1 + \sum_{j \neq i}^{n} \alpha_{ji}/\alpha_{ii} \tag{27}$$

That is, ε_i represents that part of the total leakage of country i, α_{ii}, which is a leakage with the US. A value of ε_i equal to 1 means that a reserve inflow (outflow) in country i comes from (goes to) the US in its entirety. A value of ε_i equal to 0 means that a reserve flow to or from country i originates from or goes to other European countries. In the following different intermediate values of ε_i will be assumed, expressing different assumptions about the degree of economic integration between the US and country i.

Table 1   *Estimation of equation (26), 1959 I–1970 IV, (in million dollars)*

	Const.	a_0	a_1	g	ζ_2	ζ_3	ζ_4	θ
Belgium	−31.40	−0.95	0.01	0.02	123.42	24.36	77.99	
	(−2.48)	(−5.14)	(0.18)	(3.31)	(4.26)	(1.58)	(4.38)	
				$R^2 = 0.85$		$SE = 32.74$		
France	−11.46	−0.62	−0.22	0.07	58.08	79.78	336.28	
	(−0.06)	(−2.31)	(−3.75)	(0.77)	(0.18)	(0.36)	(0.98)	
				$R^2 = 0.78$		$SE = 231.2$		
W. Germany	−234.86	−0.55	−0.09	0.31	467.73	380.78	661.23	
	(−1.72)	(−3.48)	(−1.33)	(2.41)	(2.24)	(2.22)	(2.22)	
				$R^2 = 0.84$		$SE = 364.35$		
Netherlands	−27.92	−0.83	−0.12	0.01	118.60	48.26	85.61	
	(−1.86)	(−3.47)	(−1.70)	(0.32)	(3.91)	(1.82)	(3.97)	
				$R^2 = 0.78$		$SE = 48.17$		
Italy	53.27	−0.12	−0.32	0.01	1.39	290.18	181.19	371.30
	(0.74)	(−1.87)	(−4.95)	(0.26)	(0.02)	(3.24)	(1.85)	(7.77)
				$R^2 = 0.79$		$SE = 170.13$		
Switzerland*	−321.20	−1.66	0.59	0.01	480.70	232.54	556.30	
	(−7.24)	(−5.12)	(1.81)	(0.19)	(7.54)	(3.80)	(7.12)	
				$R^2 = 0.83$		$SE = 138.4$		
United Kingdom	−2.01	−0.22	−0.02	0.03	−10.60	−51.11	−14.05	431.25
	(−0.05)	(−1.69)	(−0.23)	(0.43)	(−0.13)	(−0.97)	(−0.15)	(5.63)
				$R^2 = 0.81$		$SE = 114.44$		

Figures in parentheses are t-statistics; $SE =$ standard error of the regression.

* The Swiss equation was estimated with an additional variable, namely the exogenous change of the domestic component of the Italian monetary base. This improved the statistical quality of the Swiss equation substantially (probably as a result of the close financial ties between Switzerland and Italy). The estimated coefficient of the Italian variable was 0.24, and significantly different from zero.

The only problem left is the estimation of the vector e in (8). As will be remembered, the vector e expresses the way a change in the supply of reserves brought about by a change in US monetary policies is distributed among the European countries. It will be assumed that this distribution is related to the size of the countries, in a similar way as was done in the case of the off-diagonal elements of matrices A_0 and A_1.[17] The reservations made there apply here too.

(2) ESTIMATION OF MODEL II

Using (23) and (24), the estimates of A_0, A_1 and e together with estimates of the parameter m_i can be employed to obtain estimates of $\overline{A}_0$, $\overline{A}_1$ and $\overline{e}$.

In order to estimate m_i the assumption was made that $\gamma_i = \gamma$ for all i, i.e. that the total elasticity of a country's balance of payments with respect to the dollar exchange rate is the same for all countries.[18] Given this assumption it follows from (20) that $m_i = \dfrac{R_{fi}}{E_f}$; that is, m_i expresses the initial equilibrium distribution of reserves in Europe. As an estimate of m_i, the average observed distribution during 1960–5 for the seven European countries was taken. The period 1960–5 was selected as it was a period of relatively few disturbances in European reserve flows.

Estimates for $\overline{A}_0$ and $\overline{A}_1$ can now be obtained using equation (23). The estimation of the vector e requires some additional discussion. Since e_i represents the proportion of reserves going to country i as a result of an expansionary US monetary policy the difference between e_i and m_i, i.e. $\overline{e}_i$, can be interpreted as originating from a difference in relative openness of European countries *vis-à-vis* the US. If $e_i < m_i$, the proportion of the flow of reserves going to country i as a result of an expansionary US policy is lower than the equilibrium share of reserves of country i, and country i can be said to be relatively less open to the US. The opposite is true if $e_i > m_i$. As an estimate of these differences in relative openness the difference in the share of country i in the total US – European trade flow (e_i) and country i's equilibrium share in total European reserves (m_i) was selected.[19]

IV   STERILISATION POLICIES

The two models derived and estimated in the previous sections form the framework of the analysis of sterilisation policies.

Sterilisation policies are not a new phenomenon. They were widely used in the inter-war period, by most industrialised countries, and especially by the US, the United Kingom and France.[20] Bloomfield also provides evidence that it was used during the period 1880–1914, the heydays of the international gold standard.[21] It is commonly agreed that in the period after the Second World War sterilisation policies continued to be used extensively.[22] Surprisingly, though, extensive empirical studies of sterilisation policies have been very scarce. Recently, however, Argy and Kouri estimated sterilisation equations of the kind specified in the previous section as (26), for several European countries. They found significant sterilisation parameters for three countries, West Germany, Italy and the Netherlands.[23]

In the framework of the models developed in the previous section, the sterilisation policy of country i can be formalised by the equation:

$$\Delta D_i = h_i \Delta R_i + \Delta Z_i \qquad (28)$$

where h_i = a policy parameter indicating the proportion of reserve flows the monetary authorities choose to offset by changes in the domestic component of the monetary base. It will be assumed that $-1 \leq h_i \leq 0$ (for $i = 1, \ldots, n$).

ΔZ_i = the change in the domestic component of the monetary base brought about by the monetary authorities independently from balance of payments considerations.

In matrix notation, and adding time subscripts, (28) can be written as:

$$D_t = HR_t + Z_t \qquad (29)$$

where

$$H = \begin{bmatrix} h_1 & \cdots & 0 \\ \vdots & \ddots & \vdots \\ 0 & \cdots & h_n \end{bmatrix} \quad \text{and} \quad Z_t = \begin{bmatrix} \Delta Z_{1t} \\ \vdots \\ \Delta Z_{nt} \end{bmatrix} \qquad (30)$$

(29) can now be incorporated into the models developed in the previous section. Taking model I, one then obtains

$$B_t = D_t + R_t \qquad (31)$$

$$R_t = A_0 D_t + A_1 D_{t-1} + e\Delta E_{at} \qquad (32)$$

$$D_t = HR_t + Z_t \qquad (33)$$

where A_0, A_1 and e have been estimated in the previous section. The model (31)–(33) is a system of first order difference equations. It consists of $3 \times n$ equations and $3 \times n$ endogenous variables, $\Delta B_{1t}, \ldots, \Delta B_{nt}$, $\Delta R_{1t}, \ldots, \Delta R_{nt}$, $\Delta D_{1t}, \ldots, \Delta D_{nt}$. The exogenous variables are $\Delta Z_{1t}, \ldots, \Delta Z_{nt}$, ΔE_{at} and $h_1, \ldots, h_n$. It should be noted that the endogenous character of the variables $\Delta D_{1t}, \ldots, \Delta D_{nt}$ does not imply that the monetary authorities have no control over the domestic component of the monetary base. By a suitable choice of h_i the monetary authorities can choose any value of ΔD_{it}.

In a similar way sterilisation policies can be incorporated in the model with joint floating (model II). One obtains

$$B_t = D_t + R_t \qquad (34)$$

$$R_t = \bar{A}_0 D_t + \bar{A}_1 D_{t-1} + \bar{e}\Delta E_{at} \qquad (35)$$

$$D_t = HR_t + Z_t \qquad (36)$$

So far no mention has been made of possible restrictions on the solutions of the two models resulting from non-negativity constraints on the stock of reserves. These must now be introduced, for it is clear that not all solutions of models I and II, even if they are stable in the mathematical sense, are feasible. If the system is slow to converge to a stable solution, large reserve outflows for particular countries might occur during a prolonged period of time so that the system hits the non-negativity condition of the reserve stocks.

Similarly, if a particular (stable) solution implies a constant outflow of reserves over time for one or more countries, the system is bound to hit the non-negativity constraints imposed by the reserve stocks. As a result monetary policies and/or exchange rates will have to be changed.

Reserve constraints can be introduced into the two models in various ways. In the simulations that follow, initial stocks of reserves, R_{io}, are assumed. Simulations of (31)–(33) and (34)–(36) are then run with the added condition

$$R_{it} = R_{i0} + \sum_{k=1}^{t} \Delta R_{ik} > 0 \qquad \text{for } i = 1, \ldots, n \qquad (37)$$

V   SIMULATION OF THE MODEL

In this section the results of the simulations of the two models are reported. The simulation results of the model with a fixed dollar exchange rate are discussed in detail. The simulation results of the model with joint floating are then compared with these results.

(1)   SIMULATION OF THE MODEL WITH FIXED DOLLAR EXCHANGE RATE (SYSTEM (31)–(33), (37))

The results of the simulations are discussed from two points of view: (a) the stability of the reserve flows, and   (b) the time path of the European monetary bases and European monetary independence.

Simulations are performed under alternative assumptions concerning the degree of economic integration between the United States and the European countries as compared to the degree of integration among the European countries.

The initial values in (31)–(33) are all set at zero. Since all the variables are expressed as flows, this means that the simulations start from a position of static equilibrium. The initial stocks of reserves in (37) are set at their average level during 1960–5. The results are now discussed in detail.

(a)   Stability of the Reserve Flows

The main results are summarised in Table 2. Full sterilisation by all countries leads to explosive European reserve flows when $\varepsilon_i = 0.20$ or

Table 2 Time path of European reserve flows. Dollar exchange rate fixed (*Simulation over 30 quarters*)

	Full sterilisation ($h_i = -1$)		Partial sterilisation ($h_i = -0.5$)	No sterilisation ($h_i = 0.0$)
	All countries	France and Germany	All countries	All countries
Exogenous supply of reserves = $750 million				
$\varepsilon_i = 0.20$	Explosive	Slow convergence (beyond simulation period)	Convergence after 4 quarters	Convergence after 2 quarters
$\varepsilon_i = 0.40$	Explosive	Slow convergence (after 25 quarters)	Convergence after 3 quarters	Convergence after 2 quarters
$\varepsilon_i = 0.60$	Slow convergence (beyond simulation period)	Slow convergence (after 19 quarters)	Convergence after 3 quarters	Convergence after 2 quarters
Exogenous supply of reserves = 0				
$\varepsilon_i = 0.20$	Explosive	Slow convergence (beyond simulation period)	Convergence after 4 quarters	Convergence after 2 quarters
$\varepsilon_i = 0.40$	Explosive	Slow convergence (after 28 quarters)	Convergence after 4 quarters	Convergence after 2 quarters
$\varepsilon_i = 0.60$	Slow convergence (beyond simulation period)	Slow convergence (after 20 quarters)	Convergence after 3 quarters	Convergence after 2 quarters

Note: The exogenous changes in the domestic component of the monetary base were set equal to their 1965–70 averages.

0.40. For a value of $\varepsilon_i = 0.60$ the reserve flows cease to be explosive. However, the extremely slow convergence to equilibrium levels of reserve flows makes the system unfeasible. Italy, for example, runs out of reserves in the eighth quarter of the simulation (assuming an exogenous supply of reserves to Europe, ΔE_a, of \$750 million per quarter).[24]

If sterilisation is undertaken by two countries only (France and Germany), the system is mathematically stable. However, the convergence to equilibrium levels of reserves is extremely slow. One or more countries run out of reserves in a relatively short time span.

Additional simulations confirm what can be expected: the larger the number of countries engaging in full sterilisation, the slower the convergence of reserve flows to equilibrium in the stable case, and the more explosive these same flows become in the unstable case.

If all countries abstain from sterilisation practices altogether, the flows of reserves attain their equilibrium level after two or three quarters. The same is true if all countries use partial sterilisation where the rate of sterilisation h_i was set at -0.50. However, additional simulations show that if this rate of sterilisation is increased for all countries, the speed of convergence to equilibrium flows of reserves decreases, and at a certain point the reserve flows become explosive. For example, at $h_i = -0.95$ for all countries, the stability characteristics of the system are found to be very similar to the case of full sterilisation.

In the absence of sterilisation or with partial (but 'moderate') sterilisation, no problems arise due to non-negativity constraints on the reserve stocks, except when the exogenous supply of reserves is assumed to be zero. In that case some countries (France and Italy) experience steady reserve losses. The non-negativity constraint, however, is hit beyond the simulation period of 30 quarters.

These various results can be given the following interpretation. A policy of full sterilisation used by a particular country implies that this country pegs its monetary base to a target value in disregard of the balance of payments. If no other countries engage in full sterilisation, the balance of payments disequilibrium of the sterilising country will be absorbed by a change in the monetary base of the non-sterilising countries. In other words, sterilisation by one country results in an adjustment of the monetary base in all the other countries to whatever level is determined by the monetary policy of the sterilising country.[25] However, if other countries refuse to let their monetary base adjust to changes in monetary policies of the first country, i.e. if they too engage in sterilisation operations, policy conflicts will emerge. Instability in reserve flows will then occur, if the burden of adjustment cannot be shifted, in a significant way, to other non-sterilising countries. But even if this can be done, as for instance in the case where only two countries use sterilisation policies, and if, as a result, reserve flows converge to equilibrium levels, the speed at which convergence occurs is very slow. Thus, instability or slow convergence of reserve flows is a direct result of incompatible monetary policies in an interdependent world.[26] This must inevitably lead to changes in monetary policies, increased controls on capital movements, or changes in exchange rates of all countries considered.

The results also indicate that with a higher degree of integration of European countries with the United States as compared to the intra-European integration, the policy conflicts between European countries will be lessened and intra-European reserve flows will become less explosive.[27] However, it should be noted that for all the different degrees of integration assumed in this study it appears that sterilisation by two or more countries in Europe leads to non-sustainable levels of reserve flows in Europe.

Finally, partial sterilisation policies (assuming a 'moderate' degree of sterilisation, e.g. $h_i = -0.50$) result in stable reserve flows and may be sustainable in the long run[28] since it shifts only part of the burden of the adjustment that must occur in the monetary base of a particular country to the other countries. As a result, conflicts of policy are less acute and reserve flows will be stable. However, with an increasing rate of sterilisation, the conflicts of policy also rise.

While the rationale for the use of sterilisation policies has often been that it isolates domestic money markets from destabilising external influences, the present study shows that an important source of destabilising external influences are the sterilisation policies themselves. Their systematic use by several countries, therefore, tends to produce exactly what they were intended to avert.

Does this mean that sterilisation policies should be abandoned altogether? The results obtained indicate that sterilisation policies at a 'moderate' rate (50 per cent of reserve flows was used as an example) are compatible with stability of reserve flows. Partial sterilisation policies, therefore, can have a useful purpose in allowing monetary authorities to achieve a limited degree of independence without endangering the stability of the international monetary system.[29] How limited this independence is, is examined now.

(b) European Monetary Independence

For the purpose of this subsection, full sterilisation policies by two or more countries are not examined, as these have been shown to lead to a swift breakdown of the system.

In order to analyse the degree of monetary independence obtainable by European monetary authorities the following test was devised. First, simulations were run using the first stage estimates of ΔZ_{it} in the two-stage least-squares estimation of equation (26), and using the estimated values of ΔE_t when the latter variable was regressed on the US policy variable $\Delta D_{n+1,t}$. Second, the simulated monetary base of country i was regressed on all the exogenous variables, excluding the variable under the control of country i (i.e. ΔZ_i). The difference in R^2 obtained in this regression with the R^2 of the regression when ΔZ_i is included,[30] gives an indication of the loss of explanatory power due to the dropping of the exogenous variable. A same procedure was used to detect the explanatory power of the US-induced change in European reserves (ΔE_a). The results are presented in Table 3.

Table 3   Loss in explanation of the simulated national monetary bases due to the dropping of an exogenous variable

Exogenous variable dropped	National monetary base	$h_i = 0.0$	$h_i = -0.5$
ΔZ_B	Belgium	0.01	0.01
ΔE	Belgium	0.43	0.27
ΔZ_F	France	0.02	0.04
ΔE	France	0.39	0.25
ΔZ_G	Germany	0.21	0.60
ΔE	Germany	0.34	0.18
ΔZ_N	Netherlands	0.01	0.02
ΔE	Netherlands	0.39	0.25
ΔZ_I	Italy	0.09	0.25
ΔE	Italy	0.35	0.30
ΔZ_S	Switzerland	0.01	0.04
ΔE	Switzerland	0.42	0.42
ΔZ_{UK}	UK	0.28	0.61
ΔE	UK	0.22	0.11

B = Belgium	N = The Netherlands
F = France	S = Switzerland
G = W. Germany	UK = United Kingdom
I = Italy	

The results show that in the absence of sterilisation policies individual monetary authorities have no significant influence on their own monetary base, with the exception of Germany and the United Kingdom. They also show that the changes in European reserves induced by US monetary policies are the most important variable to explain the national monetary base for all countries except the United Kingdom. Partial sterilisation policies ($h_i = -0.50$) increase the impact monetary authorities can exert on the national monetary base in a significant way for most 'large' European countries (Germany, Italy, the United Kingdom). For the 'small' European countries (Belgium, Nertherlands, Switzerland), this is not the case: partial sterilisation at a rate of 50 per cent does not allow those countries to obtain monetary independence in any significant way.

Partial sterilisation by European countries significantly reduces the overwhelming influence of the US monetary policy on the national monetary base. However, US monetary policy remains the most important factor in the explanation of the national monetary bases in five out of seven countries (the exceptions are Germany and the United Kingdom). The case of France is worth a few additional comments. It is rather surprising to find that in this simulation France's monetary authorities are no more successful to exert an influence on their own monetary base than, for example, Switzerland. The reason for this can be found in the fact that over the period considered (1960–68) exogenous changes in France's domestic component of the monetary base have on the average moved in the opposite direction with the exogenous changes in the supply of reserves to Europe. The correlation coefficient between both variables was found to be -0.63.

This result for France shows that a country whose monetary policies are substantially out of line with monetary policies elsewhere in the system will find the effectiveness of its monetary policies in controlling its monetary base greatly reduced. It also indicates that the effectiveness of monetary policies cannot be judged from the size of a country's leakage (a_0 and a_1) alone. It has to be evaluated in the context of an interdependent system, where the actions of other countries' monetary authorities help to determine the effectiveness of monetary policies in a particular country.[31] The actions of the US monetary authorities seem to be the most important in this context.

(2) SIMULATION OF THE MODEL WITH VARIABLE DOLLAR EXCHANGE RATE
(SYSTEM (34)–(36), (37))

(a) Stability of the reserve flows and the dollar exchange rate
The results are summarised in Tables 4 and 5. A comparison of Table 4 with Table 2 (the case of fixed dollar exchange rate) shows almost identical results. This means that the introduction of a joint floating of all European currencies *vis-à-vis* the US dollar does not change the stability characteristics of the system as far as reserve flows are concerned. In other words, if sterilisation policies lead to explosive reserve flows in Europe in the absence of joint floating, the same policies will lead to explosive reserve flows when joint floating occurs.

This result means that the introduction of joint floating does not substantially alter the policy conflicts in Europe implied by the use of sterilisation policies by two or more countries. Variations in the dollar exchange rate cannot eliminate intra-European conflicts of policies, in the same way as variations in the total level of European reserves cannot eliminate intra-European conflicts of policies when the dollar exchange rate is fixed. The use of sterilisation policies will lead to the same kind of instability, whether the dollar exchange rate is fixed or flexible.

Table 4   Time path of European reserve flows under joint floating (Simulation over 30 quarters; US monetary impulse = $750 million)

	Full sterilisation ($h_i = -1$)		Partial sterilisation ($h_i = -0.5$)	No sterilisation ($h_i = 0.0$)
	All countries	France and Germany	All countries	All countries
$\varepsilon_i = 0.20$	Explosive	Convergence beyond simulation period	Convergence after 5 quarters	Convergence after 2 quarters
$\varepsilon_i = 0.40$	Explosive	Convergence beyond simulation period	Convergence after 4 quarters	Convergence after 2 quarters
$\varepsilon_i = 0.60$	Convergence beyond simulation period	Convergence beyond simulation period	Convergence after 4 quarters	Convergence after 2 quarters

The results of Table 5 indicate that instability of reserve flows and instability of the dollar exchange rate occur simultaneously. Policy conflicts induced by the use of sterilisation policies will lead to unstable reserve flows and an unstable dollar exchange rate.

However, the instability of intra-European reserve flows dominates the instability of the dollar exchange rate. Whereas in the extreme case of full sterilisation by all countries, several countries run out of reserves after six quarters, the quarterly variations of the dollar exchange rate attain significant proportions (more than 10 per cent) after twenty quarters.

These results can be explained as follows. Unstable reserve flows resulting from conflicts of policies in Europe offset each other on an aggregate European level, so that the aggregate European variables follow a perfectly stable path. However, the leakages of individual European countries with the US are not the same; for example, an expansionary monetary policy in Germany may have a relatively higher impact on the dollar exchange rate than a same expansionary monetary policy in France. As a result changes in monetary policies in different European countries which on an aggregate European level may exactly offset each other will have a net (positive or negative) effect on the dollar exchange rate. Therefore instability of the system will ultimately be reflected in an unstable dollar exchange rate.

(c) European Monetary Independence

It will be clear from the theoretical model developed earlier in this chapter that the existence of joint floating of the European currencies *vis à vis* the dollar effectively insulates the European monetary base from outside disturbances, *in casu* from US monetary policies.

Table 5 Time path of dollar exchange rate (Simulation over 30 quarters; US monetary impulse = $750 million)

	Full sterilisation ($h_i = -1$)		Partial sterilisation ($h_i = -0.5$)	No sterilisation ($h_i = 0.0$)
	All countries	France and Germany	All countries	All countries
$\varepsilon_i = 0.20$	Explosive	Convergence after 20 quarters	Convergence after 4 quarters	Convergence after 2 quarters
$\varepsilon_i = 0.40$	Explosive	Convergence after 18 quarters	Convergence after 4 quarters	Convergence after 2 quarters
$\varepsilon_i = 0.60$	Convergence beyond simulation period	Convergence after 15 quarters	Convergence after 4 quarters	Convergence after 2 quarters

The question, however, arises to what extent the US monetary policies may affect the monetary base of individual countries. As has been shown in Section II, structural differences in the relations between individual European countries and the US reintroduces the US monetary policy as an exogenous variable in the explanation of the monetary base of individual countries.

The tests performed here were identical to the ones performed in the previous subsection, where they have been described in detail.[32] The results are presented in Table 6. They show that despite joint floating the US monetary policy variable remains an important variable in the explanation of the monetary base in individual countries. In four out of seven countries (Belgium, France, Netherlands, Switzerland) the dropping of the US monetary policy variable leads to a substantial loss in explanation of the simulated national monetary base. In these four countries the introduction of joint floating does not significantly increase the control monetary authorities have over the national monetary base.[33] Only in three countries (Germany, Italy and the United Kingdom) does the introduction of joint floating allow these countries to increase the control over their monetary base at the expense of the US monetary policy variable.

Table 6   Loss in explanation of simulated monetary base due to the omission of an exogenous variable (joint floating)

Variable dropped	National monetary base	$h_i = 0$	$h_i = -0.5$
ΔZ_B	Belgium	0.01	0.01
ΔE_a	Belgium	0.39	0.41
ΔZ_F	France	0.03	0.03
ΔE_a	France	0.29	0.35
ΔZ_G	Germany	0.70	0.76
ΔE_a	Germany	0.07	0.05
ΔZ_N	Netherlands	0.01	0.01
ΔE_a	Netherlands	0.37	0.40
ΔZ_I	Italy	0.25	0.25
ΔE_a	Italy	0.05	0.03
ΔZ_S	Switzerland	0.01	0.01
ΔE_a	Switzerland	0.45	0.52
ΔZ_{UK}	United Kingdom	0.39	0.49
ΔE_a	United Kingdom	0.10	0.04

These results can be interpreted as follows. Assuming, as we have done, that the elasticities γ_i are equal for all European countries a difference in the vectors e and m in (24) is the result of differences in relative openness of European countries *vis-à-vis* the US. As long as such differences exist expansionary (contractionary) US monetary policies are not neutral as far as their effect on the distribution of reserves in Europe is concerned. In fact, since Europe as a whole cannot gain or lose reserves due to the joint floating, any change in US monetary policy must lead to a net reserve loss for some countries and a corresponding reserve gain for other countries.[34] As a result a change in US monetary policy will be inflationary for some and deflationary for other European countries when they jointly float their currencies *vis-à-vis* the dollar.

VI   CONCLUSION
The main results of this study can be summarised as follows. First, the systematic use of sterilisation policies by two or more countries in order

to offset the monetary effects of balance of payments disequilibria may lead to explosive reserve flows and, therefore, to the breakdown of the system. Second, in the cases where those policies do not lead to unstable reserve flows (i.e. in the cases of partial sterilisation policies) their effectiveness is extremely limited. Third, although some larger European countries may gain some degree of monetary independence by the use of these policies, it appears that this is only true if the course of the monetary policies in these countries is not too far out of line with monetary policies in the rest of the system, and especially with US monetary policies. Therefore, attempts to use sterilisation policies in situations where a country wants to pursue substantially different monetary policies than in the rest of the system have to fail.

These conclusions are not substantially altered by the introduction of joint floating of European currencies. Attempts by national monetary authorities to insulate their money markets by sterilisation policies lead to explosive reserve flows. In addition, although joint floating insulates the total European monetary base from external (US) influences, it does not do so for individual European countries. Finally, although larger European countries do gain some degree of monetary independence by the device of joint floating, small countries (Belgium, Netherlands, Switzerland) do not increase their control over the monetary base in any significant way.

NOTES

1. De Grauwe (1975).
2. More on this inverse relationship between domestic and foreign component of the monetary base below.
3. In the absence of sterilisation policies. It should also be pointed out that if commercial banks can substantially change the total domestic liquidity by their borrowing and lending activities in foreign currencies, the concept of the monetary base as consisting of high-powered money issued by the monetary authorities becomes less useful. This problem will be disregarded here, mainly because most national monetary authorities have long since taken steps to control the net foreign position of commercial banks. See *Annual Report on Exchange Restrictions* by the International Monetary Fund.
4. If the European monetary authorities acquire US Treasury securities in the open market (through the Federal Reserve Bank of New York), there will be no effect on the US monetary base. The open-market transaction restores the liquidity position of the US banking system which had declined as a result of the accumulation of deposits by European monetary authorities at the Federal Reserve Bank of New York. However, if the US deficit is financed by the issue of US Treasury bills to European monetary authorities *and* if the US Treasury uses the proceeds from this sale to *increase* its deposits at the Federal Reserve, the US monetary base will be affected (Burger and Balbach (1972) p. 13).
5. If the Federal Reserve does not neutralise these changes.
6. Without loss of generality one can assume that the $n+1$ currencies relate to each other as one to one.

7. See Mundell (1962), Sohmen (1967), Johnson (1965).

8. In the absence of speculation it will be assumed that $-1 \leq \dfrac{\partial R_i}{\partial D_i} \leq 0$. If speculation occurs, a situation could arise where $\dfrac{\partial R_i}{\partial D_i} < -1$.

9. Strictly, $E_j = \dfrac{\partial E}{\partial D_j}$ where $E = \sum\limits_{i=1}^{n} R_i$. Therefore E has to be interpreted as the level of net European reserves. It is a function of the same variables as R_i, i.e. $E = E(D_1, \ldots, D_n, D_{n+1})$.

10. Assuming that the European currencies relate to each other as one to one, the dollar exchange rate is the same for all countries.

11. $E_f(\quad)$ is the equivalent of the function $E(\quad)$ in the model with fixed dollar rate. See note 9.

12. $\sum\limits_{i} m_i = \dfrac{1}{1+\gamma} \sum\limits_{i} \left(1 + \gamma_i\right) \dfrac{R_{fi}}{E_f} = \dfrac{1}{1+\gamma} \left(1 + \dfrac{K}{E_f} \sum\limits_{i} \dfrac{\partial R_{fi}}{\partial K}\right) = \dfrac{1}{1+\gamma} \left(1 + \dfrac{K}{E_f} \dfrac{\partial E_f}{\partial K}\right) = 1.$

13. The results of the simulations have been subjected to a sensitivity test so as to find out to what extent they change with changes in the numerical values given to the coefficients of the model.

14. For some detail about the bias this procedure introduces see De Grauwe (1975), pp. 212–13. It is shown there that this procedure *under* estimates the true interdependence.

15. This variable is introduced here as an approximation of ΔE_{at} in (8). Since the US monetary policy variable can be expected to be the most important variable explaining the observed changes in total European reserves, during the sample period, the bias introduced here is probably small. In any case, it does not affect the estimation of a_{i0} and a_{i1}. See, e.g. Christ (1966) p. 389.

16. A statistical description of the data can be found in De Grauwe (1975) p. 227.

17. An extensive sensitivity analysis was performed in order to find out how the results of the simulations, reported in the next section were altered by different assumptions concerning the off-diagonal elements of A_0 and A_1, as well as the vector e. Different alternative indicators of relative size were chosen such as money supplies, stock of foreign reserves. In addition, substantial changes in the structure of these matrices were introduced, e.g. to reflect the relative importance of Switzerland as a financial centre. These changes, however, did not alter the basic results as reported in the next section.

18. This assumption is made here for purposes of simplicity. A sensitivity test indicated that it did not substantially change the simulation results reported in Section V. For instance, using the Houthakker and Magee (1969) estimates of the regional US export and import elasticities as proxies for γ_i, the simulation results were basically unaltered.

19. This procedure implies a different estimate of e_i than in model I.

20. See Nurkse (1944) for extensive evidence, pp. 73–88.

21. See Bloomfield (1959) pp. 47–51. The author suggests that during this period sterilisation was mainly of the passive kind and not the result of deliberate intervention of the central banks; Bloomfield (1959) p. 50.

22. See, e.g., Michaely (1971) p. 40; also Katz (1969) pp. 32–3.

23. See Argy and Kouri (1972). The fact that estimates of the sterilisation parameters for other countries turn out to be insignificant does not mean that sterilisation policies were not used. Non-significant estimates may be the result of variations in the degree of sterilisation through the sampling period. In general attempts at estimating policy reaction functions such as sterilisation functions, fail to produce significant estimates because of the unstable character of these functions.

24. If the quarterly exogenous supply of reserves is put at a lower value, Italy will run out of reserves even faster, as will France.

25. This result is similar to a result obtained by Swoboda (1970) in a Keynesian-type two-country model. Swoboda finds that the sterilising country determines the 'world'

interest rate. The non-sterilising country cannot influence the 'world' interest rate nor its own income. See also Aghevli and Borts (1973).

26. See Cooper (1969) for a general statement of instability resulting from policy conflicts in an interdependent world.

27. This would be compensated by a higher instability of reserve flows between the US and the European countries, if the relation between the US and the European countries were symmetrical rather than asymmetrical, as has been assumed.

28. Provided, of course, that domestic monetary policies are not too divergent. In the simulation average changes in the domestic component of the monetary base during the period 1965–70 were used. These did not reveal problems arising from the non-negativity constraints on reserve stocks, except when the exogenous supply of reserves was set at zero. But even in the latter case the quarterly reserve losses of France and Italy were found to be relatively low, so that no immediate danger of running out of reserves exists. It is clear, though, that in this case an adjustment of some kind (exchange rates, monetary policies) must occur sooner or later.

29. See McKinnon (1973) for a similar suggestion.

30. This R^2 is equal to 1 since the simulated model is deterministic.

31. It may be noted here that for other periods one may find that say Germany's monetary authorities have particularly failed to control their monetary base. In 1969–71, for example, when the German authorities tried to have domestic interest rates substantially out of line with the rest of the world, this failure is blatant (for evidence see McClam (1972) pp. 11–13).

32. See Section V 1(*b*).

33. Compare Table 6 with Table 3 (p. 196).

34. This may not be the case if Europe creates its own reserves. However, the US monetary policy would still influence the distribution of reserves in Europe.

REFERENCES

Aghevli, B. B. and G. H. Borts, 'The Stability and Equilibrium of the Balance of Payments under a Fixed Exchange Rate', *Journal of International Economics* (Mar 1973) 1–20.

Argy, V. and P. Kouri, 'Sterilisation Policies and the Volatility in International Reserves', preliminary draft IMF (1972).

Bloomfield, A. J., *Monetary Policy under the International Gold Standard, 1880–1914* (New York 1959) 62 pp.

Burger, A. E. and A. Balbach, 'Measurement of the Domestic Money Stock', *Review*, Federal Reserve Bank of St Louis (May 1972).

Christ, C. F., *Econometric Models and Methods* (New York 1966) 705 pp.

Cooper, R., 'Macroeconomic Policy Adjustment in Interdependent Economies', *Quarterly Journal of Economics* (Feb 1969).

De Grauwe, P., 'The Interaction of Monetary Policies in a Group of European Countries', *Journal of International Economics*, 5 (1975) 207–28.

—*Monetary Interdependence and International Monetary Reform. A European Case Study* (Saxon House, Westmead, 1976).

Houthakker, H. and Magee, S., 'Income and Price Elasticities in World Trade', *Review of Economics and Statistics* (May 1969) pp. 121–5.

International Monetary Fund (various issues), *Annual Report on Exchange Restrictions*.

Johnson, H. G., 'Some Aspects of the Theory of Economic Policy in a World of Capital Mobility', *Rivista Internazionale di Scienze Economiche e Commerciali*, no. 6 (1965).

Katz, S., 'External Surpluses, Capital Flows, and Credit Policy in the European Economic Community, 1958 to 1967', *Princeton Studies in International Finance*, no. 22 (1969).

McClam, W., 'Credit Substitution and the Euro-Currency Market', *Banca Nazionale del Lavoro Quarterly Review* (Sep 1972).

McKinnon, R., 'On Securing a Common Monetary Policy in Europe', *Banca Nazionale del Lavoro Quarterly Review* (Mar 1973).

Michaely, M., *The Responsiveness of Demand Policies to Balance of Payments: Postwar patterns*, National Bureau of Economic Research, (New York 1971).

Mundell, R. A., 'The Appropriate Use of Monetary and Fiscal Policy for Internal and External Stability', *IMF Staff Papers* (Mar 1962).

Nurkse, R., *International Currency Experience*, League of Nations (1944) 249 pp.

Sohmen, E., 'Fiscal and Monetary Policies under Alternative Exchange Rate Systems', *Quarterly Journal of Economics*, vol. LXXXI (1967).

Swoboda, A. K., 'Reserve Policies Currency Preferences, and International Adjustment', *Yale Economic Essays* (Spring 1970).

Viner, J., *Studies in the Theory of International Trade*, (New York 1937) 650 pp.

12 International Reserves and Capital Mobility

K. L. Mahar and M. G. Porter*

The behaviour of holdings of official reserves in western economies has long been influenced by a theoretical approach which, while relevant to the world economy in the 1940s and 1950s, is increasingly deficient. This theoretical view was one which regarded capital movements as highly 'disequilibrating' and as not being part of an efficient adjustment process. This assumption was accepted as valid in the post-war period no doubt because international capital markets were imperfect and distorted, partly because of the official acceptance of the 'disequilibrating' hypothesis. It may be useful to contrast this dominant view with an approach which takes into account both the increasing integration of national capital markets and the monetary approach to balance of payments theory. It is the major purpose of this paper to consider some of the consequences of this 'new' view for domestic and international economic policy.

The 'old' view may be summarised as follows:

(1) Official reserves are used to finance current account fluctuations, e.g. reserve fluctuations represent a manifestation of an excess demand for *goods*.

(2) There exists a desired level, or range, of official reserves which is a function of the level and variance of current account payments, reflecting transactions and precautionary needs.

(3) The composition, but not the level, of reserves is determined by relative rates of return on alternative foreign securities.

(4) It is appropriate to use fiscal and monetary policies to adjust the level of GNP so as to keep the level of reserves in this desired range.

* Priorities Review Staff, Australian Government, on leave from the Reserve Bank of Australia and the Australian National University, respectively.

(5) Capital flows are a major source of reserve and exchange rate instability.

(6) There is a need for conscious international policy aimed at creating optimal reserves through controlled variations in the stock of, say, SDRs.

This 'old' view is not to be taken lightly since, for example, the symposium on international reserves held by the IMF (1970), made it quite apparent that it continues to dominate official and academic thinking, with significant exceptions at that conference being the articles or comments of McKinnon, Salant, Johnson and Sohmen. The role of the capital account in the adjustment process has been virtually ignored in most recent literature. For example the literature on international reserves as summarised by Hipple (1974), Williamson (1973) and Grubel (1971), implicitly rejects the possibility that efficient capital markets may obviate most of the demand for official reserves. Most empirical studies also appear to ignore the importance of capital mobility; see, for example, IMF (1970), Frenkel (1974).

The extent to which this view directs controlled changes in GNP to adjustments in the desired level of reserves is exemplified in the Clark (1970) model, which we take to be a representative and rigorous statement of the 'old view'. In its simple, non-stochastic form the Clark model argues that there is a desired level of reserves, and the level of GNP is a 'control' exercised via fiscal or monetary policy by which the government regulates imports, so adjusting reserves:

i.e. $S_t^* = (R_t^* - R_{t-1})$
and $S_t^* = X_t - mY_t$

where R^* is desired level of reserves;
         R is actual level of reserves;
         S^* is required adjustment in trade balance;
         S is actual adjustment of reserves;
         X = exports (assumed exogenous);
and mY = imports (m is also exogenous).

Solving this model yields a desired level of GNP at which the government should presumably direct its expenditure-changing monetary and/or fiscal policies.

i.e. $(R_t^* - R_{t-1}) = X_t - mY_t$
hence $Y_t = \lambda[(R_{t-1} - R_t^*) - X_t]/m$

Thus the 'desired' adjustment of the domestic level of GNP depends on: (1) the discrepancy between desired and actual reserves, (2) the (expected) flow of exports, (3) the marginal propensity to import and (4) the 'adjustment coefficient'. This coefficient λ in turn, reflects both the willingness of the government to allow a greater variance in income and the returns from holding reserves. The higher the aversion to fluctuations in income, the slower the speed of adjustment. The higher is the yield on reserves then the lower the adjustment cost, and hence the more rapid should be the response of expenditure-adjusting policies. The essence of the old view is that it involves the real economy adjusting to the existing exchange rate, at speeds reflecting the willingness of the authorities to sacrifice or create jobs so as to adjust international reserves. The tail wags the dog.

STOCHASTIC ELEMENTS
The old view typically insists that capital flows are a nuisance which cause undesired fluctuations in the level of reserves. Kenen and Yudin (1965) postulate that fluctuations in reserve holdings can, like other inventory holdings, be described by a simple Markov process:

$$\Delta R_t = \rho \Delta R_{t1} + \varepsilon_t$$

where $\quad 0 < \rho < 1$

and $\quad \varepsilon_t \sim N(\bar{\varepsilon}, b_\varepsilon^{\,2})$

The empirical evidence in favour of this statistical hypothesis is at best shaky; however adaptations of this methodology continue to dominate the literature in this field. Archibald and Richmond (1971) modify the procedure so as to allow for heteroscedasticity (since there is a presumption of non-constancy in the variance of the residual term over time) and they also direct attention to the probability of running out of reserves.

Hipple in his useful summary of the 'disturbances' approach to reserves, postulates a demand function for reserves of the form:

$$E(R) = R(Q, H, A, W)$$

where $\quad Q$ = measure of disturbances
$\qquad\;\; W$ = national wealth
$\qquad\;\; H$ = cost of holding reserves
$\qquad\;\; A$ = cost of adjustment to disturbances.

He refines the model by allowing for lagged adjustment, etc., but, never really questions the behavioural assumptions.

While all the above authors are conscious of the purely statistical, as opposed to behavioural, nature of their hypothesis they nevertheless suggest that the analysis has implications for the determination of the desired level of actual reserves. It cannot be denied that reserves *are* an inventory that enable their holders to 'buy time' rather than impose other socially expensive policies, and that, therefore, inventory theory such as that of Whitin (1953) is applicable. However by ignoring the more basic determinants of reserve fluctuations it is clear that this approach may offer misleading guidance as to the desired level of reserves. The extent to which this approach may mislead is illustrated by its application in the Clark (1970) model.

In terms of the simple version of the Clark model, the required or preferred adjustment in reserves (via imports) is:

$$S_t = S^*_t + \varepsilon_t$$

where the random element, ε_t, is taken to be short-term capital flow. Clark analyses 'optimal' policies, according to the nature of the assumptions regarding the probability distribution of ε_t, costs of adjustment, etc. There is a search for policy rules which reduce the probability of running out of reserves below x per cent, where x reflects the maximum acceptable risk. The view of the residual is that there is a strong *positive* correlation between the trade balance $(X_t - mY_t)$ and ε_t or ε_{t-1}, so that a trade deficit implies capital *outflow*; thus correction of current account behaviour is seen as critical to the maintenance of desired reserves. However, it is the essence of what we would label the 'new view' that if the exchange rate is at its equilibrium value, as assumed by the 'old viewers', then ε_t has an expected value which is not only non-zero, but equals $-(X_t - mY_t)$, so long as capital markets are not distorted.

i.e. $E(X_t - mY_t + \varepsilon_t) = 0.$

We will return to the theoretical and empirical evidence for this below. For the present it is perhaps sufficient to argue that the 'old view' made no proper allowance for capital flows nor for the intertemporal implications of free trade, since it was rooted in the 'Keynesian' adjustment process by which all conscious adjustment of the balance of payments was through expenditure-changing strategies.

THE NEW VIEW

By contrast, proper consideration of both the impact of efficient capital markets and the appropriate assignment of monetary policy suggests a view along the following lines:

(1) Observed changes in reserves reflect an excess demand for *money* balances, rather than goods – i.e. changes in the net holdings of foreign money balances reflect changes in domestic money supply and demand, and can be corrected by monetary policy, e.g. by changing the domestic monetary base, the domestic interest rate or the domestic price of foreign money.

(2) Trade fluctuations will, in Fisherian style, tend to be automatically financed if no capital restrictions are enforced. *Private* reserve holdings or private capital flows will, if allowed, do the work currently assumed by official institutions.

(3) Observed fluctuations in reserves reflect either (i) restrictions on capital flows or interest rates; (ii) monetary policy incorrectly assigned to domestic stabilisation when fixed exchange rates are maintained; or (iii) an incorrect exchange rate – although almost any fixed rate is incorrect when (i) and (ii) occur.

(4) In the case of perfect integration (i.e. of total fixity of the exchange rate and perfect capital mobility) the need for official reserves approaches zero apart from the need for a 'war chest' to provide security against particular shortages. Such a chest need not include holdings of foreign exchange; real security, at a price, could be also obtained from a diverse portfolio of grains, fibres, minerals, etc. The need for such a 'war chest' is in any case largely independent of whether fixed or floating rates are adopted. Thus, contrary to the old view in which the choice was between a flexible exchange rate regime without reserves, and a fixed rate with reserves, the new view would insist that so long as international capital markets are allowed to do their work then the truly random component in reserves will have a low mean and variance, and the resulting need for official reserves may be very modest, under *either* fixed or floating exchange regimes.

(5) The optimal portfolio of a central bank involves a choice between foreign and domestic assets based on estimated risks and expected rates of return on *all* assets, whether gold, dollars or uranium, at home or abroad.

Varying theoretical support for such a new view can be extracted from Machlup (1966), Clower and Lipsey (1968), Mundell (1968), McKinnon (1969) and, in particular, from the monetary theory of the balance of payments (as summarised for example in Johnson (1972)). One aspect of the 'monetary' view is that fluctuations in *observed* reserves are an ex post reflection of an excess demand for money which, in many instances, is simply the outcome of misguided monetary and/or exchange rate policies. A feature of this approach is that fluctuations in the current account are a lagged response to excess demand for money and that they, in turn, tend to be offset by capital movements. As a result, foreign reserve movements will tend to adjust so that the preferred quantity of money is obtained. This is a quite different state of affairs from that set out under the old view.

THE MONETARY APPROACH TO RESERVE FLUCTUATIONS

Under this model an exogenous current account surplus, for example, increases the money supply, moderates any excess demand for money and so reduces capital inflow. Using quarterly data and with a fixed and believable exchange rate, the model predicts that capital flows will tend to offset the monetary impact of the current account unless restrained by official controls. Evidence on this for a number of countries may be found in Kouri and Porter (1974). Proponents of the new view would argue that the observed changes in reserves are equal to the gap (adjusted proportionately for the money multiplier, κ) between the domestic demand for money (assumed, for simplicity, to be a simple function of income and the level of the world interest rate) and the money supply

i.e. $\qquad \kappa(R_t - R_{t-1}) = L(Y_t, i_t) - Mo_t + \varepsilon_t$

In the short run (one quarter) the current account can be taken to be independent of monetary policy so that we can, using the Kouri – Porter (1974) model, modify the above equation so that capital flows are a function of all exogenous sources of change in the excess demand for money in the quarter. This provides the following equation:

$$C_t = \alpha\Delta NDA_t + \alpha(X_t - M_t) + \beta\Delta Y + \gamma\Delta i^* + \varepsilon_t$$

where C = net capital inflow
ΔNDA = change in domestic component of the monetary base
$X - M$ = current account
Y = GNP
i^* = world interest rate.

Thus we have capital flows offsetting any excess demand for money. Where $\alpha > -1$, i.e. where trade fluctuations are not completely offset, it does not necessarily follow that reserves should be correspondingly higher, since monetary policy may be assigned to maintaining reserves.

If $\alpha > -1$ it also follows that monetary policy, such as changes in NDA, allows some independent variation in the money supply and hence the interest rate. However, for every \$1,000m sales (or purchases) of bonds by the central bank there will be induced capital inflow (outflow) of about \$500m in the case of estimates for Australia and \$800m in the case of Germany. Thus a period of monetary expansion (restriction) can rapidly cause a loss (gain) of reserves, which in turn may induce destabilising speculative flow of capital.

The above example does spell out one role for international reserves – namely that in the short run they buy time to facilitate an independent monetary policy in those countries still 'blessed' with offset coefficients (α) which are small. The only question is the length of this 'short run' and the true marginal offset coefficients. Increasingly, the empirical evidence suggests that, with a fixed exchange rate and fluctuating conditions in international money markets, reserves and capital market restraints are an inferior substitute for the alternative policy of flexible exchange rates, and a genuinely independent monetary policy.

In the case where the authorities allow freedom of capital movement and investors view securities as being perfect substitutes, then the offset is perfect, i.e. $\alpha \rightarrow -1$, and reserves are unnecessary to finance trade fluctuations. But on the other hand monetary policy is no longer available as a tool of domestic stabilisation. Of course, within currency areas, such as nations, it is self-evident that fixed exchange rates make reserves unnecessary and monetary policy infeasible, but this lesson appears far from understood in countries which are increasingly approximating the conditions of full financial integration but for government interference. Thus under a fixed exchange regime we continue to live with the 'knife-edge' problem of destabilising speculation and reserve instability, where domestic interest rates are prevented, by sterilisation policies, from reflecting the effect of reserve changes on the money supply.

STOCHASTIC ELEMENTS

Let us consider random fluctuations in exports, imports, income, the demand for money and the official supply of money, ΔNDA. In all of these cases random fluctuations will, given capital mobility, tend to induce capital movements which reduce the excess demand for money to zero. Inserting the error terms we obtain:

$$
\begin{aligned}
C_t = &\alpha(\Delta NDA_t + \mu_{1t}) + \alpha(X_t - M_t + \mu_{2t}) \\
&+ \beta(\Delta Y_t + \mu_{3t}) + \gamma(\Delta_i{}^* + \mu_{4t})
\end{aligned}
$$

where μ_1, μ_2, μ_3 and μ_4 represent unanticipated fluctuations in the official domestic source of money, the current account, income and the world interest rate, respectively. In each case capital flows respond to the aggregate excess demand for money – which incorporates the aggregate of the random elements μ_1 to μ_4. Thus capital movements will, unless distorted by controls, *stabilise* the domestic economy in those instances where fluctuations in the excess demand for money would otherwise disrupt the real economy. This is in accordance, for example, with the evidence of McKinnon (1972) that openness tends to be a source of stability in the domestic economy.

If the disturbance term is the fluctuation in foreign interest rates, Δi^*, then there is a choice between sharing the world experience, i.e. adjusting the domestic component of the money supply, ΔNDA, such that capital flows do not occur, or adjusting the (rate of change of the) exchange rate. Since the fluctuation in the world interest rate has two components, real and nominal
(i.e. $\Delta i^* = \Delta r + \Delta \rho^{\cdot e}$, where r = real interest rate, $\rho^{\cdot e}$ = expected percentage change in world prices), it can be argued that optimal policy, for a small economy with a goal of price stability, would be to adjust domestic interest rates, i, *only* to Δr, since the fluctuations in the actual (and expected) world price level should be reflected in the spot (and forward) exchange rate.[1] Where the exchange rate is fixed, the impact of such an independent interest rate policy would be self defeating, and would involve destabilising flows of international capital.

If, then, increasing capital market integration implies the possibility of dispensing with a reserve oriented approach to domestic economic policy, and if fluctuations in current account movements are largely irrelevant to desired reserve holdings, what should determine the policy of the domestic authorities with respect to their behaviour in international capital markets?

THE PORTFOLIO APPROACH TO INTERNATIONAL RESERVES

The present state of the traditional view is well presented by Makin (1971) in an article which considers a portfolio model for reserve asset holdings, and suggests that central banks are not indifferent to the composition of their international reserves. Such an approach is valuable, but is excessively constrained. The assumption remains, in this literature, that the size of the total resource portfolio of the central bank, is or should be, set by the expected behaviour of the current account. Britto and Heller (1973) relax this constraint, but still constrain reserves to be non-negative, and restricted to financial assets, i.e. the portfolio manager is constrained to be a net holder of securities in *each* market. The importance of these limitations become clearer if we re-examine the concept of reserves.

In at least one sense, global reserves of any financial asset are always equal to zero since any financial asset is always the financial liability of the issuer. In this sense, the reserve currency countries are holding negative reserves. Again, the reserve position of any country may alter as the definition of reserves is extended to include financial assets which mature over longer or even indeterminate periods. Thus a positive short-term position may be completely offset by long-term liabilities even if the private sector's holdings or liabilities are ignored; and as soon as we drop the emphasis on official holdings we may have a total picture which both conflicts with, and exceeds by some orders of magnitude, the official statistics.

If corresponding liabilities are neglected all countries will of necessity be holding positive reserves, but these figures will be relatively meaningless – for example, world reserves could be doubled by a swap between Haiti and the Dominican Republic. The above points are obvious, and have been made in the past by Machlup (1966) and others, but it is unfortunately necessary to reiterate them in order to draw attention to the relevance of official and unofficial liabilities for the international capital market.

In so far as the authorities of any country are concerned with the problem of minimising the transactions and information costs of international trade, they are concerned at bottom with the costs and availability of credit on international financial markets and the predictability of prices, including foreign exchange.[2] The fundamental problem, when considering the optimal level of international reserves, is the determination of the optimal level of net foreign reserves, official and private, for the society as a whole – or the net financial indebtedness or credit of the society relative to the rest of the world. In a society which is attempting to maximise the combined utility derived from all resources, over time, the most relevant variables are going to be the expected real rates of return (allowing for transactions costs) which may be obtained by investment of resources within the society or elsewhere, and the relative risks and covariances attaching to those rates of return.

While portfolio theory allows for a simple solution to the problem of utility maximisation when rates of return and risk (variance) are given for several markets, the answer is usually constrained to non-negative holdings in each market. An answer can also be obtained when borrowing on *any* or *all* markets is permitted. The portfolio in this case consists of the entire resource set available to the society: we have that the expected end period value of a portfolio $x_1 + x_2$ is

$$u = x_1(1 + r_1) + x_2(1 + r_2)$$

where x_1 is the amount invested at home, at rate r_1
               x_2 is the amount invested abroad, at rate r_2.

The variance of u is

$$\sigma_u^2 = x_1^2 \sigma_1^2 + x_2^2 \sigma_2^2 + 2 x_1 x_2 \sigma_1 \sigma_2 \rho_{12}$$

where σ_1^2 is the variance of r_1
               σ_2^2 is the variance of r_2
               ρ_{12} is the correlation coefficient of r_1 and r_2.

For the portfolio manager we have a (reduced form) utility function of the form:

$$U = U(u, \sigma^2)$$

where $\dfrac{dU}{du} > 0, \dfrac{dU}{d\sigma} < 0$

so that the manager is a risk averter who seeks to maximise his utility, given uncertainty. We now introduce the possibility that while $x_1 + x_2 = 1$, that x_1 or x_2 may exceed 1; i.e. of borrowing at r_1 and lending at r_2. Optimal foreign reserves would be negative if the preferred mix of portfolio yield and variance required $x_1 > 1$, financed by net central bank borrowing. This outcome is not allowed in the conventional model. In terms of Figure 1, A and B define the risk and return from the investment of his equity in either market A or B yielding r_1 and r_2 respectively. Our quite simple point is that the possibility frontier facing any nation, goes through B, and is not constrained to points in ACB. The curve is linear through B if $\rho = 1$ (i.e. ABD)

The interesting point arising out of this is that, given a likely utility function, it may become attractive to move *more* than net equity into any one market. This point is highly relevant to the game of international reserve management. Suppose we consider market A to represent the market for US securities, market B the financial market for investment in either Australian minerals, grain and wool. The correlation between Australian and foreign yields is likely to be positive, and may be quite high. There is thus no reason to believe that optimality necessarily consists, for the society, in balancing resources between domestic investment and foreign securities in such a way that each section of the portfolio is positive; i.e. we shuld not constrain investment to the interior of *ACB*. As an example Australia might hold negative official balances of foreign exchange, with our real stock of claims on foreign commodities being the market value of realisable *claims* against tradeable reserves such as coal.

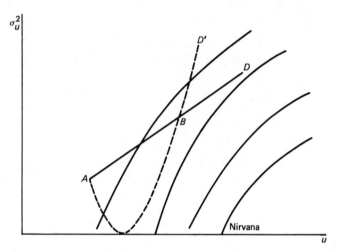

Figure 1

OFFICIAL VERSUS PRIVATE RESERVES

Suppose then that the best return to the society, in terms of its own risk-return preferences, is a position in which it is a net debtor on world financial markets. In a non-controlled foreign securities market, the bulk of the borrowing and reserve holding might still be done by the private market. But this situation could be complicated by a number of factors. There may be costs of intermediation, causing the borrower to face higher rates than the lender. This will serve to kink each portfolio possibility frontier at *B*, increasing the slope above that point, and lowering the risk-return point at which constrained maximisation occurs. Larger official institutions, such as central banks, may, through economies of scale, particularly as regards information costs, be able to reduce the costs of intermediation. It is also possible that large official holdings of reserves may indicate credit worthiness and allow borrowing at superior terms when it is needed. More interestingly, a central bank or official holder/disburser of reserves may be able to correct for divergence between the private rate of return and the social rate of return on either market. Thus a desirable situation might be one in which the only intervention of the central bank in the international finance market occurs to correct for differences between private and social rates of return through open-market operations, say, in uranium futures. These would be justified if the private market were viewed having a distorted view of future relative to current prices for uranium.

Some further complications arise if we increase the size of the central bank portfolio (or the social portfolio the central bank seeks to adjust) relative to the markets considered. In the Australian case, the impact on market A (US securities) is likely to be small – major shifts in Australian holdings would have relatively little impact on rates of return there. However the rate of return in B (domestic investment) would be likely to fall as resources were shifted massively into this market. Thus we have the rather more realistic yield function, based on

$$r_1 = f(x_i),$$

of the form $\quad u = x_1(1 + f(x_1)) + x_2(1 + f(x_2))$
where $f(x)$ reflects the saturation and floor rates in each market.

THE WAR CHEST
Governments may also intervene to hold financial assets, easily bartered commodities (e.g. gold) or strategic resource stockpiles when they fear that political developments will prevent the normal market mechanisms from operating effectively. We could rephrase this to state that national governments may have a very high expected own rate of return on certain resources, or that their view of the future differs markedly from that implied by the spot and futures markets.

TRANSACTIONS BALANCES
Given a solution to the major portfolio problem of the society, i.e. our correct mix of stocks of financial and real assets, and assuming that the central monetary authority is able to correct for the deficiencies of the private sector, there is the secondary and narrower problem of the extent to which liquid financial assets should be held to minimise transactions costs. This is the problem which Kenen and Yudin (1965), Archibald and Richmond (1971) and Clark (1970) have analysed, without considering the broader implications of capital markets' financing of trade fluctuations.

One consequence of the 'new' view is the recognition of the fact that, with fixed rates and free capital markets, this problem is analogous to the transactions balance that, say, California faces in its dealings with the rest of the United States.

There is, in principle, no reason why all transactions could not be financed on a credit base, each transaction immediately having attributed a financing price reflecting credit rating and prevailing interest costs. In practice, such a system (given finite velocities arising out of administrative complexities) is unattainable. The usual system within an economy is a mix in which some transactions balances are held to cover the very short periods over which the administration of financing is more expensive than the opportunity cost of holding transactions balances. In a system in which there exists no 'outside' money, e.g. in the international monetary system, the cost of holding the transactions balance translates into the opportunity cost of resources sold to acquire balances (Australia's case) or the cost of inducing foreign countries to advance a loan (the US case).

The period in which the capital market is likely to respond will be fairly short, if we are to judge from the behaviour of capital flows as estimated in Kouri and Porter (1974), so the necessary or desirable transactions balance is likely to be only a fraction of present reserve holdings. If, then, increasing financial integration of capital markets reduces the transactions demand for reserves, what are the likely consequences of existing reserves for the international monetary system?

EXCESS RESERVES
Over the last few decades we have witnessed a predictable increase in world velocity of payments, except that the trend has been reversed since 1969. Since then a considerable expansion of the ratio of real reserves to trade has occurred, partly as a result of US payments deficit, partly as a result of SDR creation, partly as a result of the rapid increase in the value of gold holdings, and partly through Eurodollar credit creation. Table 1 gives world reserves, (unadjusted, and adjusted for the market valuation (Table 2) of gold stocks), world imports and velocities relevant to both measures of reserves. A trend line for velocity, calculated from 1959 to 1969, was extrapolated to give a rough approximation to desired reserve holdings; for 1970–3, and these data are presented in columns 6 and 7 for the alternative reserve valuation assumption.

A real balance approach, i.e. the assumed existence of a stable demand function for real international reserves, would suggest that countries would attempt to run down these excess real reserves to trend values. In a world in which the reserve currency nations were already operating at or near capacity this appears possible only by a world inflation, since (competitive) revaluation of currencies does not serve to remove excess balances. Other options include floating since this could remove the problem of excess reserves if private demands for foreign balances turn out to exceed (earlier) official demands (and perhaps this would be the case given the presence of economies of scale in holding money balances). Another possibility is that the reserve currency countries pay a sufficiently large interest bill to increase the demand for reserve holdings. Devaluation by reserve currency countries implies a higher level of net exports in these countries and a tight domestic fiscal – monetary mix to sterilise the monetary inflow. Either course of action must of necessity involve a reduction in domestic standards of living in the reserve centre. The national political costs of such action would appear to rule out these alternatives as potential policies.

Table 1   *Actual and trend reserves*

	1	2	3	4	5	6	7
	Reserves US\$ billion (notional)	Reserves adjusted for gold price	Imports US\$ billion	Velocity (a) $3 \div 1$	Velocity (b) $3 \div 2$	'Trend' reserves using (a)	using (b)
1950	49.0	49.0	58.2	1.19	1.19		
1955	54.0	54.0	88.6	1.64	1.64		
1959	57.4	57.4	106.7	1.86	1.86		
60	60.3	60.3	119.4	1.98	1.98		
61	62.3	62.3	124.6	2.00	2.00		
62	62.9	62.9	132.4	2.10	2.10		
63	66.3	66.3	143.5	2.17	2.17		
64	68.5	68.5	160.8	2.35	2.35		
65	70.3	70.3	175.1	2.49	2.49		
66	72.7	72.7	192.5	2.65	2.65		
67	74.3	74.3	202.6	2.73	2.73		
68	77.4	84.8	225.2	2.91	2.65		
69	78.3	78.3	256.7	3.28	3.28		
70	92.7	95.0	294.3	3.18	3.10	92.0	94.3
71	130.6	140.0	329.0	2.52	2.35	98.8	101.5
72	158.7	191.5	385.0	2.43	2.01	111.3	114.6
73	183.1	277.5	521.0	2.85	1.88	145.1	149.7

Source: I.F.S. 1967 and 1974

Table 2   *London gold price US\$ per fine oz (end of year)*

1967	\$35.20
1968	41.90
1969	35.20
1970	37.38
1971	43.62
1972	64.90
1973	112.25

Source: I.F.S. 1974

The remaining alternatives are non-market sterilisation or inflation. The extent to which excess reserves, once created, translate into excess demand for goods and services will depend on the monetary strategies adopted at national levels. If the authorities continue to expand the money supply until reserves 'run out', or if the wage – price spiral flowing from earlier monetary expansion is sufficient, then the adjustment of real reserves should be fairly rapidly achieved through world inflation. The alternative of sterilisation does not seem politically feasible. But either sterilisation or inflation implies the loss of real reserves by all countries which are net creditors; and thus a tax is imposed on those countries by the reserve currency countries. The tax will be equal to the total depreciation of any increment in reserves from the date of the increment to the date at which equilibrium is reached, less interest paid on that increment (and also less the initial value of the monetary gift implied by the creation of the excess reserves, in the case of SDRs.)

SUMMARY

It is central to the established view of international reserves that capital flows are basically a nuisance from the viewpoint of foreign reserve management. What we have termed the 'new view' accepts the old idea that current account fluctuations are largely self financing, so long as capital markets are allowed to function efficiently. Thus variations in current account do not automatically create a need for official reserves.

The real blame for reserve instability is seen to lie in distortion of capital markets, and misguided monetary policy. To allow free 'spot' trade while constraining 'futures' trade, i.e. capital transactions, is contradictory, and distorts the balance of payments so creating the illusion of need for greater reserves. By imposing capital market distortions officials thus can in a sense be accused of having contrived the need for their own 'official' reserves.

The one valid case we do find for sizeable international reserves is when the 'offset coefficient' – the extent to which monetary policy induces offsetting capital movements – is small. Our difficulty is with the quantification and interpretation of this coefficient. Evidence for developed economies suggests that the offset coefficient is not small enough to allow successful independent monetary policies to be maintained for significant periods such as eighteen months. Yet monetary policies typically take that long to work, unlike the period it takes for expectations to form regarding a change in the exchange rate. Thus we would argue that the supposed independence of monetary policy which is facilitated by reserve holding is likely to be feasible only by allowing the exchange rate to vary. But this negates most of the purpose of reserves.

NOTES

1. A more complete statement of the connection between the expected time path of the exchange rate and the equilibrium term structure of interest ratios is given in Porter (1972).

2. It is barely worth reiterating that 'fixed' exchange rates do not necessarily improve the predictability of prices; some would argue they have a comparative disadvantage here.

3. In the case of minerals in the ground this yield, r_1, would reflect the expected rate of increase in mineral prices.

REFERENCES

G. C. Archibald and J. Richmond, 'On the Theory of Foreign Exchange Reserve Requirements', *Review of Economic Studies* (1971).

R. Britto and H. R. Heller, 'International Adjustment and Optimal Reserves', *International Economic Review* (Feb 1973).

P. B. Clark, 'Optimum International Reserves and the Speed of Adjustment', *Journal of Political Economy* (Mar 1970).

R. Clower and R. G. Lipsey, 'The Present State of International Liquidity', *American Economic Review* (May 1968).

J. A. Frenkel, 'The Demand for Reserves by Developed and Less Developed Countries', *Economica* (1974).

H. G. Grubel, 'The Demand for International Reserves: A Critical Review of the Literature', *Journal of Economic Literature* (Dec 1971).

F. Steb Hipple, 'The Disturbances Approach to the Demand for International Reserves', *Princeton Studies in International Finance*, No. 35 (May 1974).

International Monetary Fund, *International Reserves: Need and Availability* (IMF, Washington, D.C. 1970).

H. G. Johnson, 'The Inflation Crisis', *International Currency Review*, vol 3 (1971) and 'The Monetary Approach to Balance of Payments Theory', *Journal of Quantitative and Financial Analysis* (Mar 1972).

P. B. Kenen and E. B. Yudin, 'The Demand for International Reserves', *Review of Economics and Statistics* (Aug 1965).

P. J. K. Kouri and M. G. Porter, 'International Capital Flows and Portfolio Equilibrium', *Journal of Political Economy* (May/June 1974).

F. Machlup, 'The Need for Monetary Reserves', *Banca Nazionale del Lavoro Quarterly Review* (Sep 1966).

R. I. McKinnon, 'Portfolio Balance and International Payments and International Payments Adjustment', in R. A. Mundell and A. Swoboda, *Monetary Problems of the International Economy* (University of Chicago Press, 1969) and 'Sterilisation in three Dimensions: Major Trading Countries Eurocurrencies and the United States', in R. Z. Aliber (ed.) *National Monetary Policies and the International Monetary System* (University of Chicago Press, 1974).

J. H. Makin, 'The Composition of International Reserve Holdings: A Problem of Choice Involving Risk', *American Economic Review* (Dec 1971).

R. A. Mundell, *International Economies* (Macmillan: London, 1968).

M. G. Porter, 'A Theoretical and Empirical Framework for Analyzing the Term Structure of Exchange Rate Expectations', *IMF Staff Papers* (Nov. 1971).

T. M. Whitin, *The Theory of Inventory Management* (Princeton University Press, 1953).

J. H. Williamson, 'International Liquidity: A Survey', *Economic Journal* (Sep 1973).

13 World Inflation, International Relative Prices and Monetary Equilibrium under Fixed Exchange Rates *

Michael Parkin

The questions which this paper addresses are easier to state if we begin by considering some stylised facts about the inflationary and monetary behaviour of the world's major industrial countries over the post-war years. Figure 1 sets out for sixteen countries,[1] the mean and standard deviation[2] (unweighted) inflation, domestic credit expansion and reserve change rates. The average inflation rate displays the well-known features of a short rapid spurt associated with the Korean War followed by an at first gentle but subsequently more rapid acceleration. The dispersion of inflation across countries shows a strong decline from 1950 to 1953 which (with the exception of 1958 which is entirely due to a once-and-for-all departure from its normal course of French inflation) never rose above 2 per cent. The well-known trends of monetary expansion are clear from the averages of domestic credit expansion and reserve changes. What is more interesting and not so widely appreciated are the movements in dispersion. It is clear that domestic credit expansion rates were becoming

* This paper is part of the University of Manchester SSRC Research Programme, 'Inflation: Its Causes, Consequences and Cures' and is a revised version of an earlier draft presented at the University of Chicago conference on The Political Economy of Monetary Reform, Racine, Wisconsin, 24–27 July 1974.

I am grateful to David Laidler, Chung Lee, Alvin Marty, Michael Sumner and George Zis for valuable criticism and comment, and to Robert Ward for research assistance.

Figure 1   Inflation, domestic credit expansion and reserve rate changes of sixteen countries

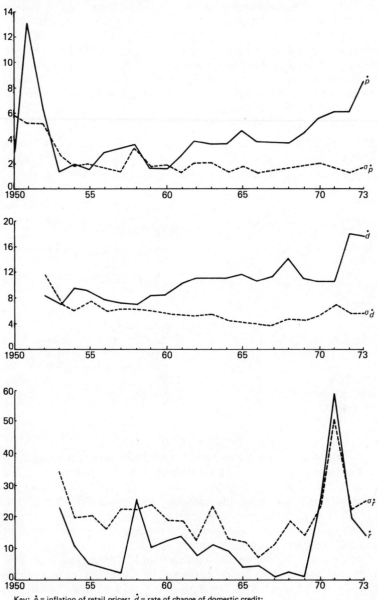

Key: $\dot{p}$ = inflation of retail prices; $\dot{d}$ = rate of change of domestic credit; $\dot{r}$ = rate of change of foreign exchange reserves; continuous line is arithmetical average; broken line is standard deviation.

more equal, virtually without halt, from 1955 to 1967. Despite these convergences of inflation and domestic credit expansion rates, there were substantial national differences. Table 1 highlights these for the sixteen western economies for the period 1958 (the start of full convertibility) to 1970 (the end of the Bretton Woods system). What is striking about these facts is first the spread in inflation rates from Germany (2.3 per cent per annum) to France (5.0 per cent per annum), and second, the lack of a negative association and the hint of a positive association between the ranking of a country's inflation rate and its balance of payments strength as measured by reserve changes.

Table 1   Inflation, domestic credit expansion and reserve changes in sixteen countries

(Average annual rates, 1958–70)

Country	Inflation	Domestic credit expansion	Reserve changes
Australia	2.4	7.6	4.2
Austria	3.1	12.8	10.2
Belgium	2.4	9.1	8.1
Canada	2.5	8.3	7.9
Denmark	4.8	9.0	11.4
Eire	4.1	11.7	7.4
France	5.0	11.6	20.5
Italy	3.4	14.1	12.5
Japan	4.9	19.3	16.0
Netherlands	3.8	11.3	10.4
Norway	4.1	7.8	11.9
Sweden	3.9	8.3	4.3
Switzerland	2.8	10.1	8.1
United Kingdom	3.5	6.6	2.9
United States	2.6	7.6	–
West Germany	2.3	14.1	11.4

To summarise: the post-war world saw inflation rates converging up to 1954 but thereafter experienced a roughly constant dispersion with a range across major countries from 2.3 to 5.0 per cent; domestic credit expansion rates converged but remained highly unequal throughout; balances of payments were highly unequal and increasingly so; there was a slight *positive* association between the ranking of countries' inflation rates and balance of payments strengths.

Can the above facts about the fixed exchange rate world up to 1970 be explained? More importantly, can they be explained with a *simple monetary* model which does not have to rely on a plethora of national socio-political factors? This is the major question which this paper seeks to answer. Additionally, it sets out the rules which countries operating a fixed exchange rate system would have to follow if that system was to work successfully, as well as the implications of following such rules for the behaviour of national price levels.

Thus, this paper is concerned with the fixed exchange rate world which, in most essentials, was abandoned in 1971. It may be objected that concern with this past era is misplaced and now that we are liberated from the constraints of the IMF rules all our effort should be spent in understanding and 'improving the functioning of the superior flexible exchange rate system which now prevails. However, against this it should be noted that there is increasing dissatisfaction with the present monetary set-up (a dissatisfaction shared strongly by the author) and likely to be strong pressure to return to a more rigid monetary system. If, and when, such a system emerges it will be important to equip it with subsidiary rules for stability which ensure that the world avoids the worst features of the Bretton Woods arrangements. The analysis presented here, while in many ways incomplete, does nevertheless provide useful insights which will guide the specification of such rules.

Some of what the paper has to say is not novel. Indeed, the main novelty consists of bringing together, in an integrated way, two pieces of analysis which have hitherto been kept separate. These are the monetary analysis of the determination of the balance of payments under fixed exchange rates of Hume (1752), Mundell (1971) and Johnson (1973) and a simple analysis of relative price determination based on the so-called 'Scandinavian' or EFO (Edgren, Faxen and Ohdner (1969)) model of the determination of the inflation rate of an open (and implicitly fixed exchange rate)[3] economy. In the next section (I) the Johnson and EFO analyses are briefly presented and integrated to provide a simple model of the determination of the balance of payments and rate of inflation relative to a given world rate of inflation in a small fixed exchange rate economy. The model is also used to determine the rate of inflation and foreign exchange rate change of a small flexible exchange rate economy. This latter analysis serves to highlight the limited applicability of the EFO model as a theory of inflation. In Section II a parallel analysis is presented for the country (one only by assumption) whose money is used as the international reserve. That country, along with n small countries, are then analysed simultaneously to determine the world rate of inflation. We then return to the individual country analyses to examine the 'ultimate' determinants of their inflation rates and payments balances under fixed exchange rates. We also examine the capacity of the analysis to explain in broad qualitative terms the stylised facts presented above. In the final section (III) we ask the central policy questions which the analysis is capable of addressing.

The main conclusions are easy to state in summary form. First, in confirmation of the earlier contribution by Balassa (1964) productivity growth differentials are the main factor underlying differences in national measured inflation rates. Second, the balance of payments of fast inflating (fast growth) countries has a tendency to be strong because their domestic credit expansion rates have been too slow (or those of others too fast) for the attainment of a full, multicountry, payments equilibrium. Third, for the attainment of a zero inflation rate with balance of payments equilibrium, whether at the world level or at the less ambitious level of monetary union (such as within Europe), it is necessary to achieve a target growth rate both for the aggregate money supply and for each individual country's domestic credit expansion rate.

I A COMBINED MONETARY AND RELATIVE PRICE ANALYSIS OF INFLATION, THE BALANCE OF PAYMENTS AND THE EXCHANGE RATE IN AN INDIVIDUAL COUNTRY

The well-known monetary analysis of inflation and the balance of payments in a small economy has four propositions:[4]

(*a*) There exists a stable demand for money function which may be written[5]

$$m^d = \alpha y + p \tag{1}$$

where m^d = nominal money balances demanded
y = real income
p = price level
α = income elasticity of demand for money.

(*Note*: all lower-case letters are logarithms throughout.)

(*b*) The supply of money is defined as

$$m^s = \delta(r + \varepsilon) + (1 - \delta)d, \tag{2}$$

where m^s = nominal money balances supplied
r = gold and foreign exchange reserves in units of numeraire currency
d = domestic credit
δ = fraction of money supply backed by gold and foreign exchange
ε = foreign exchange rate (units of domestic currency per world unit of account)

(*c*) Equilibrium prevails in the money market, i.e.

$$m^d = m^s. \tag{3}$$

(*d*) Commodity arbitrage ensures that prices are equal across countries, i.e.

$$p = \varepsilon + \pi, \tag{4}$$

where π = index of prices in world unit of account (constructed on same weights as domestic index)[6]

For a fixed exchange rate economy, these four propositions imply:

$$\dot{p} = \dot{\pi} \tag{5}$$

$$\dot{r} = -\left(\frac{1-\delta}{\delta}\right)d + \frac{1}{\delta}\left(\alpha\dot{y} + \dot{\pi}\right), \tag{6}$$

[where a dot $\equiv d/dt$],
i.e. the country inflates at the same rate as the world and its balance of payments *ceteris paribus* varies directly with its growth and inflation rates, and inversely with its rate of domestic credit expansion.

For a flexible exchange rate economy in which either $\delta = 0$ or $\dot{r} = d$ so that δ is maintained as a constant,[7] the four propositions imply:

$$\dot{p} = d - \alpha\dot{y} \tag{7}$$

and $\quad \dot{\varepsilon} = d - \dot{\pi} - \alpha\dot{y}, \tag{8}$

i.e. the rate of inflation in the economy is independent of the world rate and depends only on the rate of domestic credit expansion and the real growth rate, the exchange rate doing the necessary adjustment to maintain constant relative prices in the world as a whole.

It is immediately clear that this model cannot, in the form stated above, account for the stylised facts presented at the beginning. Its worst failure is that it predicts equal inflation rates for fixed exchange rate countries, a feature which the world does not seem to display.[8] It may be argued that the above model is intended only as a long-run equilibrium model and will fail to fit the facts because we are always observing a world which is off its long-run equilibrium path but tending towards it. However, this objection is hard to accept for two reasons. First, there was remarkable constancy in the dispersion of inflation rates across countries for the seventeen years after 1954 with no tendency for that dispersion to vanish. Second, modifying the above model to allow for short-run disequilibrium adjustment does not permit an explanation of all the facts presented at the beginning. In Parkin (1974) the above model was extended to analyse the disequilibrium interactions of the money, foreign exchange, labour, tradeable and non-tradeable goods markets. The analysis showed that a fixed exchange rate country's inflation rate could indeed depart from the world inflation rate if domestic credit expansion departed from its balance of payments equilibrium rate. It also showed that the Johnson predictions were stable long-run equilibrium paths. Further, however, it predicted that an economy which inflates faster than the rest of the world would have a balance of payments deficit and vice versa. Thus, allowing for disequilibrium adjustments we are able to account for different rates of inflation, but are not able to account either for the persistence of differences or for the fact that some of the fastest inflating countries have had strong balances of payments and some of the slowest inflating countries weak ones.

One way of overcoming these problems is to allow explicitly for *relative* price changes between countries. There are many alternative detailed ways in which this could be done ranging from a completely general analysis to ones based on highly restrictive assumptions. Because the focus of attention in this paper is not the general equilibrium determination of relative prices and quantities, but the integration of relative price and monetary analysis, it seems appropriate to adopt a simple and highly restrictive model. That chosen is the widely known analysis of Edgren, Faxen and Odhner (1969) (EFO). The strong assumptions implicit in that analysis about labour supply, commodity demand and technology are not discussed here but are explored by Branson and Myrman (1974), Baumol (1967) and Kierzkowski (1975).

The basic EFO model is based on two related propositions:[9]

(*a*)   The price index of an economy is a weighted average of prices of individual goods. For simplicity, focus on two goods, one internationally tradeable and one non-tradeable. Then,

$$p = \beta p_T + (1 - \beta) p_N \qquad (9)$$

where p_T = price of tradeable good

p_N = price of non-tradeable good

β = value weight of tradeable good,

i.e.

$$\beta = \frac{P_T Q_T}{P_N Q_N + P_T Q_T}$$

(*Note:* capital Qs and Ps are measured in natural units and a logarithmic price index is used for algebraic simplicity.)

(*b*)   There is a competitive labour market with one homogeneous (or composite) labour which is paid its marginal product and has a constant share of value added. There is also a competitive goods market, i.e.

$$w = p_T + q_T \qquad (10)$$

$$w = P_N + q_N, \qquad (11)$$

where q = output per head, T tradeable, N non-tradeable.

Equations (9), (10) and (11) imply that[10]

$$p = p_T + (1 - \beta)(q_T - q_N)$$

or $$\dot{p} = \dot{p}_T - (1 - \beta)(\dot{q}_T - \dot{q}_N)$$

This says what is fairly obvious, namely that the general level of prices relative to the price of tradeables (and their rates of change) will depend on the difference between productivity (and their rates of change) in the two sectors. The faster the productivity growth in tradeables relative to non-tradeables, the faster the country's rate of inflation relative to the rate of inflation of tradeables prices. The reason for this result is that a faster productivity growth rate for tradeables implies higher wages everywhere and hence higher costs and therefore higher prices in the competitive non-tradeables sector. However, it needs emphasis that this is only a model of *relative* prices. Equations (9), (10) and (11) equally imply

$$\dot{p} = \dot{p}_N + \beta(\dot{q}_T - \dot{q}_N) \tag{12}$$

or, more honestly,

$$\dot{p}_N - \dot{p}_T = \dot{q}_T - \dot{q}_N. \tag{13}$$

What this analysis lacks is a method for determining the *level* of prices or the rate of inflation. This is of course a monetary matter and can only be achieved if we combine the relative price model with a monetary sector. This is both simple to do and rich in insights.

From Johnson's monetary analysis, we retain the first three propositions, i.e.

$$m^d = \alpha y + p. \tag{1}$$
$$m^s = \delta(r + \varepsilon) + (1 - \delta)d. \tag{2}$$
$$m^d = m^s. \tag{3}$$

From the EFO analysis we have the domestic price index definition and the constant relative shares competitive markets wage, price and productivity relations

$$p = \beta p_T + (1 - \beta)p_N. \tag{9}$$
$$w = p_T + q_T. \tag{10}$$
$$w = p_N + q_N. \tag{11}$$

Additionally we have a definition of real (*per capita*) income as

$$y = \beta q_T + (1 - \beta)q_N. \tag{14}$$

Finally, we use a modified version of Johnson's proposition (equation (4) above) and assume that commodity arbitrage ensures that prices of tradeables are equal across countries when expressed in the international unit of account, i.e.

$$p_T = \pi_T + \varepsilon, \tag{15}$$

where π_T = price of tradeables in the international unit of account.

The propositions contained in the above eight equations may now be used to determine, for a fixed exchange rate economy, its rate of inflation and balance of payments, and for a flexible exchange rate economy, its inflation rate and rate of change of its exchange rate. For the fixed exchange rate case we obtain the following results:

$$\dot{p} \equiv \dot{\pi}_T + (1-\beta)(\dot{q}_T - \dot{q}_N). \tag{16}$$

$$\dot{r} = \left(\frac{1-\delta}{\delta}\right)d + \frac{1}{\delta}\left[\dot{\pi}_T + (1-(1-\alpha)\beta)\dot{q}_T - (1-\alpha)(1-\beta)\dot{q}_N\right]. \tag{17}$$

Several features of these results are worthy of comment, and one feature requires a clarifying explanation. First it is now clear that for a small country for which $\dot{\pi}_T$ is exogenous, its inflation rate is determined as that world determined rate of inflation of tradeables prices plus (or unlikely minus) an adjustment, $(1-\beta)(\dot{q}_T - \dot{q}_N)$ which picks up the effect of that country's relative price movements. The balance of payments depends, as in the Johnson case, inversely on the rate of domestic credit expansion, but unlike Johnson, directly on the world rate of inflation of tradeables prices rather than the country's inflation rate and a productivity adjustment more complex than the real growth rate. It is this last feature of the result which needs explanation. Inspection of the above $\dot{r}$ equation shows that a rise in $\dot{q}_T$ unambiguously improves the balance of payments, but the effect of $\dot{q}_N$ is ambiguous and depends on the elasticity of demand for money. Formally,

$$\frac{\partial \dot{r}}{\partial \dot{q}_N} \gtrless 0 \text{ as } \alpha \gtrless 1.$$

The Johnson analysis predicts that a rise in productivity improves the balance of payments, hence this result, that a rise in productivity in non-tradeables will, if $\alpha < 1$, worsen the balance or, if $\alpha = 1$, have no effect on the balance, needs explanation. To see how this arises let us examine the derivation of the crucial expression contained in the $\dot{r}$ equation,

$$\dot{\pi}_T + (1-(1-\alpha)\beta)\dot{q}_T - (1-\alpha)(1-\beta)\dot{q}_N.$$

This expression starts out in equation (1) as

$$\alpha\dot{y} + \dot{p},$$

i.e. the demand for money. Substituting (14) for $\dot{y}$ and (16) for $\dot{p}$ yields

$$\alpha[\beta\dot{q}_T + (1-\beta)\dot{q}_N] + \dot{\pi}_T + (1-\beta)(\dot{q}_T - \dot{q}_N).$$

It is immediately clear that both $\dot{q}_T$ and $\dot{q}_N$ have *two* effects on the demand for money: one on real income (output) and one on the price level. Now a rise in $\dot{q}_T$ has the same sign effect (positive) on the rates of increase of both real income and the price level and hence raises the rate of growth of the demand for money and, *ceteris paribus*, improves the balance of payments. However, a rise in $\dot{q}_N$ raises the growth rate of real income but lowers the rate of inflation; hence its effect on the rate of change of the demand for money and on the balance of payments depends on the relative strength of the two effects. The homogeneity postulate incorporated in (1) makes the price level elasticity of the demand for money unity; hence, if the income elasticity is also unity, a change in $\dot{q}_N$ has no effect on either the demand for money or the balance of payments and has a positive (negative) effect as the income elasticity exceeds (falls short of) unity.

Although the above results differ from Johnson's, they may be expressed in terms which make them entirely equivalent to his. This is clear by noticing from the above discussion that

$$\dot{\pi}_T + (1 - (1-\alpha)\beta)\dot{q}_T - (1-\alpha)(1-\beta)\dot{q}_N \equiv \alpha\dot{y} + \dot{p}. \tag{18}$$

The virtue of the left-hand side of identity (18) is that it gives more information than the right-hand side by decomposing the two variables, $\dot{y}$ and $\dot{p}$ into their independent and exogenous constituents, $\dot{\pi}_T$, $\dot{q}_T$ and $\dot{q}_N$.

Since the EFO model is often presented with the implication that a fast tradeables productivity growth economy must inevitably inflate faster than the world average, it is worth considering the predictions of the system described by equations (1), (2), (3), (9), (10), (11), (14) and (15), under flexible exchange rates. Either with $\delta = 0$ or $\dot{r} = \dot{d}$, the flexible exchange rate system yields the following predictions:

$$\dot{p} = \dot{d} - \alpha[\beta\dot{q}_T + (1-\beta)\dot{q}_N] \tag{19}$$

and $\quad \dot{\varepsilon} = \dot{d} - \dot{\pi}_T - [(1-\alpha)(1-\beta)\dot{q}_T - (1-\alpha)(1-\beta)\dot{q}_N]. \tag{20}$

Thus, with a flexible exchange rate, inflation is determined by what it always was, the rate of monetary (equals domestic credit) expansion, the elasticity of demand and the real growth rate, and is independent of the *relative* productivity growth rates of auto-workers and hairdressers! The exchange rate, however, depends in a predictable and unambiguous manner on $\dot{d}$, $\dot{\pi}_T$ and $\dot{q}_T$, but ambiguously on $\dot{q}_N$ as $\alpha \gtrless 1$, for identical reasons to those discussed above.

The above analysis is incomplete in that it takes the world rate of inflation of the price of tradeables as given. We now turn to an analysis of the determination of that variable and to an analysis of the (equilibrium) interactions of the reserve issuing country and the other countries which comprise the world monetary system.

II INFLATION AND THE BALANCE OF PAYMENTS IN THE RESERVE CURRENCY COUNTRY AND THE WORLD AS A WHOLE

This section abstracts from the details of the world by assuming there to be only one reserve currency which constitutes part of the liabilities of a national economy.[11] There is an additional reserve asset, g, which may be thought of as gold or a world central bank liability such as SDRs. The reserve currency country is a small economy in the limited sense that its producers are like those of any other country, price takers in world markets for tradeables. The economy may be thought of, in terms of the IMF world, as the United States. In subsequent analysis it will be necessary to subscript variables to identify countries. The subscript i will denote the individual economy, and $i = 0$ will be the reserve currency country and $i = 1, 2, \ldots, n$, the other countries.

The basic model presented as equations (1), (2), (3), (9), (10), (11), (14) and (15) in the previous section requires modification in two places to capture what may be regarded as the essential features of the reserve currency economy. First, its demand for money consists of two parts: (*a*) private demand and (*b*) the foreign exchange component of reserveholdings by the central banks of other countries. Thus,

$$m_o^d = \mu_o m_{op}^d + \sum_{i=1}^{n} \mu_i m_{oi}^d, \tag{21}$$

where μ_i is the fraction of the reserve currency country's total money supply held in the foreign exchange reserves of country i and μ_o is the fraction held domestically. The demand for money in the reserve issuing country, m_{op}^d is determined in exactly the same way as in other countries, and is therefore given by an equation identical to (1). The second modification concerns the money supply. For the reserve country, it is assumed the money supply is backed by a primary reserve, g, (gold or SDR) and domestic credit, d, i.e.

$$m_o^s = \delta_o g_o + (1 - \delta_o) d_o. \tag{22}$$

These modifications of equations (1) and (2) together with $m_p^d = \alpha_o y_o + p_o$ and equations (3), (9), (10), (11), (14) and (15) yield the following expressions for the rate of inflation and balance of payments of a fixed exchange rate (the only interesting case) reserve currency economy:

$$\dot{p}_o = \dot{\pi}_T + (1 - \beta_o)(\dot{q}_{To} - \dot{q}_{No}) \tag{23}$$

and
$$\dot{g}_o = -\frac{(1 - \delta_o)}{\delta_o} \dot{d}_o + \frac{\mu_o}{\delta_o} [\dot{\pi}_T + (1 - (1 - \alpha_o)\beta_o)\dot{q}_{To}$$
$$- (1 - \alpha_o)(1 - \beta_o)\dot{q}_{No}] + \frac{1}{\delta_o} \sum_{i=1}^{n} \mu_i \dot{m}_{oi}. \tag{24}$$

The relation between the country's inflation rate and $\dot{\pi}_T$ is exactly the same as for any other country and needs no comment except to note that it becomes less plausible to treat $\dot{\pi}_T$ as independent of the country's monetary actions. We return to this below. Also, the expression for the behaviour of the country's gold stock ($\dot{g}$) is unsatisfactory since it contains both the rate of inflation of tradeables and a direct dependence on other countries' reserves behaviour about which we ought to be able to say something. First, let us turn to an analysis of the world as a whole to determine the world average rate of inflation and inflation rate tradeables goods prices. Then we will return to consider the 'ultimate' determinants of the reserve currency country's inflation and balance of payments.

It is convenient to begin by writing the monetary equilibrium for each country not in logarithmic form but measuring monetary variables in international units of account, thus:

$$G_o + D_o = M_{op}^d + \sum_{i=1}^{n} M_{oi} \tag{25}$$

is the monetary equilibrium condition for the reserve currency country and (defining the exchange rate implicitly as unity),

$$M_{oi} + G_i + D_i = M_i^d \tag{26}$$

defines monetary equilibrium for country i with

$$R_i \equiv M_{oi} + G_i. \tag{27}$$

Aggregating over all countries, and noting the cancelling of M_{oi} terms, gives the *world* monetary equilibrium condition as

$$\sum_{i=0}^{n} G_i + \sum_{i=0}^{n} D_i = \sum_{i=0}^{n} M_i^d \tag{28}$$

or $\quad G_w + D_w = M_w^d, \tag{29}$

where the subscript w denotes world aggregates.

Since we are interested in inflation and payments balances, we want to consider the rates of change of the variables while satisfying the above equilibrium conditions, i.e.

$$\dot{G}_w + \dot{D}_w = \dot{M}_w^d. \tag{30}$$

Now $\quad \dot{M}_w^d = \sum_{i=0}^{w} \dot{M}_i^d, \tag{31}$

but since the logarithmic form of the demand for money is written in (1) as $m^d = \alpha y + p$, in natural units we have

$$M_i = Y^\alpha P \tag{32}$$

therefore $\dot{M}_i = M_i(\alpha \dot{y}_i + \dot{p}_i). \tag{33}$

Using (33) in (30), we have

$$\dot{G}_w + \dot{D}_w = \sum_{i=1}^{n} M_i(\alpha_i \dot{y}_i + \dot{p}_i) \tag{34}$$

or, dividing both sides by M_w and defining $\lambda_i \equiv \dfrac{M_i}{M_w}$ and $\delta_w \equiv G_w/M_w$ becomes

$$\delta \dot{g}_w + (1-\delta)\dot{d}_w = \Sigma \lambda_i(\alpha_i \dot{y}_i + \dot{p}_i). \tag{35}$$

It will be recalled that

$$\alpha_i \dot{y}_i + \dot{p}_i \equiv \alpha_i \dot{y}_i + \dot{\pi}_T + (1 - \beta_i)(\dot{q}_{Ti} - \dot{q}_{Ni}),$$

from which it immediately follows that the rate of change of the price of tradeables, $\dot{\pi}_T$, is determined as

$$\dot{\pi}_T = \delta_w \dot{g}_w + (1 - \delta_w)\dot{d}_w - \Sigma \lambda_i \alpha_i \dot{y}_i - \Sigma \lambda_i \dot{\phi}_i, \tag{36}$$

where

$$\dot{\phi}_i \equiv (1 - \beta_i)(\dot{q}_{Ti} - \dot{q}_{Ni}). \tag{37}$$

The role of the $\dot{g}_w$ and $\dot{d}_w$ terms is clear; a *ceteris paribus* rise in the rate of world money supply growth raises the rate of inflation of tradeables by the same amount. The third term, $\Sigma \lambda_i \alpha_i \dot{y}_i$, is the weighted aggregate absorption of additional money balances resulting from real income growth and the last term is a relative price effect. Basically, it says that the faster are non-traded goods prices rising (for given monetary and real income growth rates) the slower must tradeables prices rise.

We may now see directly how the world equilibrium inflation rate is determined. First, substituting (36) for $\dot{\pi}_T$ into (16) country i's $\dot{p}$ equation and using the definition of ϕ_i given in (37) gives the 'ultimate' determinants of the individual country's inflation rate as

$$\dot{p}_i = \delta_w \dot{g}_w + (1 - \delta_w)\dot{d}_w - \sum_{i=0}^{n} \lambda_i \alpha_i \dot{y}_i + \{\dot{\phi}_i - \sum_{i=0}^{n} \lambda_i \dot{\phi}_i\} \tag{38}$$

and the world inflation rate weighted according to λ_i is

$$\dot{p}_w = \delta_w \dot{g}_w + (1 - \delta_w)\dot{d}_w - \sum_{i=0}^{n} \lambda_i \alpha_i \dot{y}_i. \tag{39}$$

This is of course an extremely familiar expression and is a world level version of the standard quantity theory equilibrium inflation rate. The one feature of the result which is new and interesting is that for relative price effects to cancel out, the weights for computing the world inflation rate need to be money supply shares, λ_i, and not such weights as real of nominal income shares.

Now it is apparent that an individual country may 'inflate' faster, slower, or at the same rate as the world average since

$$\dot{p}_i - \dot{p}_w = \dot{\phi}_i - \Sigma \lambda_i \dot{\phi}_i \gtrless 0. \tag{40}$$

This difference is of course purely a relative price effect. A country with a rapid real growth rate may be presumed to have a large ϕ_i since non-tradeable goods are primarily services whose productivity growth is typically low. Hence, we may expect, for fixed exchange rate countries, growth and measured inflation rates to be positively correlated.

Let us now turn to the 'ultimate' determinants of a country's balance of payments. Recall that treating $\dot{\pi}$ as given, we obtained equation (17) together with definition (37) above

$$\dot{r}_i \equiv -\frac{(1-\delta_i)}{\delta_i}\dot{d}_i + \frac{1}{\delta_i}\{\dot{\pi}_T + \alpha_i\dot{y}_i + \dot{\phi}_i\}. \tag{41}$$

But we now know (equation (36)) that $\dot{\pi}_T$ is determined as

$$\dot{\pi}_T \equiv \delta_w\dot{g}_w + (1-\delta_w)\dot{d}_w - \Sigma\lambda_i\alpha_i\dot{y}_i - \Sigma\lambda_i\dot{\phi}_i. \tag{36}$$

Using this to eliminate $\dot{\pi}_T$ from (41) above yields the following expression for the balance of payments of a non-reserve issuing country,

$$\dot{r}_i \equiv -\frac{[(1-\lambda_i)(1-\delta_i)]}{\delta_i}\dot{d}_i + \frac{[(1-\delta_w)-\lambda_i(1-\delta_i)]}{\delta_i}\dot{d}_{w-i} + \frac{\delta_w}{\delta_i}\dot{g}_w$$

$$+ \frac{1}{\delta_i}[(1-\lambda_i)\alpha_i\dot{y}_i - \sum_{\substack{j=0 \\ j\neq i}}^{n}\lambda_j\alpha_j\dot{y}_j + (1-\lambda_i)\dot{\phi}_i - \sum_{\substack{j=0 \\ j\neq i}}^{n}\lambda_j\dot{\phi}_j], \tag{42}$$

where the subscript $w-i$ refers to the world excluding the ith country and the subscript j refers to individual countries excluding country i.
The balance of payments for the reserve issuing country is simply,

$$\dot{g}_o = \frac{\delta_w}{\delta_o}\dot{g}_w - \sum_{i=1}^{n}\frac{\delta_i}{\delta_o}\dot{g}_i. \tag{43}$$

Several features of these results are worthy of comment. First let us look at the effects of domestic credit. For a non-reserve issuing country the balance of payments will depend inversely on its rate of domestic credit expansion and directly on the rate of domestic credit expansion in the rest of the world. The degree of dependence will depend on the country's share of world money supply,[12] λ_i. If the country is very small so that $\lambda_i \to 0$, then its own domestic credit creation worsens its balance of payments by the usual $-(1-\delta_i)/\delta_i$ times any rise in the rate of domestic credit expansion. Domestic credit creation in the rest of the world has a symmetric effect, improving the individual country's balance of payments by $(1-\delta_w)/\delta_i$ times any increase in domestic credit expansion. If the country is large, the adverse effects of its own domestic credit creation and helpful effects from the rest of the world both diminish. As $\lambda_i \to 1$, the extreme case of a one-country world, it is clear (with obvious interpretation) that the effects on the balance of payments of domestic credit creation on the balance of payments disappears. In the case of the reserve currency issuer the effect of its own and other countries credit expansion washes out completely, not because of size but because its domestic credit in part backs the reserves of others. A rise in its domestic credit expansion rate increases the world rate of inflation but also provides extra domestic money for its own citizens and foreign exchange for the rest of the world. Only if foreign central banks in aggregate decide they want more g (gold or SDR) than is being produced is there a loss of g from its reserves.

Next consider the effect of increasing the rate of creation of primary reserves, g. This unambiguously improves all countries' payments balances *ceteris paribus*.

Finally, consider the effects of real growth and relative price changes. Again, in the case of the reserve issuer, these have no effects. They have important effects however on the other countries. It is clear from (42) that a rise in the country's growth rate or inflation rate, relative to the rest of the world, will improve its balance of payments. Again, this effect will depend on size, being greater the smaller the country, i.e. greater as $\lambda_i \to 0$. The effect of these factors in the rest of the world is opposite to this and again depends on size. Both the growth rate and the relative price change rate depend, of course, on the growth rates in the tradeables and non-tradeables sectors and hence the discussions of these effects in the preceding section are directly applicable here. The effect of a rise in the productivity growth rate in the tradeables sector of the economy unambiguously improves the country's balance of payments, whilst a similar improvement in the rest of the world worsens it. The effects of a rise in the rate of productivity growth of non-tradeables is ambiguous for reasons identical to those set out in the previous section.

One of the stylised facts presented at the beginning of this paper was the lack of association between rates of inflation and payments balances. We have shown above how countries' inflation rates may differ because of relative price effects and also discussed the 'ultimate' determinants of their balances of payments. It is now possible to show how these are related to each other. Dealing only with non-reserve currency countries, it is clear that a strong balance of payments requires that $\dot{r}_i \geqq 0$. Since (equation (42) repeated here for convenience)

$$\dot{r}_i \equiv \frac{[(1-\lambda_i)(1-\delta_i)]}{\delta_i} d_i + \frac{[(1-\delta_w)-\lambda_i(1-\delta_i)]}{\delta_i} d_{w-i} + \frac{\delta_w}{\delta_i}\dot{g}_w$$
$$+\frac{1}{\delta_i}\left[(1-\lambda_i)\alpha_i\dot{y}_i - \sum_{\substack{j=0\\j\neq i}}^{n}\lambda_j\alpha_j\dot{y}_j + (1-\lambda_i)\dot{\phi}_i - \sum_{\substack{j=0\\j\neq i}}^{n}\lambda_j\dot{\phi}_j\right] \qquad (42)$$

then a positive rate of reserve change requires that domestic credit growth, d_i, must be sufficiently small. Specifically, for $\dot{r}_i \geq 0$, it is apparent that domestic credit growth must satisfy the inequality,

$$d_i < \frac{1}{(1-\lambda_i)}\left\{\left[\frac{(1-\delta_w)}{(1-\delta_i)}-\lambda_i\right]d_{w-i} + \frac{\delta_w}{(1-\delta_i)}\dot{g}_w\right.$$
$$\left. + \frac{(1-\lambda_i)}{(1-\delta_i)}[\alpha_i y_i + \dot{\phi}_i] - \frac{1}{(1-\delta_i)}\left[\sum_{\substack{j=0\\j\neq 1}}^{n}\lambda_j(\alpha_j y_j + \dot{\phi}_i)\right]\right\}.$$

If we treat $\dot{g}_w$ as being negligible and focus on the rest of this expression several important things become clear. First, the longer the country's share of the world money supply (λ_i) the greater may its rate of domestic credit expansion ($\dot{d}_i$) be without causing reserve losses. Second, and very obviously, the more domestic credit is being created by the rest of the world, the more may country i create. Third, and for present purposes most interestingly, the larger is a country's growth rate and relative inflation rate (i.e. the faster is its growth rate per head in the tradeables sector) the faster may be its rate of domestic credit expansion.

It is now clear that the factors which affect a fixed exchange rate country's inflation rate relative to the world average, namely the productivity growth rate in its tradeable sector relative to that in its non-tradeable sector, is also one of the key factors determining its balance of payments strength. It is not, however, the only factor affecting the balance of payments; hence it is possible, with a sufficiently disequilibrating domestic credit policy, to have either an external surplus or deficit with the inflation rate either above or below the world average.

To summarise we may have

$$\dot{p}_i \gtrless \dot{p}_w \text{ as } \phi_i \gtrless \sum_{i=0}^{n} \lambda_i \phi_i$$

and
$$\dot{r}_i \gtrless 0 \text{ as } d_i \lessgtr \frac{1}{1-\lambda_i} \left\{ \left[\frac{(1-\delta_w)}{(1-\delta_i)} - \lambda_i \right] d_{w-i} + \frac{\delta_w}{(1-\delta_i)} \dot{g}_w \right.$$
$$+ \left(\frac{1-\lambda_i}{1-\delta_i} \right) [\alpha_i \dot{y}_i + \phi_i]$$
$$\left. - \frac{1}{(1-\delta_i)} \left[\sum_{\substack{j=0 \\ j \neq 1}}^{n} \lambda_i (\alpha_j \dot{y}_j + \phi_i) \right] \right\}.$$

Thus, it is clear that countries may be in any of four positions, $\dot{p}_i \gtrless \dot{p}_w$ and $\dot{r}_i \gtrless 0$. However, if the d_is tend to move closely together (and that apparently did happen under the IMF system) while ϕ_is are very different, then surplus countries will be high-growth and high-inflation countries while deficit countries will tend to have low growth and low inflation.

Let us now return to the stylised facts with which this paper began and see how, if at all, the above analysis can interpret them. First, we must recognise that the analysis presented in this section deals with countries on fixed exchange rates. If exchange rates change then, according to the results in Section I above, their inflation rates differ from those of the rest of the world over and above what they otherwise would have done by an amount equal to the change in the exchange rate. It is not differences in inflation rates reflected by changes in exchange rates that are in need of explanation, hence it is appropriate to net out such differences. This is done in the first three columns of Table 2 which presents, for our sixteen countries, the rate of inflation, exchange rate changes and 'as if' fixed exchange rate inflation, on the average, between 1958 and 1970. The final column gives the average growth rate of industrial production over the same period. The analysis presented above predicts that 'as if' exchange rate fixed inflation rates will differ as $\dot{\phi}_i \gtrless \dot{\phi}_j$ where $\dot{\phi} = (1 - \beta)(\dot{q}_T - \dot{q}_N)$. If we suppose that $\dot{q}_N$ is relatively small and roughly equal across countries

Table 2   Inflation and Growth – Sixteen Countries
(Average annual rates 1958–70)

Country	Inflation rate	Exchange rate change	Inflation as if on fixed exchange rate	Productivity growth
Australia	2.4	0.0	2.4	5.7
Austria	3.1	0.0	3.1	5.8
Belgium	2.4	0.0	2.4	4.3
Canada	2.5	0.2	2.3	5.5
Denmark	4.8	0.6	4.2	6.3
Eire	4.1	1.1	3.0	6.7
France	5.0	2.0	3.0	5.7
Italy	3.4	0.0	3.4	7.8
Japan	4.9	0.0	4.9	13.8
Netherlands	3.8	−0.4	4.2	7.3
Norway	4.1	0.0	4.1	5.1
Sweden	3.9	0.0	3.9	6.2
Switzerland	2.8	0.0	2.8	5.8
United Kingdom	3.5	1.1	2.4	3.1
United States	2.6	0.0	2.6	4.4
West Germany	2.3	−1.1	3.4	6.2

and that the β weights are similar across countries, then there should be a direct association between average inflation rates and average productivity growth rates. Of course, to the extent that the βs and $\dot{q}_N$s do differ, this direct and simple association will be weakened. Figure 2 illustrates the actual relationship between production (as a proxy for productivity) growth and inflation adjusted for exchange rate changes for the sixteen countries. It is clear that whilst the relationship is by no means perfect there is a positive association. Further, for the big six (USA, UK, West Germany, France, Italy and Japan) the relationship is an extremely close one. Further its slope is almost exactly what would be predicted from the assumption that productivity growth is the same in all countries in non-tradeables and the tradeables share of total output (β), is the same in all countries and is approximately 0.75. It is interesting that the outliers from this relationship between the big countries are the Scandinavian countries and the Netherlands. While an explanation for this is offered, it would be fruitful to explore the detailed differences in the

$\dot{p}_i$ weights and $\dot{q}_{Ni}$ growth rates in these countries as compared with the others.

The above analysis can then, in broad terms, account for national measured inflation rate differences (netting out the effects of exchange rate changes) largely as relative price effects. In this respect, the results presented here are in line with an earlier important study by Balassa (1964). Why though has there been a tendency (although a loose one) for balance of payments strength to be correlated *positively* with inflation?

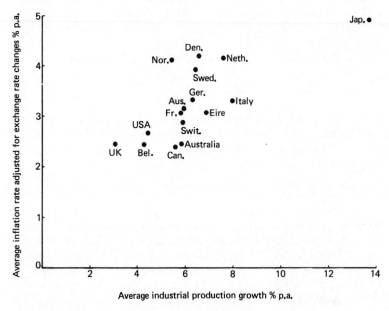

Figure 2   The relation between production growth and 'as if' fixed exchange rate inflation rates in sixteen countries, 1958–70

This seems explicable in terms of the above analysis as a result of the tendency of fast growth economies to run *relatively*, but (see Table 1) clearly not *absolutely*, tight domestic credit policies. The increasing tendency for domestic credit growth rates to equalise, apparent in Figure 1 (but obscured in Table 1) strengthens that interpretation. Since balance of payments equilibrium requires rates of domestic credit expansion to be unequal and in greater degree the greater the tradeables productivity growth differential, then a general tendency to equalise domestic credit expansion rates will bring bigger surpluses for the fast growth countries and bigger deficits for the slow growth countries and thereby create additional strain and pressure for exchange rate realignments.

This suggests that, aside from all the problems caused by the behaviour of the United States in the late 1960s, the world monetary system was coming under greater strain as a result of inconsistent domestic credit policies being pursued by the other major members of the fixed exchange rate club.

What are the rules which need to be obeyed if a fixed exchange rate system is to work? We now turn to that question.

III   SOME POLICY RULES

What policy rules does the above analysis suggest should be set for a world consisting of many countries each of which wish to maintain a fixed exchange rate system with balance of payments equilibria and a stable world price level?

First, at the world aggregate level, for (39) above, we have,

$$\dot{p} = \delta_w \dot{g}_w + (1 - \delta_w) \dot{d}_w - \sum_{i=0}^{n} \lambda_i \alpha_i y_i. \tag{39}$$

For $\dot{p}_w = 0$ it is clearly necessary to control $\delta_w \dot{g}_w + (1 - \delta_w) \dot{d}_w \equiv \dot{m}_w$, i.e. the *world* money supply. In a recent paper, Parkin *et al.* (1975) showed that this is likely to require control of *both* $\dot{g}_w$ and $\dot{d}_w$. The rate at which $\dot{m}_w$ should grow for price stability is of course

$$\sum_{i=0}^{n} \lambda_i \alpha_i y_i.$$

However, this is not enough. Rules must be specified for individual countries' d_i in order that the required d_w emerges. What should such a rule be? To answer this it should first be noted that each country needs a balance of payments target to which it should be held. This, for simplicity, will be taken as $\dot{r}_i = d_i$, i.e. the gold standard rule of constant fractional backing. Then, since from (42),

$$\dot{r}_i \equiv \frac{[(1 - \lambda_i)(1 - \delta_i)]}{\delta_i} \dot{d}_i + \frac{[(1 - \delta_w) - \lambda_i(1 - \delta_i)]}{\delta_i} \dot{d}_{w-i} + \frac{\delta_w}{\delta_i} \dot{g}_w$$

$$+ \frac{1}{\delta_i} \left[(1 - \lambda_i)\alpha_i \dot{y}_i - \sum_{\substack{j=0 \\ j \neq 1}}^{n} \lambda_j \alpha_j \dot{y}_j + (1 - \lambda_i)\dot{\phi}_i - \sum_{\substack{j=0 \\ j \neq 1}}^{n} \lambda_j \dot{\phi}_j \right]$$

Then $\dot{r}_i \equiv \dot{d}_i \equiv \dot{d}_i^*$ for all countries require that

$$\dot{d}_i^* \equiv [\alpha_i \dot{y}_i + (\dot{\phi}_i - \dot{\phi}_w)].$$

That is, the individual country should set its domestic credit expansion rate equal to its real growth rate, adjusted for the income elasticity of demand for money, *plus* an adjustment for the departure of the country's movement of relative prices relative to that of the world average.

Individual country's price levels will inflate/deflate depending on the sign of $\phi_i - \bar{\phi}_i$, fast growth countries experiencing rising prices and slow growth countries falling prices. It is worth noting that if countries followed the quasi-Friedman rule[13] of making $\dot{m}_i = \alpha_i \dot{y}_i$ then fast growers would develop surpluses and would have to revalue while slow-growth countries would develop deficits and have to devalue. In such cases, country prices would have zero inflation rates, but at the expense of multiple moneys and moving exchange rates.

The analysis presented here does not pretend to be exhaustive and has only aimed to be suggestive of further useful empirical work which needs to be undertaken. It ignores completely short-run adjustment problems. Its main virtue, perhaps, is that it sets out in the simplest conceivable terms the long-run requirements of a successful fixed exchange rate system which avoids both inflation, balance of payments disequilibria and exchange crises. As such, it has probably more to say about monetary unions such as proposals for European Monetary Union than it has about global monetary reform, at least for the immediate future.

NOTES

1. The sixteen countries are: Austria, Australia, Belgium, Canada, Denmark, Eire, France, Holland, Italy, Japan, Norway, Sweden, Switzerland, UK, USA and West Germany. See Appendix on data sources and methods.

2. Some writers have used the coefficient of variation as a measure of dispersion (see, e.g., Pattison (1975)). Such a measure shows a dramatic reduction in dispersion over the 1960s. My view is that the standard deviation is a more appropriate measure since one wants to know about movements in the dispersion of relative price levels. Since the rate of inflation is a (logarithmic) first difference of the price level, only a zero standard deviation of the inflation distribution implies constant relative prices. At a time when the rate of inflation is rising, it is possible to create the impression of convergence of inflation rates and stable relative prices by 'normalising' on the inflation rate. However, the convergence is illusory.

3. The monetary conditions which are necessary for the EFO analysis to be valid are rarely discussed although by implication, a fixed exchange rate economy is being assumed.

4. The best exposition of this theory is Johnson (1973).

5. It may be objected that this demand for money function is inappropriate because it does not include and opportunity-cost variable. Such a variable is omitted purely because the focus of analysis is equilibrium (fully anticipated and constant) inflation; hence the opportunity cost of holding real balances will be constant.

6. It is possible that one of the reasons why inflation rates differed in the fixed exchange rate world which prevailed up to 1970 is the difference in weights in the national price indices. However, casual empiricism suggests that there are substantial price differences which would still remain.

7. These two assumptions are alternative ways of ensuring full domestic insulation. If both were violated, the resulting expression would involve δ, be a little more complicated and the world inflation rate would have some (small) effect on the national rate.

8. But see note 6 for a qualification.

9. The summary presented here is almost identical to that found in Prachowny (1971) and Jackson *et al.* (1972) and embraced by Jones (1972).

10. It may be objected that the equation immediately below (p.000) is inappropriate since, with relative prices changing, β will vary. In general, β will of course vary and such variation could be allowed for at the expense of considerable loss of simplicity. Throughout the paper, β is treated as constant mainly for simplicity but also on the grounds that *a priori* β could be constant; alternatively it may be regarded as approximately constant for small enough changes. The papers by Baumol (1967), Branson and Myrhman (1974) and Kierzkowski (1975) give more general treatments which imply the conditions on which β will be constant.

11. To allow each and every currency to serve as a potential reserve asset for each and every other central bank raises difficulties which I have not been able to resolve and appears to me to require an explicit analysis of central bank portfolio behaviour if determinate solutions are to be obtained.

12. This result is of course well known; see Swoboda (1973).

13. *Quasi*-Friedman because Friedman recognises the need for flexible exchange rates if his rule is to be followed successfully. See Friedman (1968).

REFERENCES

Balassa, B., 'The Purchasing-Power Parity Doctrine: A Reappraisal', *Journal of Political Economy*, 72 (6) (Dec 1964) pp. 584–96.

Baumol, W. J., 'Macroeconomics of Unbalanced Growth: the Anatomy of Urban Crises', *American Economic Review*, 57 (3) (June 1967) pp. 415–26.

Branson, W. H., and Myrhman, J., 'Inflation in Open Economies: Supply-Determined versus Demand-Determined Models', paper presented to the Conference on Inflation in Small Economies (Vienna, 1974).

Edgren, G., Faxen, K. O., and Odhner, G. E., 'Wages Growth and the Distribution of Income', *Swedish Journal of Economics*, 71 (3) (Sep 1969) pp. 133–60.

Friedman, M., 'The Role of Monetary Policy', *American Economic Review*, 58 (1) (Mar 1968) pp. 1–17.

Hume, D., 'Of the Balance of Trade' (1752). Excerpts in R. N. Cooper (ed.) *International Finance* (Harmondsworth: Penguin Books, 1969).

Jackson, D. S., Turner, H. A., and Wilkinson, F., *Do Trade Unions Cause Inflation?* (Cambridge University Press, 1972).

Johnson, H. G., 'A Monetary Approach to Balance of Payments Theory' in *Further Essays in Monetary Economics* (London: Allen & Unwin, 1973).

Jones, Aubrey, *The New Inflation: the Politics of Prices and Incomes* (London: Penguin Books and Deutsch, 1972).

Kierzkowski, H., 'Theoretical Foundations of the Scandinavian Model of Inflation', forthcoming in *The Manchester School* (1976).

Mundell, R. A., *Monetary Theory, Inflation, Interest and Growth in the World Economy* (California: Goodyear Publishing, Pacific Palisades, 1971).

Parkin, J. M., 'Inflation, the Balance of Payments, Domestic Credit Expansion and Exchange Rate Adjustments', in Aliber, R. Z. (ed.) *National Monetary Policies and the International Financial System* (Chicago and London: University of Chicago Press, 1974).

Parkin, J. M., Richards, I. M. and Zis, G., 'The Determination and Control of the World Money Supply Under Fixed Exchange Rates, 1961–71', *Manchester School*, vol XLIII (3) Sept. 1975, pp. 293–316.

Pattison, J., 'The International Transmission of Inflation' in Parkin, J. M., and Zis, G. (eds) *Inflation in the World Economy* (Manchester University Press, 1975).

Prachowny, M. F. J., 'The Inflationary Process in Open Economies', Queen's University Kingston, Ontario Discussion Paper no. 52 (Sep 1971).

Swoboda, A. K., 'Monetary Policy Under Fixed Exchange Rates: Effectiveness the Speed of Adjustment and Proper Use', *Economica* (n.s.) 60 (158) (May 1973) pp. 136–54.

APPENDIX

SOURCES AND DEFINITIONS OF DATA USED

The source for all data was the IMF publication *International Financial Statistics*. The latest data were taken from the May 1974 issue and earlier data from the July 1968 issue and the supplement to Volume 19 1966/67.

Annual data for the sixteen countries, Austria, Australia, Belgium, Canada, Denmark, Eire, France, Italy, Japan, Netherlands, Norway, Switzerland, Sweden, UK, USA and West Germany, were collected for the period 1949–73.

All rates of change were calculated on the basis:

$$X_t = ((X_t - X_{t-1})/X_{t-1}) \times 100,$$

where X_t is the annual figure.

The item numbers in *International Financial Statistics* were as follows:

Prices: no. 64 average of monthly cost-of-living indices
Domestic credit: no. 32 domestic credit (end of year)
Industrial production: no. 66 average of monthly indices of production

Exchange rate: no. 1 dollar value of national currency (spot rate) (end of year)

International liquidity: *gold reserves plus special drawing rights plus foreign exchange reserves (end of year).

*separate from country notes

Summary of the Discussion

An initial question involved the breakdown of the Bretton Woods system. At the 1966 Conference in Chicago, there was some concern – but not a great deal – with the lack of flexibility in the exchange rate mechanism. Nevertheless, the Bretton Woods system worked reasonably well for twenty years; so an explanation is needed for twenty years of reasonable exchange rate stability. Was it because the currencies of many other countries were slightly undervalued relative to the dollar and constantly absorbing reserves? If so, is there an analogy for the future should there be a return to pegged rate? Has the economic structure of the world changed, perhaps because of the integration of world capital markets? Is the similarity of the phasing of the business cycle around the world evident for the first time in the last several years a new and permanent feature of the international economy?

Robert Gordon offered two hypotheses about the sustainability of the pegged rate system for twenty years. One was that a pegged rate system has a natural life of twenty-five years; and while the Bretton Woods system was still operating in 1966, there was a persistent dis-equilibrium. The accumulation of dollars by Germany and other surplus countries was not entirely voluntary, as suggested by Despres–Kindleberger–Salant intermediation hypotheses; rather it did not lead to revaluation because of domestic factors in the surplus countries, political and competition for exports. The second hypothesis is that there is a direct relationship between the acceleration of inflation in the late 1960s and the breakdown of the system. Gordon favoured the second view – the acceleration of inflation and the changes in relative inflation rates in different countries were the crucial element in the breakdown. Until October 1973 when the oil crisis started, there was a managed *de facto* float. After February 1974, the yen floated quite naturally without much intervention from the government authorities. The Japan experience shows that the system is in the process of transition to a rather reasonably behaved semi-managed floating rate. One problem involves the interval for a stock adjustment; when the Bank of

Japan bought large amounts of dollars, should it do so over a short or a long period.

Makin took issue with Kouri's point that the rate of inflation would not be effected by the choice between fixed exchange rates. The rate of inflation cannot be predicted without information on the rate of growth of the money supply and a theory of the demand for money. Theories of the demand for private international reserves under floating exchange rates are scarce. One hypothesis is that an increase in exchange rate flexibility increases the private demand for reserves; another, that it decreases the private demand for reserves. Someone has suggested that the decreased demand for private liquidity under floating exchange rates has contributed to world inflation. There is greater need for analysis of both official and private demands for international liquidity under the different exchange rates regimes, both under completely floating systems and under managed floating.

Anne Krueger replied that by the mid-1960s there was already a great deal of concern that the pegged rate system was performing poorly. The official view was that the US dollar could not be devalued, and so there was a lot of frustration. Moreover Gordon's second hypothesis can be turned around, the dollar deficits led to increase in the world liquidity, to world inflation and to an increase in velocity – so that the breakdown was inevitable; the higher US inflation may have speeded up the breakdown by several years.

Robert Aliber noted that economists fell into two groups in the 1960s – one group was constitutionally for floating rates and had been since year one, regardless of the nature of the shocks and disturbances in the system. The second group wanted to increase the flexibility of the adjustable peg system. There were a variety of proposals for crawling pegs, and for widening support limits around parities. Williamson said he was surprised at the contents of the first Chicago Conference in that there was not more concern with exchange rate flexibility.

Michael Parkin asked whether the breakdown of the Bretton Woods system was inevitable, regardless of the US monetary policy. Or did they mean that since the United States would be monetarily irresponsible from time to time, that such system is going to breakdown? Krueger replied that she meant the former.

Williamson countered that the US inflation was not the central issue. With an adjustable pegged system and discrete movements in the exchange rates, people will learn about the system and the inevitability of changes in exchange rates. Then the whole system becomes more and more destabilising. That would have been just as true if the United States had been in the centre of the system behaving responsibly, and if from time to time, Germany had appreciated and Great Britain had depreciated.

Parkin replied that it was difficult to be very confident when trying to interpret such recent historical events. Looking at the broad trends in demand management, the dominant feature of key indicators of excess demand in Europe and America over the period from the middle fifties to the seventies was that the United States steadily lowered its unemployment rate and steadily added to demand. The broad trend of world excess demand, as measured by a weighted average indicator across the world, seems to have been pretty well in equilibrium until the early part of the sixties. The indicator then moved into a state of overall excess demand by 1966, primarily as a result of US events. While Europe did not want inflation as a result of overall demand pressure, the European countries independently attempted to resist the inflation by inappropriate monetary policies. Nevertheless the inflation was inevitable given the commitment to fixed exchange rates. The US inflationary movement that began in a gentle way and then accelerated in the late 1960s was the dominant factor in explaining the breakdown. Although the Bretton Woods system was not perfect and had many inflexibilities, it would not have broken down, provided the major countries behaved sensibly with their domestic monetary policies. Parity changes would have occurred a little more frequently with smaller jumps.

Gordon turned the argument back to Williamson's proposition, and asked why, if the recurrent British crisis before 1966 had not caused the system to break down, the system could not handle the US crisis in 1970 and 1971. The transmission mechanism of the world inflation involved the movement of dollar balances to Europe. If these balances were being created at the rate that was roughly equal to the increase in German demand for money in the early sixties, then the system was stable. But when the US inflation rate increased, particularly stepping it up at a variable and irregular rate with a stop–go monetary policy, the system could no longer cope.

Krueger noted Germany had had problems, with capital inflows in the early 1960s. There was an excess demand for dollars prior to 1966, and the system coped with the imbalances for a while with the move to an excess supply of dollars. Increasingly a few currencies such as the mark had problems, then more did. The underlying mechanism had to do with this gradual shift from a dollar shortage to a dollar glut. While the dollar problem was central to the breakdown, the US inflation was not its cause, but just one factor contributing to the acceleration.

John Makin suggested that the behaviour in the real sector should be considered. The approximate cause of the breakdown was the sloshing of funds in the Eurocurrency system, which mirrored the excessive rate of inflation in the United States. The real cause of the breakdown of the system was that the United States decided it wanted either a balance of payments equilibrium or a surplus, in response to producers of tradeable goods in the United States who claimed that they were being taxed out of existence by an overvalued dollar. In 1971 the United States wanted a large balance of trade surplus to finance the long-term capital outflows. Increased capital mobility, by itself, was not responsible for the breakdown of the Bretton Woods system, although it may have been the necessary condition. The sufficient condition was that balance of payments goals were inconsistent. The major shock to the consistency of balance of payments goals in the late 1960s and the early 1970s was the US desire for a balance of payments equilibrium. As long as the United States was passive and would accept its deficits, the Bretton Woods system would have survived.

Capital market integration facilitated a very fast offsetting response of capital flows to domestic monetary policy. The attempts of the central banks to sterilise capital movements aggravated the situation. Their insistent attempts of sterilisation led to huge levels of reserve build-ups, which fed speculative flows, causing the system to blow up. The source of the problem is not fixed exchange rates *per se* but independent monetary policy under fixed rates; fixed rates are fine with the appropriate monetary rules. Floating exchange rates were necessary if there is to be independence from US inflation coming out of the Vietnam war.

Gordon asked Makin which US policy actions were in reaction to political pressure? Makin replied the pressure that the United States put on other countries to absorb more dollars; their only other option was to revalue.

Stanley Fisher asked if the United States had behaved, would the system have held up given that other countries were also misbehaving. The British maintained an overvalued exchange rate from 1964 to 1967 at a substantial cost to themselves. He doubted they would behave that way again for very long. If any fairly large country is going to follow inappropriate monetary policies, it cannot maintain a pegged rate. If there are sufficient discrepancies among rates of growth of the various currencies, the retention of the pegged rate system is untenable over long period.

Michael Porter said that the independent monetary policy did not cause any difficulties for Australia in the 1960s. But in 1970–1, when there was an attempt to be independently restrictive, massive capital movements occurred within a very short period of time; Australia suddenly found itself with reserves of $4 to 5 billions. This was unprecedented, since the restrictive monetary policy had not operated for very long. The system may have changed, in that the degree of capital market integration had increased even before academic thinking recognised the change.

Porter continued that the monetary theory of balance of payments has been agnostic regarding changes in balances on capital and current accounts. In the world economy there has been an increase in the rapidity of capital movements, more so than with regard to trade movements. Countries that are reluctant to change their parities are left with a disequilibrium exchange rate, which then provides the incentive for massive movements of money. What is not understood is the role of capital movements in thi; whole process and what is not understood theoretically is the role of these movements in the monetary theory of the balance of payments.

Helliwell responded that an alternative explanation for the Australian case is that the 1970 situation was triggered by heavy resource investment that was really unrelated to the monetary policy. The pattern of resource distribution across the world is uneven and changing. The financial system must be flexible enough to digest large, exogenous capital flows, which have substantial trade consequences.

Horst Böckelmann said the rapid decline in the US gold stock meant that the system could not have survived for very long, given the unwillingness of the United States to see the stock decline much further. The adoption of the two-tier gold system in 1968 was clearly a crisis signal. Gold was important in the system in that the other countries would support the dollar in the exchange market given the US obligation to maintain the convertibility of the US dollar into gold. Once it was clear that the United States could no longer meet this obligation, the whole system got into danger.

Michael Mussa suggested that it is necessary to specify what we mean by 'the system' before the controversy about its breakdown could be clarified. If 'the system' means that the major countries, except the United States, can change their parities then clearly action on the part of other countries, an attempt to discipline the United States, is required for a breakdown. Two factors made the system more and more unstable. One was the increasing integration of the capital markets and the more rapid movement of short-term funds. The second was the decline in the relative size of the US economy in comparison with those of Germany and Japan, which made it less and less easy for the United States to play the dominant centre role.

Paul De Grauwe said that since 1959 there was increasing integration of the world economy, and especially of the European economies. Consequently they could not follow the same policies as before. So there was increasing intra-European instability which occurred at a time when the inflation originated in the United States. The Eurodollar market resulted because the monetary authorities tried to resist this inflation and put controls on capital flows, which led to the problems of the seventies.

Williamson agreed with Porter that the increasing capital flows and increasing capital mobility led to the breakdown of the system. However, it did not lead to the breakdown of the fixed rate system because increasing capital mobility stabilises a fixed rate system. Rather it led to the breakdown of an adjustable peg system. An adjustable peg system is not compatible with a high degree of capital mobility.

Krueger said the rapid increase in capital mobility occurred partly in response to incentives which were built into the fixed rate system which made it highly profitable to shift, and therefore paid for these institutions to develop. Capital flows forced the breakdown. Nothing about the behaviour of floating rates has cast doubt on the system – but we have not achieved the world we thought we were going to get with floating rates. The current system is better than the old system, but there are still many problems.

John Spraos disagreed; he felt that the pegged system was going to breakdown but that there will eventually be an even worse breakdown with floating rates.

The discussion turned to the operation of the floating exchange rate system since March 1973. Aliber observed that the participants at Wingspread II seem less enamoured of floating rate system than those at Wingspread I. Perhaps the difference reflects only a change in the mix of participants; perhaps it reflects some disenchantment with the way the floating rates have worked.

One possible criticism of the behaviour of floating rates of the last two years, centres on speculation, the sharp movements in the mark and the pull of the mark on the other European currencies. Another is that the floating rate system led to far less monetary independence than had been anticipated, as shown in quite similar rates of inflation.

Rachel McCullough noted that there had been frequent comments that while floating exchange rate systems might be advisable in the long run, the changeover to the floating system could be catastrophic. Yet the adjustment to the new system does not seem bad. Private individuals and firms are learning how to operate in the new environment; as they learn, there should be less rather than more variance in exchange rates.

Jeremy Siegel said that the behaviour of floating rates in several years had been smoother than he had expected. The floating rate system would not isolate business cycles in several countries; no one had said that. If on an *ex ante* basis the capital account balances differs from the current account balance, there is no way that the economy can be isolated under a floating exchange rate system from a foreign business cycle. The independence afforded by a floating rate system involves the choice of the trend rate of inflation; the authorities can choose any trend rate they want. He said he had not been disappointed that there has not been greater isolation of monetary events in one country from those. If one is going to talk about the success of the floating rate system, there is bound to be an over-reaction immediately when the rate begins to float after twenty years of pegging. The exchange rates were less volatile in the first half of 1974 than in the previous six months. Moreover any comparison of floating and pegged rates should include an index of tariffs rates and capital controls adopted for balance of payments adjustment; given some of the underlying major disturbances over the last years, this index has been surprisingly low. Controls on capital outflows have been relaxed.

And the oil crisis led to a smaller imposition of tariffs and controls, than would have occurred under a regime of fixed exchange rates. He noted that the floating rate system was not a clean float, but central bank intervention did not greatly concern him, even though it led to a consistency problem.

Kouri responded that a number of empirical developments and a number of theoretical developments have led to some questioning of the floating exchange rate system. There have been arguments for floating exchange rates in terms of monetary independence and isolation of cyclical developments in one country from those in other countries. The discussion of the Canadian experience in the 1950s was that Canada might isolate itself from US cyclical fluctuations. The two major empirical phenomena of today, the oil problem and the problem of world inflation, would be more or less the same, regardless of whether exchange rates were pegged or floating. The adjustment to higher oil prices is exactly the same with or without pegged exchange rates. The problem of world inflation, in aggregate terms, would be the same, if monetary expansion rates in various countries are believed given. In the present situation, there is no way to stabilise exchange rates by pegging them since the national inflation rates differ.

Kouri continued that if one begins to analyse what it is that makes the flexible exchange rate system a good system, the arguments in terms of monetary independence are that countries can have different rates of secular inflation. If capital markets are integrated there is very little national economic independence. Rational behaviour and integrated markets suggest there is little scope for such independence; transactions costs of having different secular rates of inflation in various countries must be considered.

Kouri modified Makin's earlier observation that the inconsistency in the balance of payments current accounts targets destroyed the fixed exchange rate system; no system could survive under those circumstances. A conflict on current account targets would destroy the floating exchange rate system in the same way, as the adjustment to the oil crisis may show. The exchange rate is an inefficient instrument for bringing about major changes in the current account balances in response to an oil crisis.

Jacob Frenkel spoke to Kouri's point that given the same policies, we should not expect much difference in the results between the two exchange rate regimes. On the theoretical level, this statement is a reflection that the system is homogeneous of degree zero in money prices, the quantity of money, and the exchange rate. The critical question is how national policies are endogenous to the alternative exchange rate systems; it is risky to assume the same kind of reaction function under the two exchange rate systems.

Helliwell said that the views of economists about exchange rate systems had developed in the absence of empirical information about their behaviour, and these views have been maintained unchanged, even as the data developed. Some economists may change their views as evidence starts to accumulate on how the new system works. The evidence in Wingspread I was about the 1950s Canadian experience, based largely on assumptions that models people had of the kind of independence Canada had with flexible exchange rates, were purely irrational models with a number of unrealistic assumptions. Some important facts, which were empirically important, were ignored in these models. The pegged rate system was not a materially different system in terms of the adjustment process from a floating exchange rate system. The floating exchange rate system moves to keep basic balance on a regular basis but had built in substantial private stabilising short-term capital flows. The pegged exchange rate system and the floating exchange rate system are two fairly adjacent systems in a spectrum of systems and they were not that different, in the Canadian case, from each other. Economists tend to say you cannot look at the evidence from two countries that are highly interdependent in order to judge how countries, which are much less interdependent will behave.

Böckelmann said there is a kind of disillusion with one aspect of the floating rate system, in that the trade response to changes in the exchange rate have been very small. No one expected that once a country had revalued, subsequent revaluations might be necessary. A more flexible system was supposed to protect a country from the need for these successive changes. From the German point of view, the need to appreciate further has not been so drastic that one would say that Germany should not have moved to floating exchange rates, for under this system, the central bank is in a position to make certain decisions which it could not make before.

Koichi Hamada noted that the system of the last several years was better described as managed-floating rather than free-floating. It is too early to conclude what its disadvantages may be. The yen began to float in February 1973, but after the initial adjustment had been made in April to about 265 yen to the dollar, Bank of Japan held the exchange rate to a very narrow range, even narrower than under the adjustable peg system.

The discussion turned to the transitional problems of stabilising the world economy. The key problem involves the approaches that countries might take towards reducing the inflation rates, and the appropriate international rules.

Dornbusch discussed the re-entry problem in a stabilised monetary system. Because countries have different inflation rates, and different potential for stabilisation, a flexible exchange rate system is required. Expectations about movements in the price levels must be stabilised. For four years, each country should stabilise its current rate of inflation and thereby gain credibility, and then all countries together should reduce their inflation rates to zero.

Böckelmann replied that no country has been able to stabilise its inflation rate. While it has frequently been said that once individuals have accepted a particular rate of inflation and the system could be in equilibrium at this rate, this argument does not appear to hold. If a country is prepared to accept a 4 per cent inflation rate, within a relatively short time-span, it will have an 8 per cent rate of inflation; if it accepts the 8 per cent inflation rate, it will soon have a 16 per cent rate. As long as the country tries to get away from its current inflation rate, it may be able to stay at the same rate of inflation because it is not succeeding. But if the country tries to stablise its inflation rate, it will not succeed.

Gordon noted the analogy between the alleged downward rigidity of prices and the asymmetry in the fixed and flexible exchange rate system. Depreciation pushes up the domestic rate of inflation while the subsequent appreciation does not have any effect in reducing prices. Thus there is a ratchet effect under the price level. At any one time, some countries are appreciating, others are depreciating; half are always depreciating. The statement that it is impossible to stabilise the rate of inflation at a particular figure is essentially this problem. Political pressures are such that any mistake, any shock like the oil crisis that puts a country into a higher level temporarily, leads to political pressure to validate that price level with monetary policy so as to avoid the unemployment Unemployment would occur because of the downward rigidity of prices and wages. Commodity prices are very flexible, and not subject to this asymmetry; there is plenty of historical evidence that commodity prices fall as well as rise. One way to make this problem concrete is to ask how much flexibility we can get in the world's inflation rate if we have very flexible commodity prices, primarily in traded goods, and at the same time rigidity in the downward adjustment of wages. The US experience suggests wages are slow to react to price changes.

McKinnon seconded Böckelmann's view that a zero rate of inflation is the only rate around which private expectations can coalesce. In addition, the price index must be defined. The long-run Phillips curve either is vertical with respect to given rates of inflation or more probably, backward bending. Thus if the monetary authorities try to stabilise the economy at an 8 per cent rate of inflation instead of a zero per cent rate, private expectations will not coalesce around this rate for the reasons Böckelmann mentioned. Various groups will try to protect their real wages against a possible further debasement of the currency. Hence, the level of employment will be lower on an inflation path that averages to 8 per cent compared with a path that averages at zero.

McKinnon continued that the difficulty with the re-entry proposal of Dornbusch is that the monetary authorities in every country except Germany have lost credibility. An international monetary agreement might stabilise domestic expectations; the monetary authorities might sign a protocol about their intended monetary behaviour. Newspapers would write up the protocol. Then they could deflate in the relatively happy situation where individual inflationary expectations would be reduced when the protocol is signed, rather than be forced in the situation of trying to deflate when inflationary expectations are very high, which would be very painful in terms of unemployment.

Parkin noted that the surveys of inflationary expectations indicated that the standard deviation of those expectations is higher, the higher the rate of inflation. Thus the higher the rate of inflation, the larger the disagreement about the future rate. The implication is that zero might be a better number around which to coalesce than eight or some higher number. He then went to place the re-entry problem in a historical perspective. We are not going to move back to price stability on this deflationary swing of the cycle. And so, it is best to re-enter after the next swing of the cycle or perhaps after the one after that. The next few years are going to be extremely unpleasant and uncomfortable in economic terms. The mid-1974 stance of monetary and fiscal policy in the United States, Germany, Japan, Great Britain and France is extremely strongly deflationary. These economies have reacted very strongly to the inflation over the last few years, and are not experiencing monetary expansion rates close to zero, even though inflation rates in some countries are in the range of 10 to 25 per cent a year. By the end of 1974, a recession is likely to be deeper than anything the world economy has had since the Second World War. If the British response is not typical, the political reaction will be strong. Monetary expansion rates and fiscal policies will be reversed, leading to a stagflation. The subsequent inflation rates will make those of 1973–4 look relatively pleasant. The international differentials in inflation rates may become larger; even though we have had higher rates of inflation, on the average, the standard deviation across countries has not gone up very much in the last year.

To get out of this mess, the re-entry problem is much bigger than it now appears; the question is which of the three alternative re-entry ways is preferable. Method I is gradualism. Each country gradually attempts to reduce its inflation by slowing its rate of monetary expansion in a controlled and steady way. At some stage, perhaps fifteen or twenty years from now, this policy will bring it into the magic number that will stabilise prices that the inflation rate would require. A floating exchange rate is required; there is no alternative. Re-entry method II is the Dornbusch formula to stabilise existing inflation rates for a period so as to gain credibility about the rate of inflation and then to reduce the rate of inflation in each country simultaneously and thereafter to move sharp immediate deflations in various countries. This approach involves international protocols, press reports, and the rest; this procedure is required for an immediate move to a fixed exchange rate system. Dramatic measures would be required to make it clear that individual countries have no discretion in their inflation rates.

The problem of choosing among these alternatives in the face of uncertainty is the standard choice-under-uncertainty problem. The expected gains and the risks attached to each of the three alternatives must be determined. There seems to be a strong preference for gradualism to slow down monetary expansion rates in each individual country at a modest rate, and allow exchange rates to float in the meantime. At some stage, if price stability is achieved in all countries, five, ten, fifteen years on, we might then think about Parkin Wingspread I-type rules, with monetary expansion rates co-ordinated among countries with different inflation rates. The dangers in the other two formulas are great; large economic risks in terms of changing expectations would be incurred. We do not know enough about how expectations react in such situations. But the variance attached to the experiment seems to be high and therefore in terms of mean-variance optimising, the cautious gradual approach is preferable.

Dornbusch asked how an international agreement might help stabilise expectations. It seems unlikely that Germany would find it in its interest to pair up with Britain or Italy in such an agreement. Much more benefit is derived from having some country actually demonstrate that it can achieve price stability and thereby build up support for this policy. That is why it is preferable that each country goes by itself rather than compromise and average its inflationary rates with those of other countries with higher inflationary rates.

Fischer asked Böckelmann to indicate the pressures on a central bank that make it hard to stabilise the rate of price increase at any value other than zero. Theoretically, there is no particular reason to choose a zero rate; yet it is probably the only rate the central bank can choose. Once there is a move from zero, there are pressures to keep increasing the inflation rate. Some years ago, it was argued that Japanese experience suggested that a country could maintain a steady inflation of 6 per cent for ten years. A policy of gradualism may not be maintainable because of the strong pressures in each country to react to recurrent short-run disturbances. This year, the oil price increase provides a reason to relax on monetary growth and on fiscal policy and to absorb the shock with a temporary increase in the price level. The increase in the price level occurs because it never seems worth while to incur the unemployment costs to obtain a reduction in the current rate of inflation. So expansionary monetary policies are taken to avoid the present costs of unemployment; we shall worry about inflation next year when the policy of gradualism will be adopted. There have been a lot of disturbances; disturbances will keep happening. The policy of gradualism may not be politically feasible.

Parkin asked Fischer what measures or approach was politically feasible.

Frenkel addressed the political realism of the policies. In three of the formulas for re-entry – those of Parkin, Dornbusch, and McKinnon – the question is how can we arrive at a system in which there is stable rate of inflation, whatever this rate is. He then asked whether we want stable inflation. And the designation of the 'we' – does it refer to the tax payers or the tax collectors? The individuals or the government? The inflation at whatever rate it is running is determined not by individuals but by the government. And hence this leads me to the political side. Governments have a high rate of time preference, and cannot resist some measures. When we speak about what we want, we want to understand 'want' in terms of a framework, subject to some constraints that are moving us. This leads to the question the kind of institutions we want – do we want a system that collapses once inflations cease to be stable phenomena? Taking experience and some realism, we need to know whether it might not be preferable to create an institution that takes it for granted that inflations are not going to be stabilised, not at least for some period. And given these constraints, we might then ask what kind of institutional arrangement is second best or third best.

Mussa noted the asymmetry of upward and downward movements of prices. The United States was in the Vietnam war from 1965 through 1968, and it took three or four years to get the world inflation rate moving. Then, when the Fed began to clamp down on the rate of monetary expansion, the rate of price increase began to fall within eighteen months. This does not suggest a strong asymmetry. The unemployment rate reached the 6 per cent level, which is not extraodinarily high. There has been a great deal of exaggeration about asymmetry and about the unemployment costs. He supported the view that each country should go it alone on the stabilisation of inflation. The US Administration in mid-1974 does not possess the political power to embark on deflationary policy; any significant change in US macroeconomic policy may have to wait for the next election and the advent of the new administration in 1977. Given the confused US political situation, other countries, particularly Germany and Japan would be well advised to pursue their own stabilisation policies.

Kouri agreed that each country should go on its own but disagreed that current rates of inflation in each country should be stabilised, given the high current inflation rates, because of a number of special and temporary factors, especially the boom in the world commodity markets and the increase in the oil price, have become less severe since the spring. He offered an alternative re-entry formula, which involved a tightening of monetary policy. The structure of financial markets in many countries cannot take a very sharp monetary contraction. An expansionary fiscal policy should be used to offset the deflationary impact of current account deficits or surplus. And wages should be completely indexed to eliminate the perpetration of inflation through inflationary expectations. Public institutions should be devised to intermediate oil money to those countries which do not have an adequate private developed capital market. He emphasised that countries should not now attach signific-ance to current account targets as they have in the past, given that there is a deficit that the oil-consuming countries together have to share; if there are quantitative targets for the current account balance, a very serious conflict problem may be created.

Gordon directed his comments and the issue of time-preference in choosing between the merits of sudden sharp deflation versus gradualism in terms of working out what our rates of time preference are. He disagreed with Mussa's interpretation of the 1969–78 experiment with gradualism in the United States in 1969 and 1970. The rate of growth of wages did not decline, despite the increase in the unemployment rate to 6 per cent. Gradualism accomplished nothing. The slight slowdown of prices was unsustainable, given the failure of wages to decline and there is no evidence that 6 per cent unemployment rate would not have had to last five or ten years.

He then asked about the possible surprises. One is that he found there was not a world depression, from 1974 to 1976. The downward flexibility of prices might surprise us. There may be the same kind of structural mistake in our models of the price-wage mechanism analogous to our mistakes in the late sixties, but in reverse. A second is that the oil price collapses and the third is that monetary authorities do not maintain their contractive policies, because they are not willing to live with the long period of unemployment; then we shall not get world recession, but we shall not get price stability either. And we will end up essentially where we are.

Böckelmann said he thought Parkin was over-dramatic about the escalation of inflationary expectations. He was much more optimistic than he had reason to be about the acceleration of inflation, because Germany had had a $2\frac{1}{2}$ per cent rate for so long that he had been hopeful that it could return to this rate. Only about three years ago some people tried to convince the German public that they had to accustom themselves to a 4 per cent inflation rate because that was the price for monetary union in Europe and the other countries wanted it this way. No one in Germany now takes the same view with respect to 8 per cent. It was a shock to see how quickly we moved from 2 to 4 per cent, from 4 per cent to 8 per cent. What was really behind this were the expectations; the trade unions in the beginning of 1973 were prepared to give the government and the authorities a chance. They said that they did not want accelerating inflation and so the union agreements were relatively moderate. But from mid-1973 there were wildcat strikes and renegotiations of wage agreements, much as in 1969. The trade unions at the beginning of 1974 felt strongly that this was not going to happen again and so they asked for an increase in real growth and a redistribution of income. They wanted the increase in wages to be large enough to cover the inflation of 1973 and the expected inflation of 1974, that is the increase in taxation which goes with a progressive income tax structure. So if the inflation is not checked, then with 8 per cent inflation wage settlements push the inflation rate to 12 per cent. This is the mechanism which makes for the acceleration of inflation.

Williamson began by reflecting on his two years in the IMF and used that experience to consider how discussions at this type of conference might be more relevant. One of the participants in the Committee of Twenty (C–20) exercise had remarked on the remarkably little input from the academic side in the various C–20 discussions. Very little academic work was useful to the negotiations on issues like the reserve indicator system, asset settlement arrangements and the system of the valuation of the SDR. We in the Fund thought the guidelines for floating were of major importance to reduce the dangers of potential conflict. The academic input to the discussion of guidelines was small. And finally the problem of the multi-currency intervention system is of considerable importance, but there has not been much academic discussion of it. The only issue the C–20 discussed on which there is an academic literature is the 'link'. An issue which people at this conference have been concerned with, such as co-ordination of domestic rates of credit expansion, was not considered by the C–20 at all; it is difficult to visualise international discussions on that subject. The official discussions are lacking because they do not take account of some relevant academic work; that central banks are interested in the yields on their portfolios seems to be fairly well-established empirical conclusion. And yet there are people in the C–20 who seem capable of discussing at indefinite length the assumption that central bankers should not and do not take any account of yields in determining their portfolios.

Williamson then asked why this gulf exists between the officials and the academicians. The striking characteristic of academic discussions which partly may explain why they are not closely related to what is going on is the official world predeliction for taking extreme cases and having intellectual revolutions.

CONCLUSIONS

Mussa began by noting that the experience under the floating exchange rates system has been better than if we had tried to continue to operate with pegged rates. Flexible rates are not a panacea for the world's ills. Most of the real economic problems that exist under a pegged exchange rate system would also exist under a floating exchange rate system. Rules for operation of the system are required whether we have a fixed exchange rate system or a flexible exchange rate system. Yet even though rules are required, it is not necessary that those rules always be written down. What is required is that there be some relatively well-defined understandings about acceptable modes of behaviour. Since countries have not intervened against their own currency under the floating rate system, the problem of competitive depreciation has not been experienced. That rule of the game that countries should not depreciate their currencies has been followed.

A set of rules will evolve over time. He recommended that the policy of developing this rule should follow his favourite architectural policy for campus planning; rather than design nice architectural patterns for the walkways, the architects should wait to see where everybody walks and then pave it. The best approach to structuring the international monetary system is to see what works, and then, after some period, to codify that behaviour.

The final point deals to some extent with analytical issues for further research. The monetary approach to the balance of payments in its early presentations focused on the proposition that the balance of payments and the exchange rate are essentially but not exclusively monetary phenomena. This conference has focused on the question that the problems of the world economy are to some extent real problems as well as monetary problems. A number of papers have attempted to penetrate that veil and to shed some light on issues relating to the real economy; that line of research which can and must continue to go forward.

Michael Porter said the elements of the monetary model which remains at the heart of this conference have still not been empirically researched. Economists at Chicago stress that empirical research complements theoretical ideas. While the monetary approach of the balance of payments now dominates the discussion, there has been very little supporting empirical work. Governments cannot be expected to adopt policies consistent with the model until there is more evidence. Similarly when governments are to be advised on the need for floating exchange rates, evidence is needed; if they are advised not to sterilise the domestic impact of payments imbalances, evidence is needed on what might happen if they do sterilise.

Porter continued that governments tend not to adhere to policy advice because the instruments are not available. Fiscal policy has not been available for domestic stabilisation in Europe. So countries use monetary policies, even though they know difficulties will result. These countries have been reluctant to adopt floating exchange rates, which is necessary if monetary policy is to be effective, because of income distribution impacts. Changes in exchange rates may not work because the change in distribution of income between the traded goods sector and the non-traded goods sector would be unacceptable; in some countries the traded goods sector may be agriculture or sections of manufacturing industries. Those groups whose share of income is sensitive to changes in exchange rate are organised politically. Hence the income distribution aspects of the exchange rate policy should be analysed.

Another subject for future research is the demand for international reserves under floating exchange rates. In Latin America, when monetary brakes have been applied very rapidly, a chronic excess demand for real balances has emerged and economic downturns have been produced. The demand for international money balances in a world with general floating rates is still unsettled; we continue to refine the model but do not bother to estimate the parameters. Rules versus discretion is another misspecified problem. If we have explained to the governments why discretionary monetary policies involving stop–go policies have not achieved their goals, then they would exercise their discretion and choose steady rates of monetary expansion as a rule, without understanding the rule. The politicians should be provided with the basic empirical studies which show why their discretionary monetary policies do not work. We need a state of full information so the policy-makers know the full implications of their choices and thereby choose steady monetary expansion rather than stop–go approaches.

We also need models of the disequilibrium system. Most exchange rate changes occur in the context of disequilibrium. They are attempts to get back to an equilibrium trajectory, and so the equilibrium models are irrelevant. If prices are sticky in the open economies then a way to restore equilibrium relative prices is through a change in the exchange rate, which can move very rapidly to a decision.

Three instances came up in the conference. One involves the monetary theory of the balance of payments, and its use to get people to accept the view that the money supply had something to do with the balance of payments. He said he was more at home in Wingspread II than in Wingspread I, largely because people have got away from the extreme type of monetarist model in which all the interesting questions get suppressed. A large number of the officials get turned off by these rather extreme models and assertions, which leave out a lot of things that are clearly important in their regular work. If one wants to appeal to the official audience, one runs grave dangers by telling them that everything they have been doing for the last twenty years is nonsense. A second example, again from Wingspread I, is the Swoboda – Johnson fixation on complete rigidity of exchange rates versus absolute flexibility without intervention. The system that was abandoned in March 1973 was an adjustable peg, not a fixed rate system. The debate which goes on, at least in official circles, is almost entirely in this middle ground. Maybe one has to change this debate in the long run, but if academic discussions are to be relevant, then they must be concerned with systems crawlings pegs, managed flexibility without fixed parities, systems of soft margins which have the idea of a parity but do not have any rigid bands. The third example is Porter's paper on the capital account and its conclusions that there is no need for international reserves. To assert there is no need for reserves because one could rely on automatic financing goes too far; it reduces the potential appeal to the official audience.

Discussions and conferences of this sort should not necessarily seek relevance. It is important in the longer term to think about the more extreme cases. The world of the 1980s may be one in which fixed exchange rates are a serious proposition. To repeat these exercises while simultaneously deploring that the official discussions are not guided by them is non-productive. If one has an interest in economic policy, then one has to discuss the issues that are currently under discussion and that means some compromise from the sort of extreme cases that make nice textbook examples. Some of the points that have come up at this conference will have to be injected much more into official discussions in future years; the idea of the very limited (particular in time) impacts on real variables which comes from influencing monetary variables is one example. The importance of non-sterilisation for the stability of the system is another such example.

Williamson then directed his comments to issues for research. One problem area involves models to incorporate imperfections in the goods market; another, guidelines for floating. More work is needed on the demand for reserves under floating exchange rates; if the demand for reserves is related to their use, in the sense of month-to-month changes in the level of reserves, then there appear to be no economies in the use of reserves under floating exchange rates. Perhaps this is a transitional problem and the system will settle down to a much lower level of reserve use. Some of the other topics involved the determinants of the capital account balance and the welfare implications of changes in the capital account; do private capital flows automatically optimise the world's allocation of resources. The effect of the capital account on the demand for reserves, and the effect of liabilities on the level of reserves that countries need, needs further exploring. Many LDCs hold a large level of reserves, not for the traditional reasons, but for confidence-type reasons, as collateral for borrowing. The income distributional of considerations demand more systematic attention, even though between long-run equilibrium positions the exchange rate has no effect on income distribution. It always seemed the height of absurdity for the then Chancellor of the Exchequer in the years when we were fighting to save the sacred figure $2.80 to say that we could not devalue because that would reduce the standard of living, but we should reduce the rate of growth of wages. Nevertheless, there are big impacts and if they seem to be engineered deliberately by government policy that is going to add to the rigidity of the exchange rate system.

The international aspects of income redistribution through the international monetary system deserve more attention. The adjustable peg system in its final years became a way of subsidising international companies; there was a systematic subsidy from the tax-payers of European countries to the shareholders of American companies. There is a danger of severe deflation and adjustment in the near future, but it is not clear that some of that deflation is not called for. Investment in alternative energy sources will pick up quite strongly and provide an additional source of demand impetus for the world economy.

Rules may be necessary during the re-entry; they are likely to be necessary once the system has moved to stability. The rules have to be related to changes in the economic relationships and political relationships among major countries. There would appear to be some difficulties in fitting McKinnon-type rules and Parkin-type rules into the developing political relationships among major countries, especially between the United States and the major European countries. An alternative approach to rule-making is to get a handle on the developing political relationships and ask what sort of rules might fit the new and emerging political relationships.

Parkin noted that the title of the conference is 'The Political Economy and Monetary Reform'. Most of the time has been spent discussing the economics of monetary reform. We know a lot about what will happen to certain key economic variables if we assume certain well-defined monetary, fiscal and other policies; we do not have all the insights that we want from simple models. Moreover we do not yet have all the dynamic models spelled out and the empirical results that we need. Relative to our knowledge and understanding of the way in which the political process chooses particular values for the instruments of economic control, however, we know a great deal about the economics. Until we understand how the political process works, why the politicians do what they do, we will not be able to come up sensibly with monetary policy and monetary reform that we would like to live with.

Kouri said he did not think that it is necessarily a good thing to be too much aware of political constraints on monetary reform or political constraints on national economic policy. Much can be said for an economist or an intellectual taking a certain position and arguing it consistently, without regard to the political realities. When a politician listens to economic advice, he assumes he is listening to economic advice, and not an economist's anticipation of political realities.

Rachel McCullough recalled that the dilemma was like Friedman's prescription for reducing the rate of inflation. Had he taken into account some of the political limitations on the policies that he advocated, he might have given somewhat different advice. That academic economists have not made a major contribution to the day-to-day issues of international monetary reform, is maybe quite appropriate in terms of the division of labour, especially since many of the issues in reform are transient. It would not have been a good investment of resources of academic economists, who are at their best in dealing with issues that are likely to be around for a longer period of time. The international institutions should deal with the parallel task of taking theoretical and empirical findings and making them useful for day-to-day and year-to-year policy decisions. There has to be some division of labour because we in the universities are somewhat removed from the necessary institutional and empirical information to do really good work on these transient issues. Hence it is better to concentrate on longer-run considerations.

Böckelmann replied that the problem of re-entry was a day-to-day issue for central banks. It was not considered of minor importance.

McCullough replied that the C–20 deliberations focused very much on operational rules for a system that in the end was rejected. It would have a misallocation of resources if academic economists had dropped their other research to work along with the C–20 on each of these methodological issues, which later turned out not to be particularly central.

Böckelmann responded that, viewed over the whole period, the C–20 was an attempt to repeat the Bretton Woods exercise of 1944. Keynes did not feel that Bretton Woods was not something for him to get involved with. If a really dominant economist had considered it worthwhile to think about practical problems, rules and operational procedures, the chances of finding a solution would certainly have been greater. Nobody of this stature is around.

Aliber said that the rules of the new system must conform to the political relations that now prevail among major countries. In that sense, rule-making in the C–20 negotiation bears a poor analogy to the rule-making at Bretton Woods. The political relationship among the participants is sharply different.

Fischer noted that both Keynes and Harry Dexter were members of their respective Treasuries in the 1940s. We may now be complaining about the fact that governments have difficulty in attracting the leading economists of the world.

Williamson responded that it is not that Keynes and White were in the Treasuries but that those were the only two national treasurers who mattered at the time of Bretton Woods. Now there are many more divergent interests to be reconciled. Even if there were a Keynes, he would have found it more difficult.

Porter said he did not think there is much point in Keynes participating for the simple reason of Arrow's impossibility theorem. If the political theory of monetary reform is put in rigorous form, no conceivable equilibrium can be found through that process which is also compatible with underlying forces that exist in the world economy.

List of Participants

Robert Z. Aliber	University of Chicago
Horst Böckelmann	Deutsche Bundesbank
Richard N. Cooper	Yale University
Rudiger Dornbusch	University of Chicago
Stanley Fischer	Massachusetts Institute of Technology
Jacob A. Frenkel	University of Chicago
Robert J. Gordon	Northwestern University
Paul De Grauwe	University of Leuven
Koichi Hamada	University of Tokyo
John Helliwell	University of British Columbia
Pentti J. K. Kouri	Massachusetts Institute of Technology
Anne O. Krueger	University of Minnesota
Rachel McCullough	Harvard University
Ronald I. McKinnon	Stanford University
Bruce K. MacLaury	Federal Reserve Bank of Minneapolis
John Makin	University of Wisconsin, Milwaukee
Michael Mussa	University of Rochester
Michael Parkin	University of Manchester
Edmund S. Phelps	Columbia University
Michael G. Porter	Government of Australia
Grant Reuber	University of Western Ontario
Carlos Rodriguez	Columbia University
Jeremy J. Siegel	University of Chicago
John Spraos	University College, London
John Williamson	International Monetary Fund

Index

Administration, financial, 215, 216
Aghevli, B. B., 194n
Agriculture, 21, 26, 129–32, 146, 168, 257
Aliber, R. Z., ix–xiii, 3–12, 13n, 89, 244, 248, 261, 262
Almon variables, 169
Ando, A., 157n, 168
Arbitrage, international, 76, 90
Archibald, G. C., 207, 215
Argy, V., 59, 137, 149, 190, 191n
Arrow–Pratt measure, 82, 261
Asset markets, 75–91, 106–21 passim, 158
Assets
  accumulation of, 39, 101
  acquisition of, 37, 52, 114
  depreciation of, 120
  domestic, 111–18, 121, 133n, 209
  earning, 111
  income from, 158, 165
  international, 3, 39, 75, 101, 114, 116, 118, 170, 209
  liquid, 165, 166
  monetary, 16, 165, 212–15
  non–tradeable, 90, 107, 115–17
  real, 212–15
  returns on, 86, 90
  self-sufficiency, 101
  sterling, 9
  tradeable, 115, 116
Assignment rules, 97–105
Australia, 22, 149, 210, 213–16, 222, 236, 237, 241, 246, 247
Austria, 22, 222, 236, 237, 241
Azariardis, C., 130n

Baily, M. N., 130n
Balassa, B., 76n, 223, 237

Balbach, A., 181n
Balkan States, 22
Ball, R. J., 128n, 135, 157n
Bank of England, 47
Bankers, international, 37
Bankruptcy, 90
Banks
  central, x–xii, 3, 9, 15, 21, 38, 40–54 passim, 74, 84, 87, 89, 91, 99, 101, 102, 107–11, 113, 116–22, 133n, 135, 149, 169, 181, 209–14 passim, 229, 230, 234, 246, 249, 250, 253, 256, 261
  commercial, 46, 47, 50–53, 110–12, 115, 116, 135n, 180n, 181
  merchant, 51
  savings, 46, 51
Bargaining, 41
Barro, R. J., 135, 141n
Barten, A. P., 157n
Baumol, W. J., 60n, 226
Behaviour, group, 18, 19, 26, 34
Belgium, 22, 23, 188, 189, 196, 199–201, 222, 236, 237, 241
Black, F., 89
Blinder, A., 132n, 135
Bloomfield, A. J., 190
Böckelmann, H., 247, 250, 251, 253, 255, 261, 262
Boes, D. C., 67n, 68n
Bolduc, J. L., 157n
Bond markets, 76, 77, 79–89 passim, 158, 165, 166, 210
Borrowing, 8, 46, 47, 52, 75, 77–91 passim, 98, 102, 111, 116, 133n, 180n, 213, 214, 259
Borts, G. H., 194n
Boyer, R., 107n

Branson, W. H., 90, 107n, 226
Bretton Woods system, ix–xii, 3, 4, 9–11, 27, 42, 43, 74, 75, 158, 179, 180, 222, 223, 243–8, 261
Brinner, R., 128n
Britto, R., 212
Brunner, K., 106n, 149
Buchanan, J. M., 14
Bundesbank, 48, 54
Burger, A., 106n, 110n, 181n

Cambridge macroeconomics, xii, 97–105
Canada, xiii, 48, 158–78, 222, 236, 237, 241, 249, 250
Capital
　accounts, 38, 206, 246, 248, 258, 259
　assets, 76, 77, 89
　controls, 248
　cost of, 132, 165, 167
　flow, xiii, 36, 38, 40, 47, 49, 51–3, 60, 74, 102, 127, 149, 157, 159, 160, 162, 165, 167, 170, 171, 206–11, 217, 218, 248, 250, 259
　gains, 79, 80, 166
　goods, 88, 98
　human, 90
　markets, 75–91, 205, 206, 208–12, 215, 218, 255; integration of, 205, 216, 243, 246, 247, 249
　mobility, 16, 70, 71, 75, 106–24, 128, 133, 135–6, 146, 147, 150, 157, 162, 167, 195, 205–19, 245–7
　risky, 76, 84, 89, 90
　services, 131
　stock, 137, 147, 163, 165
　transactions, 15, 215, 218
Christ, C. F., 188n
Christofides, L. N., 165, 166
Clark model, 206–8, 215
Clower, R. W., 209, 219
Cobb-Douglas function, 131, 144n
Collective action, 18, 19
Commodities, demand for, 144, 146–8, 214, 215, 226
Commodity
　markets, 84, 89, 128, 131–4, 139, 140, 143, 146, 148, 254
　standard, 44, 64
Conflict, inter-nation, 10, 103

Constraints, 4–12 *passim*, 43, 47, 48, 50, 51, 78–81, 110, 116, 141, 147, 169, 182, 192, 194, 195n, 209–14, 218, 223, 254, 260
Consultation, international, 37, 40, 41
Consumption factors, 25, 59–71, 78, 80–83, 88, 89, 91, 129, 166
Contract negotiation, 134
Cook, A. C., 131n
Cooper, R., 195n
Corden, W. M., 15, 43
Cost levels, 227
Cournot solution, 26
Courtney, M. M., 59
Credit
　arrangements, 3–4, 75–91 *passim*, 180, 212, 215
　bank, 44, 46, 49, 53, 54, 111
　contraction, 150, 169
　creation, 233–5
　domestic, 23, 44, 47–9, 53, 54, 108–10, 113, 115, 116, 127, 136, 137, 140, 149, 150, 224, 225, 230, 233–5, 238
　expansion, 220–5, 228, 233, 235, 237, 238, 256
　international, 11, 54
　transfers, 4–9, 11
Currency
　accumulation, 243
　appreciation, xii, 4, 38, 127, 133, 134, 136, 162, 187, 244, 251
　conversion, 9, 15–17, 20, 42
　decimal, 21
　depreciation, xii, 38, 39, 100, 101, 136, 162, 244, 251, 257
　domestic, 119–22, 127, 134, 224
　European, 184, 248
　exchange, 16
　floating, ix, xi, 39, 42, 184–7, 192, 197–201, 216, 243, 250, 256
　foreign, 26, 208, 209
　intervention, 40, 256
　premium, 85, 86, 91
　reserve, 181, 212, 216, 218, 229–38
　unification, *see* Monetary integration
　values, 42
Current accounts, 32–41, 102, 205, 208–12, 218, 246, 248, 249, 254, 255
Customs, 20

d'Alcantara, G., 157n
Debt
  factors, 102, 108–11, 115, 116
  management, 158, 165–7
  non-traded, 107, 111–13, 115–17, 119,
    120, 122, 123, 166
  policies, xiii, 157–78
  tradeable, 111, 112, 115–17, 123
Decision-making, 5, 8–10, 18–20, 25, 41,
  250, 261
Defaulting, 77, 90
Deflation, 21, 34, 54, 101, 127, 133, 169,
  179, 200, 239, 252, 254, 255, 260
De Grauwe, P., xiii, 179–203, 247
Demand, aggregate, 97, 99
Denmark, 23, 222, 236, 237, 241
Deposits, 77, 181n
Depression, ix, 24, 137, 255
Devaluation, 11, 34–6, 38, 39, 41, 127, 134,
  136, 137, 139, 140, 147, 148, 150, 187,
  216, 239, 244, 259
Developing countries, xi, 40, 259
Dexter, H., 261
Dicks Mireaux, L. 135
Diplomacy, international, 37, 39, 41
Discounts, 43, 46, 47, 52, 53, 85, 169
Dispersion, 220n, 239
Disturbances, xii, 59–71, 75, 88, 89, 99,
  111, 248, 253
Diversification, 165
Dividend factors, 79, 165, 168
Dixit, A. K., 78
Dollar
  holdings, 39–40, 244
  overvaluation of, 34–7
Dominican Republic, 212
Dornbusch, R., xii, 59n, 60, 106–24, 137,
  250–5
Dramais, A., 157n
Dresden Convention, 20
Dufty, N. F., 131n

Eckstein, O., 128n
Economies
  closed, 17, 44, 128, 132, 133, 141n, 150,
    185
  developed, 33, 218
  growth, 45, 46, 101, 136, 232, 234, 235,
    237–9

linked, xiii, 15, 157–203
mature, 45
open, 17, 18, 44, 90, 106–22 *passim*, 128,
  133, 135, 180, 186, 188, 190, 200, 211,
  223, 258
static, 135
Economy, world, ix, x, 205, 246, 247, 252,
  257, 261
Edgren, G., 223, 226
EFO model, 223, 226, 227, 229
Eire, 222, 236, 237, 241
Employment factors, xii, 5, 17, 25, 33, 76,
  91, 97–9, 101, 103, 126, 128, 137, 138,
  141, 158, 160, 163, 164, 179, 251
Entrepreneurship, 19–21, 24, 64, 131a
Equilibrium, economic, 4, 5, 15, 24, 48, 49,
  106–14, 116, 118–22, 128, 129, 140–50,
  160, 179–201, 218, 220–40, 243, 245–7,
  251, 257–9, 261
Equity, 77, 79, 81–4
Eurocurrency market, 74, 77, 245
Eurodollar market, 169, 216, 247
European Community, 10, 11, 13, 15,
  24–6, 39, 50, 52, 157n, 179–203, 245,
  247, 260
  monetary union, 42, 239
Exchange
  controls, 3, 5, 10
  markets, xii, 3, 4, 6–9, 11, 33, 38–40, 43,
    44, 46–51, 53, 54, 159, 247
  rates, ix–xii, 3–5, 8, 11–13, 15–18, 20,
    23–6, 43, 46–9, 54, 59–71, 97–101,
    103, 126, 127, 133, 135, 136, 141,
    158–64 *passim*, 169, 171, 174–81, 192,
    195, 206–12, 218, 223, 224, 244–50,
    257–9; dollar, 46, 184–6, 190, 192,
    193, 197–9; fixed, xii, 13, 25–7, 42–9,
    59–71 *passim*, 106, 127, 136, 148, 150,
    162, 179–85, 187, 192, 208–11, 212n,
    215, 220–40, 244–9, 251, 252, 256,
    259; floating, ix–xii, 3, 8, 13, 16, 26,
    32–42, 48, 59–71 *passim*, 74–91, 99,
    127, 133, 158–60, 171, 179, 181,
    184–7, 192, 209, 210, 223, 225, 227,
    229, 235–7, 243, 244, 246, 248–53,
    256–9; pegged, x–xii, 3, 32–41, 43, 47,
    74, 158, 159, 243, 244, 246–50, 256,
    258, 259
Exploitation, 19

Export factors, 17, 36, 39, 44, 98, 99, 101, 135, 137, 147, 161, 168, 169, 171, 190n, 206, 211, 216, 243

Faxen, K. O., 223, 226
Finance Institutions, xi, 3, 4, 52
Financial markets, 75–91, 212–15, 254
Fiscal policies, xi, xiii, 4, 33, 36, 38, 64, 74, 75, 97, 98, 100, 101, 103, 106, 132, 157–78, 205, 206, 216, 252–4, 257, 260
Fischer, S., xii, 59–71, 74n, 78, 89, 246, 253, 261
Fisherian model, 79, 88, 120, 208
Fleming, M., 119
Foley, D., 88n
Forward markets, 43, 76, 85, 107, 118–22
France, 22, 24, 39, 42, 48, 137, 187–90, 193–200, 220, 222, 236, 237, 241, 252
Frenkel, J. A., 69n, 90, 206, 249, 254
Friedman, M., 42, 46, 52, 128, 132, 239, 260
Future markets, 215, 218

Gailliot, H. J., 76n
Gains, economic, 4
General Arrangements to Borrow, 3
Germany, x, xii, 20, 23, 35, 48, 54, 149, 187–9, 191, 193, 194, 196–200, 210, 222, 236, 237, 241, 243–5, 247, 250–5
Girton, L., 106n, 107n
GNE, 160–2, 170, 171, 174–8
Gold, 3, 9, 35, 36, 181, 209, 215–17, 224, 229, 230, 234, 242, 247
   standard, 4, 9, 12, 20, 22, 23, 26, 33, 47, 102, 190, 238
Goldman, S. M., 78
Goods
   demand for, 205, 217
   non-traded, 45, 78, 124, 137–46, 150, 225–8, 232, 234, 235, 257
   traded, 43–6, 49, 53, 78, 128, 133, 136, 137, 139, 140–50, 162, 225–30, 232, 234–7, 245, 251, 257
Gordon, D. F., 130n
Gordon, R. J., xii, 126–52, 243–6, 251, 255
Government
   debt, 10n, 86, 87, 89, 101, 102, 158, 165–7
   expenditure, 97–9, 105, 162, 166, 170, 171, 174–8, 206, 207

interference, 210
   policies, 206, 254, 257, 259
Gradualism, 252–5
Grassman, S., 77n
Graybill, F. A., 67n, 68n
Greece, 22, 23
Greenwood, J., 13n
Gresham's Law, 24, 75, 91
Grossman, H., 135, 141n
Gross National Product, 44, 45, 53, 54, 187, 188, 205, 206, 210
Grubel, H. G., 206

Haiti, 212
Hall, R. E., 131n
Hamada, K., xi, 13–31, 167, 250
Hanoch, G., 64n
Harrod, R. F., 131n
Heller, H. R., 212
Helliwell, J., xiii, 157–78, 247, 249
Henderson, D., 106n, 107n
Henderson, J. M., 34, 36
Herring, R., 169
Hickman, B. G., 157n
Hines, A. G., 130n
Hipple, F. S., 206, 207, 219
Hoarding, 139, 140, 143, 144
Hodjera, Z., 149
Holmes, J. M., 76n
Houthakker, H., 190n
Hume, D., 223

Import factors, 17, 39, 40, 44, 98, 99, 101, 129–31, 137, 147, 168, 169, 171, 190n, 206, 211, 216, 217
Income factors, 4, 60, 83, 107–9, 114, 116, 118, 129, 132, 134n, 139, 143, 144, 158, 160, 161, 164, 166, 206, 207, 211, 224, 227, 228, 232, 256, 257, 259
Inflation, ix–xii, 8, 17, 21, 34–7, 42, 44, 45, 54, 60, 74–91 *passim*, 99, 120, 126–52, 161, 200, 216–18, 220–40, 243–56, 260
Influence, distribution of, 4
Information costs, 214
Ingram, J., 52
Inoguchi, T., 13n
Interest rates, 4, 38, 47, 51, 52, 74–91, 102, 107–23, 127, 130n, 131–6, 139, 147–9, 158–60, 162, 164–7, 169, 171, 174–8,

194n, 197n, 208–11, 215–16, 218
pegged, xii, 160–4, 167, 174–8
Intermediation, financial, 110, 111, 116
International
  law, 15
  Monetary Fund, ix, xi, 3, 6, 9, 10, 16, 27,
    36, 206, 223, 229, 235, 241, 256; Com-
    mittee of Twenty (C–20), ix, x, 3, 256,
    261
  monetary system, 33
  relations, 97–103
Investment, 37, 74–91, 101, 160, 163, 165,
  210, 213–15, 247, 260
IS curve, 160
Ishii, Kanji, 13n
Italy, xii, 20–4, 42, 48, 137, 188, 189, 191,
  194, 195n, 196, 200, 222, 236, 237, 241,
  253

Jackson, D. S., 226n
Japan, x, xii, 10, 11, 20, 21, 23, 24, 45, 47,
  48, 52, 157n, 222, 236, 241, 243, 247,
  252–4
  Bank of, 48, 250
Jasay, A. J., 120
Job creation, 207
Johnson, H. G., 59, 75, 130n, 150, 182n,
  206, 209, 223, 224n, 225, 227–9, 253
Johnson, K., 157n
Jones, A., 226n
Jones, E. H., 131n
Jorgensen, D. W., 131n

Katz, S., 190n
Kenen, P. B., 207, 215
Keynes, J. M., 44, 120, 208, 261
Kierzkowski, H., 226
Kindleberger, C. P., 13n, 59, 74n, 76, 243
Klein, L. R., 157n
Kouri, P. J. K., xii, 49, 59, 74–91, 107n,
  149, 190, 191n, 209, 210, 216, 244, 249,
  254, 260
Krueger, A. O., xii, 32–41, 244, 245, 247

Labour
  capital substitution, 144, 145, 150
  costs, 129, 130, 134n, 169
  demand and supply, 128n, 129–32, 134,
    137–42, 144–8, 163, 225, 226
  movement of, 23, 137, 140

Laffer, A. B., 16
Lags, 36, 63, 64, 70, 98, 130n, 159, 163,
  168–70, 183, 186, 187, 207, 209
Latin America, 258
Leadership, 19, 23, 24, 27
Leakages, 100, 101, 184–6, 188, 189, 197,
  198
Lending, 37, 75, 77–91 *passim*, 98, 180n
Lester, J., 169
Levich, R. M., 90
Lipsey, R. G., 128, 130n, 209, 219
Liquidity factors, 33–7, 51, 52, 81, 116,
  180n, 181n, 242, 244
Living standards, 217, 259
LM curve, 160
Loans, 47, 110–17, 166, 167, 213, 214,
  216
London Business School, 135
Lucas, R. E. Jr., 64

McClam, W., 197n
Machlup, F., 209, 212
McCullough, R., 248, 260–2
McKinnon, R. I., xii, 42–55, 59, 79, 195n,
  206, 209, 211, 251, 254, 260, 262
MacLaury, B. K., 262
McRae, R., xiii, 157–78
Magee, S., 190n
Mahar, K. L., xiii, 205–19
Makin, J. H., 212, 244–6, 249, 262
Market clearing conditions, 143
Markov process, 207
Marston, R., 169
Mathieson, D., 54
Maxwell, T., 158, 168
Mayers, M. C., 89
Merton, R. C., 77–9, 89, 90
Michaely, M., 52, 190n
Migration, xiii, 157, 159, 163, 169, 170
Modigliani, F., 74n, 168
Monetarism, domestic/international, 135
Monetary
  agreements, 3, 6, 7, 10, 42–55, 251
  arrangements, ix, x, 3–56
  behaviour, 3, 5, 6, 11, 12, 220
  contraction, 162, 254, 255
  expansion, 4, 26, 135, 163, 190, 200, 210,
    218, 220, 229, 249, 252–4, 258
  independence, xii, 74–91 *passim*, 195–7,

199–201, 205–18, 246, 248–50
integration, benefits of, 15–20, 24–7, 34;
  calculus of participation, 15, 17–20,
    237; costs of, 15–20, 25–7, 34;
  historical perspective, 20–24;
  incentives for, 13, 14; risk elements, 26
policies, conflicting, 195, 197, 198
restrictions, 150
rules, ix–xii, 3–55, 90, 158
system, flexibility of, 179
Union, European, 48, 224; Latin, 22–4;
  Scandinavian, 23
Money
  balances, 208, 258
  chartal theory of, 24
  coinage, 20–4
  creation of, 102
  distribution of, 106
  high powered, 52–3, 111, 112, 117, 180n
  low-powered, 52–3
  markets, 90, 108–12, 116, 139, 143, 144,
    195, 201, 210
  paper, 22–4
  state theory of, 24
  stock, 158
  substitutability of, 91
  supply and demand, 59–71, 77, 81–90
    passim, 101–23 *passim*, 135, 136,
    139–43, 146, 149, 150, 158–67, 170,
    174–8, 190n, 208–11, 224, 228–35,
    238, 245, 258; growth of, 7–12, 43–54,
    120, 132, 133, 136, 148–50, 159, 217,
    232, 244, 246
  token, 22–3
Mood, A. M., 67n, 68n
Morishma, M., 157n
MPS system, 157–9, 161–3, 165, 167
München convention, 20
Mundell, R., 16, 59, 70, 88, 106, 107, 110,
  118, 119, 121, 182n, 209, 223
Murata, Y., 157n
Mushakoji, K., 13n
Mussa, M., 247, 254–6, 262
Myrhman, J., 106n, 226, 240

Nations, competition between, 4
NDA, 210, 211
Netherlands, 187–9, 191, 196, 199–201,
  222, 236, 237, 241

Nobay, A. R., 130n
Norway, 21, 222, 236, 237, 241
Nurkse, R., 190n

Odhner, G. E., 223, 226
OECD, 40
Officer, L. H., 76n
Oil, price of, 39, 127, 136, 137, 243, 249,
  251, 253–5
Olson, M. Jr., 14, 18, 27, 28
Open-market operations, 43, 46–7, 49, 53,
  54, 87–9, 107, 113, 114, 117, 119–22, 215
Output levels, 33, 59–71, 98, 101, 127–9,
  135, 136, 139, 141–4, 146, 148, 150, 161,
  163, 169–71, 174–8, 226, 228

Papal states, 22
Paretian standard, 18, 27
Parities, fixity of, 3, 15, 17, 20, 22–4, 26, 27,
  42–55, 246–7, 258
Parkin, M., xii, 130n, 220–40, 244, 252–5,
  260, 262
Patrick, H., 47
Pattison, J., 220n
Payments
  balance of, x-xii, 15, 24, 26, 33–41,
    59–71 *passim*, 75, 97, 100, 102, 103,
    126, 132, 133, 135–7, 150, 161, 180,
    184, 190, 191, 194, 205, 208, 209, 218,
    222–39, 246–9, 257, 258
  deficits, 4, 5, 8, 17, 34–7, 39, 49, 50,
    52–4, 102, 127, 136, 137, 148, 149, 179,
    181, 216, 225, 235, 239, 255
  international, 49, 53
  surplus, 4, 5, 7, 8, 11, 34–7, 49, 50, 52–4,
    98, 99, 101, 102, 127, 140, 146, 181,
    216, 235, 237, 239, 243, 245
Pearce, I. F., 131n
Perry, G., 128n
Phelps, E. S., 128, 262
Phillips curve, xii, 17, 25, 60, 64, 65, 70, 126,
  128–32, 135, 137, 140, 145, 150, 251
Political factors, 4, 9, 10, 43, 215, 217, 218,
  246, 251–4, 257, 260, 261
Population, 163
Porter, M. G., xiii, 49, 90, 107n, 149,
  205–19, 246, 247, 257, 258, 261, 262
Portfolio balance, 106–24, 160, 165, 166,
  170, 209, 212–15, 229n

Power factors, 4, 10
Prachowny, M. F., 90, 226n
Preferences, 34
Premiums, 119–21
Price
  indices, 44–6, 53, 54
  levels, ix–xii, 4, 5, 16, 25, 26, 33–6, 42–7,
    49, 53, 54, 59–71, 76, 78, 79, 81, 85, 88,
    89–91, 102, 107, 126–50, 158, 161–4,
    168, 169, 179, 180, 211, 212, 215, 217,
    249–55, 258
  theories, 14, 150, 169
Prices, relative, 220–40, 258
Primary products, 37, 148
Private
  goods, 25
  sector, 84, 85, 98–103, 111, 112, 115,
    119, 212, 214–15
Productivity
  factors, 34, 129–32, 141, 142, 146
  growth, 15, 43, 88, 223, 226–9, 232,
    234–7
Profits, 133
Project LINK, 137, 128n
Protectionism, 39
Prussia, 20
Public
  bads, 25
  goods, theory of, 14, 16–19, 24–6, 28
  institutions, 254, 255, 260
Puerto Rico, 52
Purchasing power parity, 76, 78, 79, 83, 85,
  91

Quota formula, 6

RDX 2 system, 157–9, 162, 163, 165–71
Recession, 8, 127, 131, 133, 137, 149, 150,
  252, 255
Redundancy, 147
Re-entry, 250–4, 260, 261
Research, 169, 257–9
Reserve
  assets, 3, 9, 15, 229
  changes, 116, 220–2, 259
  Federal, 48, 181
  losses/gains, 117, 120, 121, 194, 243
  targets, 37, 38, 164
Reserves
  accumulation of, 35, 37, 120, 149, 246

  acquisition of, 116
  bank, 44, 50–3, 107–11, 113, 114, 149,
    184, 234
  deficit/surplus countries, 35, 36
  demand for, 259
  disturbances, 207, 211
  domestic, 52, 114–16, 120, 133n, 146,
    148, 185
  European, 181–3, 185–201
  excess, 216–18, 246
  flow of, 136, 140, 149, 150, 179, 182
  fluctuations, 209–11
  foreign exchange, 16, 43, 230
  international, 15, 16, 43, 50, 54, 75, 102,
    111, 112, 135, 136, 181, 184, 185, 188,
    190n, 205–19, 221, 223, 224, 230, 242,
    244, 258
  inventory theory, 207
  official, 205, 206, 209, 212, 214–15,
    218
  private, 212, 214–15, 244
  stocks of, ix, 120, 122
Resources
  distribution of, 40, 149, 247, 259
  utilisation of, 24, 213–15
Reuber, G., 262
Revaluation, 35, 127, 150, 216, 239, 243,
  246, 250
Richmond, J., 207, 215
Risk factors, 81–83, 213
Robinson, J., 100
Rodriguez, C., 262

Salant, W., 107n, 206, 243
Salter, W. E. G., 137
Samuelson, P. A., 90
Sanctions, 7
Sardinia, 20, 21
Savings, 80, 102, 160, 165
Scitovsky, T., 107n
SDRs, 15, 36, 206, 216, 218, 229, 231, 234,
  256
Securities
  domestic, 49, 51, 107, 111, 118–22
  foreign, 205, 210, 212–15
  government, 46, 47, 51
  private sector, 101, 102
Shifts in supply and demand, 75
Shocks, ix, 5, 6, 10–12, 16, 60, 70, 148, 150,

159, 161, 163–6, 170, 171, 174–8, 244, 246, 251, 253
Shultz-Volcker plan, 36–8, 40
Sidrauski, M., 77, 78, 88n
Siegel, J., 248, 262
Smithsonian agreement, 3, 42
Sohmen, E., 182n, 206
Solnik, B. H., 77
Spain, 22
Special Drawing Rights, 3
Speculation, 46, 48, 50, 54, 74, 75, 90, 119, 120, 210, 246, 248
Spot markets, 76, 118–20, 211, 215, 218
Spraos, J., xii, 97–105, 120, 248, 262
Stabilisation, x, xii, xiii, 17, 43, 45, 48, 52, 54, 59–71, 74, 75, 100, 102, 159, 191n, 194, 195, 197–9, 206, 208, 210, 211, 216, 218, 220n, 223, 224, 238, 243–60 *passim*
Stagflation, 252
Stall, H. R., 76n
Stein, J. L., 59
Sterilisation, xiii, 49, 50, 52, 102, 133n, 140, 146, 180, 188, 190–201, 211, 217, 218, 246, 257, 259
Sterling, 9, 35
Strikes, 130, 136, 169, 255
Subsidies, 115, 259
Sumner, M., 130n
Swap agreements, 3, 41, 53, 212
Sweden, 22, 23, 222, 236, 237, 241
Switzerland, 22, 188, 189, 190n, 196, 197, 199, 200, 201, 222, 236, 237, 241
Swoboda, A. K., 194n, 233n, 258

Tariff rates, 248, 249
Taxation, 64, 90, 106, 115, 116, 127–33, 136, 147, 148, 166, 218, 245, 254, 256, 259
Technology, 129, 226
Tobin, J., 88, 89, 106n, 165
Tower, E., 59
Trade Unions, 130, 255
Trading factors, x-xiii, 5, 17, 23, 32, 33, 36, 39, 47, 52, 54, 75–91 *passim*, 98–102, 128, 133, 136–50, 157–71 *passim*, 190, 206, 208, 210, 212, 214–16, 246, 247, 250

Transactions, cost of, 90, 215, 216
Transfers, 64
Tripartite agreement, 26–7
Turner, H. A., 226n

Unemployment, 8, 16–18, 91, 100, 126–8, 130n, 132–4, 137–9, 149, 150, 161, 171, 174–9, 245, 251, 252–5
United Kingdom, 35, 42, 47, 48, 121, 128n, 130n, 136, 137, 187–90, 196, 197, 200, 222, 236, 237, 241, 244–6, 252, 253
United States, ix, x, xiii, 10–12, 17, 22, 27, 33–9, 47, 48, 52, 74, 84, 128, 130, 131, 134, 135, 158–78, 181–201, 213–16, 222, 229, 236–8, 241, 244–7, 251–5, 260
Uranium, 209, 215
Usury laws, 51

Valuation market, 166
Vienna Convention, 22
Vietnam war, 34, 36, 246, 254

Waelbroeck, J., 157n
Wage factors, 44, 45, 64, 128–42 *passim*, 146–50, 169, 179, 180, 217, 227, 251, 254–6, 259
War chest, 209, 215
Ward, R., 130n
Wealth factors, 79–83, 86–9, 107–9, 118, 165, 170, 207
White, 261
Whitin, T. M., 207
Wiener process, 78
Wilkinson, F., 226n
Willet, J. D., 76n
Williamson, J. H., 206, 244, 245, 247, 256, 259, 261, 262
Wingspread Conference, xi, xiii, 74n, 158, 248, 250, 253, 258

Yudin, E. B., 207, 215

Zecher, J. R., 149
Zeckhauser, R., 27, 28
Zollverein, the, 20, 22, 24